T0333428

Values in Medicine

In the age of evidence-based medicine, regard for objectivity is critical for any good practitioner. But how realisable is objectivity in the doctor/patient relationship and in the development and delivery of healthcare? The danger is to account for the difficulties in eliminating uncertainty by reference to practical obstacles embodied in isolating the truth from fiction or knowledge from hunches or opinions. Such explanations make the critical assumption that the incontrovertible truth is buried somewhere in the world of nature or human nature simply awaiting discovery.

Whilst it would be irresponsible to be careless about the truth in the quest for knowledge and in the doctor/patient relationship, the drive to eliminate uncertainty in health care settings embodies many dangers. The contribution of science to the development of modern medicine has afforded remarkable progress in the delivery of effective health care. But it has also tended to remove the patients' experience of ill health from centre stage and replace it with the insights of experts. Such a change poses serious threats to the doctor/patient relationship and to the well-being of patients.

This books sets out to examine the critical assumption in a number of areas of clinical practice and research and, in so doing, find a proper place for ethical values in health care. It argues that ethical dimensions of clinical practice do not always arise from undisputed facts. On the contrary, they are sometimes to be found at the level of the determination of the facts themselves. Recognition of this places the experience of the patient firmly back on centre stage. This does not underestimate the crucial role which science plays in modern medicine, but rather identifies its proper place in assessing and meeting people's health needs.

Professor Donald Evans, a philosopher by training, has published widely in Medical Ethics for 23 years. During that period he has directed two Bioethics Centres, one in the University of Wales and the other in the University of Otago, New Zealand. He has completed research projects for many national and international bodies and served on numerous international, regional and local ethics committees. He is currently a Vice-President of the International Bioethics Committee of UNESCO and the international member of the Stem Cell Oversight Committee of the Canadian Institutes of Health Research.

Biomedical Law and Ethics Library

Series Editor: Sheila A.M. McLean

Scientific and clinical advances, social and political developments and the impact of healthcare on our lives raise profound ethical and legal questions. Medical law and ethics have become central to our understanding of these problems, and are important tools for the analysis and resolution of problems – real or imagined.

In this series, scholars at the forefront of biomedical law and ethics contribute to the debates in this area, with accessible, thought-provoking, and sometimes controversial ideas. Each book in the series develops an independent hypothesis and argues cogently for a particular position. One of the major contributions of this series is the extent to which both law and ethics are utilised in the content of the books, and the shape of the series itself.

The books in this series are analytical, with a key target audience of lawyers, doctors, nurses, and the intelligent lay public.

Available titles:

Human Fertilisation and Embryology (2006)
Reproducing regulation
Kirsty Horsey & Hazel Biggs

Intention and Causation in Medical Non-Killing (2006)
The impact of criminal law concepts on euthanasia and assisted suicide
Glenys Williams

Impairment and Disability (2007)
Law and ethics at the beginning and end of life
Sheila McLean & Laura Williamson

Bioethics and the Humanities (2007)
Attitudes and perceptions
Robin Downie & Jane Macnaughton

Defending the Genetic Supermarket (2007)
The law and ethics of selecting the next generation
Colin Gavaghan

The Harm Paradox (2007)
Tort law and the unwanted child in an era of choice
Nicolette Priaulx

Assisted Dying (2007)
Reflections on the need for law reform
Sheila McLean

Medicine, Malpractice and Misapprehensions (2007)
Vivienne Harpwood

Euthanasia, Ethics and the Law (2007)
From conflict to compromise
Richard Huxtable

Best Interests of the Child in Healthcare (2007)
Sarah Elliston

Values in Medicine (2003)
What are we really doing to patients?
Donald Evans

Forthcoming titles include:

Medicine, Law and the Public Interest
Communitarian perspectives on medical law
J. Kenyon Mason and Graeme Laurie

Healthcare Research Ethics and Law
Regulation, review and responsibility
Hazel Biggs

The Body in Bioethics
Alastair Campbell

About the Series Editor
Professor Sheila McLean is International Bar Association Professor of Law and Ethics in Medicine and Director of the Institute of Law and Ethics in Medicine at the University of Glasgow.

Values in Medicine

What are we really doing to patients?

Donald Evans

Routledge·Cavendish
Taylor & Francis Group
LONDON AND NEW YORK

First published 2008
by Routledge-Cavendish
2 Park Square, Milton Park, Abingdon, Oxon OX14 4RN

Simultaneously published in the USA and Canada
by Routledge-Cavendish
270 Madison Ave, New York, NY 10016

*Routledge-Cavendish is an imprint of the Taylor & Francis Group,
an informa business*

Typeset in Times by
RefineCatch Limited, Bungay, Suffolk
Printed and bound in Great Britain by
TJ International, Padstow, Cornwall

British Library Cataloguing in Publication Data
A catalogue record for this book is available from the British Library

Library of Congress Cataloging-in-Publication Data
Evans, Donald, 1939–
    Values in medicine : what are we really doing to patients? / Donald
Evans.—1st ed.
      p. ; cm.
    Includes bibliographical references.
    ISBN-13: 978-0-415-42468-4 (hbk.)
    ISBN-10: 0-415-42468-2 (hbk.)
    ISBN-13: 978-0-415-42469-1 (pbk.)
    ISBN-10: 0-415-42469-0 (pbk.)

1. Medical ethics.
    [DNLM: 1. Ethics, Medical. W 50 E975v 2008]   I. Title.
    R724.E92 2008
    174.2—dc22
                                                    2007025734

ISBN10: 0-415-42469-0 (pbk)
ISBN13: 978-0-415-42469-1 (pbk)

ISBN10: 0-415-42468-2 (hbk)
ISBN13: 978-0-415-42468-4 (hbk)

eISBN10: 0-203-94042-3 (ebook)
eISBN13: 978-0-203-94042-6 (ebook)

To Ann

Contents

Preface

This book has been some twenty or so years in gestation, the first half of that time I spent in the United Kingdom and the second half in New Zealand. In each place I was stimulated to reflect on a wide range of situations in health care delivery encountered in the process of teaching Health Care Ethics to health professionals. I am particularly grateful to the University of Wales for allowing me to develop an advanced degree scheme in Medical Ethics in the mid-nineteen eighties. This teaching experience, which facilitated extended contact with senior health care professionals from a multiplicity of professions and specialities, afforded a remarkable opportunity to learn of and reflect on a wide range of problems and concerns encountered by those professionals in the course of their many collective years of practice. I shall always be deeply grateful to them for their willingness to share their accounts of these matters. I am also grateful to the University of Otago for my appointment at the Dunedin Medical School where I have faced the very different challenge of teaching medical ethics to medical undergraduates in a hospital setting. The contact with clinical colleagues, patients, policy makers, hospital administrators and students has been invaluable in bringing the complexity of health care decision making into bold relief.

During this period I have enjoyed the benefits of a wide range of contacts with research colleagues in Medicine, Bioethics and Medical Law. I acknowledge the research support of various funding agencies including the European Commission, the UK Department of Health, the World Health Organisation, the Foundation for Research, Science and Technology New Zealand, the Marsden Fund New Zealand, UNESCO and the New Zealand Health Research Council. I also wish to extend my thanks to the many academic colleagues and members of various National and International Committees in Bioethics with whom I have worked over these years and for the intellectual stimulation and collegial support which they have provided.

Many of the ideas in the book have appeared in various learned journals, books and conference proceedings over the years. It has been rewarding to bring these together in a way which will make them available to a wider audience. It has also been interesting to recognise more clearly continuing themes which have shaped and informed my intellectual development in Bioethics.

Donald Evans
Otago, New Zealand
May 2007

Acknowledgements

Chapter 1 is based on my inaugural professorial lecture published by the University of Otago in 1998 which was entitled 'Values in medicine: what are we really doing to our patients?' Some of these ideas were also presented in the paper 'Objectivity, subjectivity and truth in medicine', *Psychologische Medizin* 16(4), 2005, 39–49. The roots of these reflections on the nature of reality go back to a much earlier paper 'Photographs and primitive signs', *Proceedings of the Aristotelian Society* LXXIX (1978), 213–38.

Chapter 2 finds its roots in a very early philosophical paper entitled 'Ethical disagreements and philosophical defences: Wellman's seven ways', *Second Order* IV(2) (1975), 3–10 and is developed in the context of a current research project on Maori Perceptions of Emerging Biotechnologies funded by the New Zealand Foundation for Research, Science and Technology.

Chapter 3 was presented as a guest keynote lecture at the Australasian Meeting of Musculoskeletal Surgeons in 2000 and was later published in the inaugural edition of the *Journal of Philosophy of Surgery and Medicine* 1 (2001), 6–13 entitled 'Mystery in Surgery'.

Chapter 4 discusses ideas presented at a World Health Organisation conference on Resource Allocation in Italy in 1991 which was published in Z. Szawarski and D. Evans (eds), *Solidarity, Justice and Health Care Priorities*, Health Service Studies 8 (Linkoping: Linkoping University Press, 1993), pp. 28–41, as a chapter entitled 'Limits to Care', and further ideas published in D. Greaves and H. Upton (eds), *Philosophical Problems in Health Care* (Aldershot: Avebury, 1996), pp. 159–73 as a chapter entitled 'The Limits of Health Care'; in D.M. Evans, and N. Price, *Ethical Dimensions of the National Waiting Time Project* (Wellington, NZ: Health Funding Authority, 1999); and in a guest lecture published in the *Proceedings of the Colloquium on the Ethical Aspects of Priority Setting and Access to Healthcare* (Calgary: Western Canada Waiting List Project, October 28, 2004), 9–21.

Chapter 5 arose out of a contribution to the European Commission research project on Assisted Reproduction and was published as a chapter entitled 'The Clinical Classification of Infertility' in D.M. Evans (ed.), *Creating the Child* (The Hague: Martinus Nijhoff, 1996), pp. 47–64.

Chapter 6 began as 'The Limits of Perinatal Practice' published in *Proceedings of the First Emirates International Congress on Perinatology* (Abu Dhabi: Center for International Health, 1998), pp. 27–37 and was developed in: a presentation to a colloquium on Medically Assisted Surrogacy at the University of Auckland in 1999 which was later elaborated and published as 'The Interests of the Child in Medically Assisted Surrogacy', *International Family Law* (December 2000), 167–72; and 'Am I my patient's keeper? Some troubling questions in assisted reproduction', *The Emirates Medical Journal* 3 Suppl. (2002), 11–16.

Chapter 7 was published as a chapter in a festschrift to John Harris entitled: *John Harris, his Arguments and his Critics* (Amsterdam: Rodopi, forthcoming). This chapter drew upon ideas contained in 'Pro-attitudes to pre-embryos', a chapter published in the volume D.M. Evans (ed.), *Conceiving the Embryo* (Dordrecht: Martinus Nijhoff, 1996), 27–46, as part of a European Commission-funded research project; 'The Status of the Perinatal Patient', *Proceedings of the First Emirates International Congress on Perinatology* (Abu Dhabi, Center for International Health, 1998), 49–58; and 'Treating the Embryo' in E.V. Cosmi, G.C. Di Renzo, T.H. Bloomfield and D.F. Hawkins (eds), *Recent Advances in Perinatal Medicine* (London: World Scientific, 1999), pp.1–13.

Chapter 8 began as the result of an invitation from the Association for the Advancement of Animal Breeding and Genetics (AAABG) to address the conference on ethical issues in their field. This presentation resulted in a book chapter entitled 'Animals, Ethics and Patents' in M.F. Rothschild and S. Newman (eds), *Intellectual Property Rights in Animal Breeding and Genetics* (Wallington, UK: CABI, 2002), pp. 163–78. I drew on ideas presented there in my Cam Reid Oration 2005 at the conference of the Australia and New Zealand Council for the Care of Animals in Research and Teaching entitled 'Are Animals our Equals?' which was published in *Proceedings of the Australian and New Zealand Council for the Care of Animals in Research and Teaching Conference* (Wellington, NZ: ANZZCART, 2005), pp.15–21.

Chapter 9 is based on ideas developed for the UNESCO curriculum on Medical Ethics, and also builds on ideas included in the book chapters entitled 'Ethicist and Patient: What is their relationship?' in R. Gillon (ed.), *Principles of Health Care Ethics* (Chichester: John Wiley and Sons, 1994), pp. 387–97; and 'Clinical Decisions, Impaired Capacity and the Public Interest', *Analecta Husserliana: The Yearbook of Phenomenological Research* LXIV (2000), 223–37 and a paper entitled 'Ethical Review of Innovative Treatment' which appeared in the *Health Ethics Committee Forum* 14 (2002), 53–63 and 'Ethical Issues in Research, part I: research by stealth' (Washington, D.C.: *Science*/AAAS, 2002).

Chapter 10 is largely the result of work produced for a UNESCO Expert

Working Group on Ethics and Nanotechnology entitled 'Ethics, Nano-technology and Health', in *Nanotechnology Ethics and Politics* (Paris: UNESCO Publishing, 2007).

Chapter 11 emerged from the discussion of the conception of the useful-ness of Literature and the Arts in teaching Medical Ethics. Some of the ideas were developed in a paper in the *Journal of Medical Ethics, Medical Human-ities Edition* 27 (2001), 30–4 entitled 'Imagination and Medical Education'. Others ideas in this chapter were discussed in a keynote address to a National Gerontology Conference in Wellington, New Zealand entitled 'Ethical Issues for Older People and their Carers' published in *Proceedings of the Wellington Gerontology Conference* (Wellington, NZ: Senior Citizens Unit of the Social Policy Agency, 1999) and in a paper entitled 'Caring for the Elderly', in *New Zealand Bioethics Journal* 2(2) (2001), 19–23.

I am grateful to the editors and publishers of the following items, fully referenced above, for permission to use those pieces either as a chapter or as a contribution to a chapter in this volume:

Psychologische Medizin, 'Objectivity, Subjectivity and Truth in Medicine'.
Journal of Philosophy of Surgery and Medicine, 'Mystery in Surgery'.
University of Linkoping Press, 'Limits to Care'.
Avebury, 'The Limits of Health Care'.
Martinus Nijhoff, 'The Clinical Classification of Infertility'.
International Family Law, 'The Interests of the Child in Medically Assisted Surrogacy'.
Rodopi, 'Qualifying as a person'.
Martinus Nijhoff, 'Pro-attitudes to Pre-embryos'.
ANZZCART, 'Are Animals our Equals?'
Health Ethics Committee (HEC) Forum, 'Ethical Review of Innovative Treatment'.
UNESCO, 'Ethics, Nanotechnology and Health'.
Journal of Medical Humanities, 'Imagination and Medical Education'.

Acknowledgements are due for permission to reproduce the following:

Figures 1.3 and 1.4, Katsushika Hokusai (1760–1849), woodcut, number 8 from the One Hundred Views of Mount Fuji series, reproduced in *One Hundred Views of Mount Fuji*, G. Braziller (ed.) (London: Thames & Hudson, 1988).
Figure 8.1, Joseph Wright of Derby, *An Experiment on a Bird in an Air Pump* (1768), oil painting. Courtesy of the National Gallery, London.

T. S. Eliot, *East Coker* extract from *Collected Poems 1909–1962* by T. S. Eliot. World permission excluding US from Faber & Faber, London; US permission from Harcourt, Inc., Orlando, Florida, USA.

Philip Larkin, extract from *The Old Fools*, from *Collected Poems* by Philip Larkin. World permission excluding US from Faber & Faber, London; US permission from Farrar, Straus & Giroux Inc., New York, USA.

Louis MacNeice, *Prayer before birth.* World permission from David Higham Associates, London.

Siegfried Sassoon, *The One-legged Man* from *Collected Poems (1908–1956)* by Siegfried Sassoon. World permission from Barbara Levy Literary Agency, 64 Greenhill, Hampstead High Street, London NW3 5TZ.

Introduction

In the age of evidence-based medicine, regard for objectivity is the *sine qua non* of a good practitioner. But how realisable is objectivity in the doctor–patient relationship and in the development and delivery of health care? It is tempting to account for the difficulties in eliminating uncertainty in medicine simply by referring to practical obstacles embodied in isolating the truth from fiction, or knowledge from hunches or opinions. Such explanations make a critical assumption, viz. that the incontrovertible truth is buried somewhere in the world of nature or human nature simply awaiting discovery.

Of course, it would be irresponsible to be careless about the truth in both the quest for knowledge and in the doctor–patient relationship. But the drive to eliminate uncertainty and establish incontrovertible data in health care settings embodies many dangers. The contribution of science to the development of modern medicine has afforded remarkable progress in the delivery of effective health care. But it has also tended to remove the patients' experience of ill health from centre stage and replace it with the insights of experts who know better what their health needs are, what treatments are indicated and what constitutes successful health outcomes. Although such a change is attractive it has posed serious threats to the doctor–patient relationship and to the well-being of patients.

This book sets out to examine the critical assumption in a number of areas of clinical practice and research and, in so doing, find a proper place for ethical values in health care. In various ways it argues that ethical dimensions of clinical practice do not always arise from reflection on, or reactions to, undisputed facts. They are sometimes, on the contrary, to be found at the level of the determination of the facts themselves. Recognition of this places the experience of the patient firmly back on centre stage, not as an expert but rather as the indispensable arbiter of what the facts are which are really significant in health care delivery. But this is not to underestimate the crucial role which science plays in modern medicine. Rather it is to identify its proper place in assessing and meeting people's health needs. The book might therefore be described as an attempt to encourage a modesty in medicine which would preserve, or if necessary restore, what is best and most valuable in medical practice.

Chapter 1

What are we really doing to patients?

We have all, from time to time, experienced debilitating illness. Many of us have faced serious illness or its possibility, or faced the uncertainties and dangers of pregnancy, or of trauma and so on. Almost without exception on these occasions we have consulted our doctor wanting to know what is wrong with us, or what is the solution to our problem to ensure continued health. We have depended on the doctor's diagnostic and therapeutic skills and been assured by authoritative answers to our questions. It is not difficult therefore to succumb to the temptation to perceive the doctor as the custodian of a treasury of secure and objective knowledge about us in these extremely important areas of our life. It is also understandable that doctors too will be tempted to think that they can, with some authority, determine what we really need, and be confident of what they are really doing to us in the clinic. But are things as straightforward as this?

The search for precision in our description of the world and the related quest to secure our knowledge of the world about us started long before the beginnings of modern medicine. It characterised the history of Philosophy from its beginnings. These two enterprises are often referred to in terms of the relation between language and reality. The first concerns the question of what it is that distinguishes a meaningless jumble of marks or sounds from a written or spoken sentence. How precisely does language latch on to reality, to the world which we inhabit? The second concerns the question of whether we can be certain that our view of the world about us is authoritative. Each of these questions applies to the world of medicine in which we are specifically concerned to describe the human condition as carefully as possible and extend our knowledge of the same so as to identify its ills and develop means to provide help to those in need.

There are two reasons for approaching this quest in medicine and health care by the circuitous route of reviewing the manner in which philosophers have dealt with the general issues. The first is to avoid the impression that the philosopher is somehow prejudiced against medicine and those who profess it when he or she engages in critical reflection upon its subject matter. The philosophical worries that concern us in this chapter apply equally in all realms of human activity from shoe repairing or cobbling to administering health care. Socrates was condemned as a meddler in the business of others for asking questions about the nature of their activities. Indeed even cobblers were not beyond the range of his interests. Philosophers have, more recently, been similarly condemned by doctors for reflecting upon their practice.[1]

The second reason is to enable us to ask the correct questions about what we are doing when we describe health and illness states and prescribe interventions to deal with those states. In short it is to help us determine how much sense there is in the question which forms the title of this chapter and to explore the consequences of the temptation to think that we can or ought to endeavour to give a definitive answer to it as it stands. In particular the object will be both to illustrate how values enter inevitably into the picture and to point out the crucial importance of this dimension of the language of health care.

The innocence of language

How would we respond if asked to describe the real significance of the following images? (See Figs 1.1 and 1.2 below.)

We might imagine that it is more challenging to formulate a response to the first than to the second image. Yet, as we shall see a little later, each response runs into the same logical problems.

Philosophers are often thought to be preoccupied with language. There is a good reason for this interest for the central question of Philosophy from its beginnings has centred around how it is that sounds we utter and signs we make and write can be significant. For example, what is it that gives the two images meaning? Or more generally, when we make claims about the world around us how is it that the noises we utter or the marks we make relate to the real world? What is it which makes it possible to refer to things in the world and to make utterances which can be true or false as opposed to meaningless?

The language of facts

The most influential and enduring answer to this question goes back to Plato and has survived through Augustine to this century when many believed it

Figure 1.1

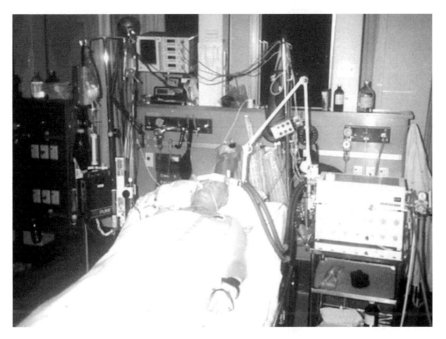

Figure 1.2

found its apotheosis in the early work of Ludwig Wittgenstein.[2] He was to go on to make fundamental criticisms of the account[3] which we shall note.[4] Despite these criticisms and as testimony to the power of the temptation to seek answers to the question: 'What are we really doing when we say something?', newer versions of the account have been espoused by contemporary philosophers.[5]

The account has an immediate appeal to common sense in that it appears to reflect the way in which we teach children to read and associate signs with things in the world about them, that is by pointing. The claim is that the fundamental activity involved in language is that of naming. A simple word or sign has an immediate relationship with what it signifies, viz. its meaning is the object it names. Of course there can be more complex signs which get their meaning from a combination of the simple signs which make them up. Hieroglyphics present us with a perspicuous model of this account where relatively simple pictures denote individual objects and they can play a part in a more complex picture enabling us to say things about the relationship between the objects referred to in the world – that is to make an assertion. However, from Plato onwards philosophers quested for even more simple signs than these primitive pictures. They wanted signs which would rule out ambiguity and somehow link with reality in an unmediated way – that is in a way which did not depend on human agency at all. This would guarantee an authentic relation with reality eliminating arbitrariness.

Perhaps one of the best approximations to this primitive relationship is found in colour words. If we wish to teach a child the meaning of a colour word then we use the word in relation to objects we point out bearing the colour – the yellow teddy bear on the page of the book, the banana on the table, the custard in the dish, and so on. We then hope that the child will catch on to the sequence and be able to go on to identify other objects which are similar in this specific regard. When it is able so to do we believe that we have established the immediate relation between the word and the colour for the child – that it has learned the meaning of the word by recognising its bearer other than by understanding a definition, as no definition (which would be something akin to a description of yellow in more basic terms) is possible. But we cannot achieve this with a blind child precisely because we cannot confront her with the object which is the bearer of the name 'yellow' and therefore we cannot establish the immediate relationship. That child is forever cut off from understanding the word. On this account, according to Plato 'the essence of speech is the composition of names'.[6]

But in order to say something it is necessary to do more than simply identify things; one has to assert something about the relation between those things. For example, to point at a cat and utter 'cat', or to a mat and utter 'mat' is not to say anything. But to link them as in 'the cat is on the mat' is to make a claim which could be true or false depending on the circumstances which prevail in the world. For this reason it is the composition of names which Plato thought was ultimately important for meaning. Here too there has been a quest for such combinations – propositions – which are absolutely unambiguous, such as Wittgenstein's elementary propositions, which were supposed to be primitive pictures of reality. But the big question philosophers had to answer was whether such activities as naming and picturing could be primitive in order to secure a link between language and the world.

There are many difficulties attaching to each of these phases of an account of meaning but before visiting them briefly let us ask what could be the relevance of such interests to the world of medicine and health care. Here too, of course, we are committed to trying to understand the world with which we are presented, identifying particular features of that world – such as biological phenomena – and making sense of them, that is seeing their significance in relation to other features of the world such as their role in determining the health state of a person presenting with the feature in question. The vastly increased influence of science in the practice of medicine over the past three centuries has led us to believe that we have made great progress in furthering our understanding of the human condition. The authority of scientific descriptions and explanations of bodily states has replaced what are now seen as rather speculative and fanciful descriptions and explanations, bringing us closer up against the realities of health and disease. Consider, as a simple example, Harvey's discovery of the function of the heart as a pump circulating the blood and thereby oxygenating the tissues of the body. It is hard for us to imagine the kind of sense made of so many physiological conditions prior to this advance in understanding or, indeed, what more accurate account of the matter could ever be given beyond more detailed information as to how such a function is facilitated in terms of electrical discharges, and so on. It is here that we have to avoid the temptation alluded to in the case of the philosopher who was concerned with the more general problems of meaning for fear of attributing more authority to our descriptions and understanding than we are entitled, as we shall later see in a number of contexts of health care provision.

What then are the problems attaching to the notion of the innocence of the language of facts which is bound up with the alleged fundamental activities of naming and picturing? Consider the first phase of naming particulars. Is the activity of pointing really an unambiguous activity and could it be the fundamental activity in language use? Wittgenstein came to see that his claim that 'a name cannot be dissected any further by means of a definition: it is a primitive sign'[7] could not stand as an account of the beginnings of language for one already has to be a master of language, in a sense, before naming is possible at all. Pointing, the activity involved in ostensive definition, is not unambiguous and the person being instructed might well misunderstand what is meant by the teacher. To take the most plausible example discussed earlier, viz. the colour yellow, we must note that pointing to a banana and saying 'yellow' does not inevitably make the link between the sign and the colour. The learner might think that we refer to the shape of the object, or to the number of objects, or to its situation of being at rest or a multitude of other things. Unless he is aware that we are referring to the colour of the object then there is no guarantee that he will take our pointing as we intend him to. But the presence of this 'colour space' at which to station the word 'yellow' assumes a whole social practice of making colour distinctions which has to be absorbed to a degree by the child before the specific naming of colours to a child will be possible. Up to a point then, what one *really* sees is determined by a whole series of expectations and shaped by familiar practices and contexts.

Let us return to our first image for a moment to illustrate the point. To ask what is it that we really see when confronted by the squiggle in isolation is puzzling. It might be something significant or not – no more than a squiggle. But now view the same squiggle in context and it takes on an unmistakable significance for the viewer who has mastered certain skills. Some of those skills are commonplace, such as our reading of two-dimensional drawings, a skill we master very early in life.

This woodcut (see p. 6), is number eight of the One Hundred Views of Mount Fuji by Hokusai.[8] It is his only drawing showing the blemish on the perfect form of the mountain – the projection on the right-hand side. This

Figure 1.3 Katsushika Hokusai (1760–1849), woodcut, number 8 from *One Hundred Views of Mount Fuji*.

was a representation of the crater formation left by the great eruption of 1707 which formed Mount Hoei. Though one might not be able to identify the background shape as Mount Fuji, nevertheless one recognises it as a mountain or a large hill pretty easily. One might be surprised to discover that our squiggle is part of the mountain profile.

Have we now discovered its significance? Can we say what we really saw earlier in the paper? The answer is no for if we place it in another context we shall see something quite different.

This electrocardiogram is one taken to trace the heartbeat of the author prior to the implementation of anaesthetic procedures for surgery (see Figs. 1.4 and 1.5 opposite). The skills which have to be mastered to invest this kind of significance in the squiggle are rarer, of course, but no less social or public in character. But we might, in a moment of revelry, note an interesting feature of the image (see Fig. 1.6).

Imagine the patient's concern if the attending clinician employing this trace at the bedside had remarked on the elegance of Mount Fuji in the patient's records. This would not merely have been highly unlikely, it would also have been a total distraction. The trace was not such a representation; rather it was made up of the T wave and the U wave in the cycle of his heartbeat – the former representing the ventricular muscle repolarisation of

Figure 1.4

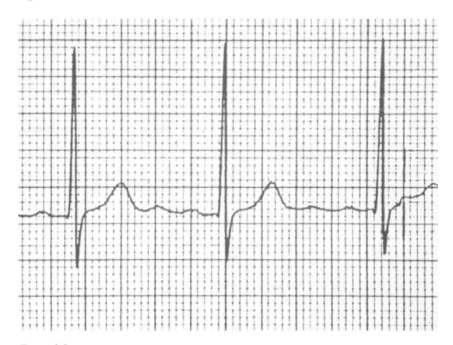

Figure 1.5

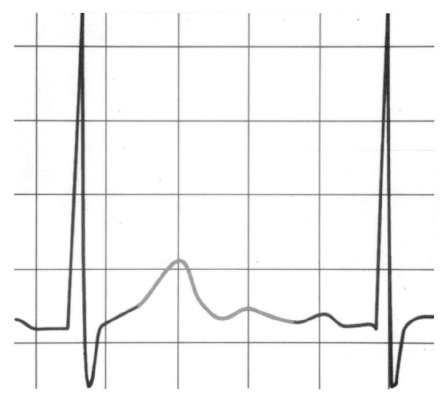

Figure 1.6

the heartbeat and the U wave being of, as yet, uncertain significance. What it was, however, could not have been recognised in the absence of other reading skills facilitating the identification of the squiggle as a phase in the heartbeat, skills attaching to the theory of muscle activity and electrical discharge as summed up in Fig. 1.7 opposite.[9]

Thus the relation between the sign and the signified is not an innocent one, is not sacrosanct and immediate, but is one which is mediated by some kind of social convention.[10]

No more could the relation of picturing be primitive as was hoped for in the case of elementary propositions. Wittgenstein came to recognise that the activity of picturing was also subject to social conventions – pictures are construed according to various rules of projection which, as we saw in our last example, can vary their significance.[11] This is even true of photographs whose causal relation to the objects before the camera lens tempted both early photographers[12] and recent semiologists to think that they were messages without a code, 'having the power to transmit literal inform-ation without forming it by means of discontinuous lines and rules of

The waves of the electrocardiogram—P, QRS, T, and U—are indicated. The measurements of the PR interval, QRS complex, ST segment, and QT interval are identified on the right.

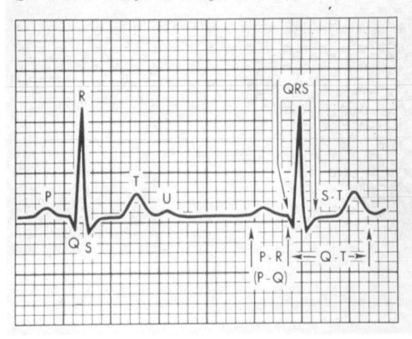

Figure 1.7

transformation'.[13] Thus, as it has been suggested, the most important feature of a photograph might be its caption in that what one reads there fixes what one sees in the image. Consider the example of the photograph of the intensive care scene presented above (see Fig. 1.2). No doubt most people would be able to say a great deal about the photograph, even to the point of recognising its intensive care context. But is there no more to it? If we view it over two quite different captions we see a radical shift in its significance (see Figs. 1.8 and 1.9).

Discussions of death with dignity and numbers of celebrated reports of patients' relatives' efforts to secure the withdrawal of 'life sustaining' efforts of the sort pictured stand in sharp contrast to the public relations activities of the medical technology industry and the enthusiasms of uncritical admirers of high tech medicine. Uncritical use of such technology was reflected in a *Lancet* editorial in the late 1970s which noted that it had become difficult to die in a UK hospital without a statutory period on a ventilator – the last rite of modern medicine. In other cases failure to provide such treatment has led

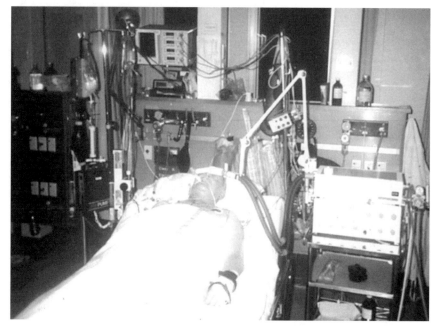

**Vex not his ghost. O, let him pass!
He hates him that would upon the
rack of this tough world stretch
him out longer.**

The Earl of Kent, *King Lear*
William Shakespeare

Figure 1.8

to cries of 'murder'.[14] Coming to the photograph from either one of these perspectives fixes the image for the viewer. Many of us, no doubt, oscillate between the two, grappling with the distinction between prolonging life on the one hand and prolonging the process of dying on the other.

The language of values

We have seen that there are considerable problems encountered in the effort to try to secure the relationship between language and commonplace properties of objects in the world. It should not be surprising therefore to discover that the problems which arise in the effort to hold on to the naming account of meaning when we come to value terms such as 'good' are much more onerous. Yet, for understandable reasons, this has been attempted. G.E. Moore was very concerned that if one moved away from the idea that

VENTILATION MANAGEMENT

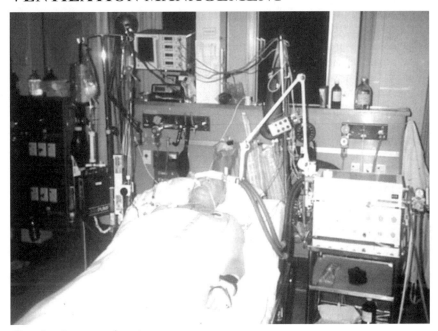

Optimize patient care

Figure 1.9

recognition of the property of goodness was involved in moral judgements then morality would become a relative matter – it would lose its absolute and authoritative character. For him this would undermine the significance of moral judgements as then things might appear good to an observer in certain connections while they might not appear good in other connections. Or some observers might regard events, and so on as good whereas others would judge them as bad. This would, he thought, be a disaster. Thus he contended that whenever we judge an action to be good we do so on the basis of having perceived the intrinsic and unanalysable property of goodness in it, not some will o' the wisp property which might attach to the action here and not there, or in this observer's view but not in that of another. He was hankering after precisely the relation we outlined earlier when we reviewed the learning of colour words by ostensive definition. Indeed he uses the selfsame example, 'yellowness', to illustrate his point.[15] As the term yellow cannot be defined in more simple terms than itself and can be learned only by confronting and naming it, so it is with goodness. To try to define goodness in simpler terms would be to commit the naturalistic fallacy – this would allow for one person to see something as good and another as bad depending on which terms they chose to define the word.

Though Moore's motive for resorting to the view that goodness is an intrinsic property – viz. to retain the objectivity and authority of moral judgements – was admirable, the attempt failed on a number of counts. Even if the meaning of 'yellow' could be secured by ostensive definition – a position we have already criticised precisely because it neglects the social context of the activity of naming – it would not help Moore's account of the significance of moral terms. For example, Moore cannot tell us how the property goodness is perceived other than to say that it is intuited. He is forced to say that goodness, unlike a colour, is a non-natural property. But, as has been pointed out by Stephen Toulmin, this is simply verbiage covering up a wrong classification as would be true of the townsman who, having mistakenly defined rams as being small bulls, tried to save his classification by claiming that he had meant non-tauroid bulls. In fact it can be shown conclusively that rams are not bulls at all. Thus there is little difference, thinks Toulmin, between calling goodness a non-natural property and saying that it is not a property at all.[16]

Though his motives were admirable, Moore created more problems than he solved by employing the analogy between moral discourse and material object language in the way he did. In pointing this out we shall see that the crucial contribution made by social context to meaning is even more marked in the use of value terms than in material object talk and that it is in this direction that the authority of moral language is to be found. Material object language of the form 'x has the property y' as in 'the ball is red' does not exhaust the language of facts. Yet Moore's choice of the colour analogy in an attempt to shore up moral discourse and establish an immediate relation between value language and the world plays into the hands of the moral sceptic as it encourages us to think, when the attempt fails, that moral discourse is not concerned with facts at all and that it is somehow hopelessly relative.

This divide between fact and value has figured prominently in philosophy since David Hume.[17] Some philosophers have been tempted to explain the use of moral terms as expressions of feeling rather than statements of fact, as prescriptive and evaluative rather than descriptive.[18] The distinction found its ultimate and most devastating expression with respect to the significance of moral language in logical positivism, most popularly articulated by A.J. Ayer.[19] On this account there are three kinds of propositions. First, logical propositions which are necessarily true and which make no claim about the world of fact, such as is the case with the proposition: 'All bachelors are unmarried.' Second, there are empirical propositions whose truth or falsity is established by rules of verification. These rules may be more or less complex, such as the rules for checking the number of chairs in a room or the rules for checking the distance of the earth from the sun. Nevertheless, no matter how complex the rules might be, to understand the proposition is to understand something of the method of verifying it. Third, there are propositions involving value terms like 'good', such as 'Promise keeping is good'. It turns out that this third group are not really propositions though they appear to be claiming that something has some property or another. They have no means of empirical verification and are thus branded as expressions of feeling. Thus 'Promise keeping is good' is equivalent to 'Hurrah for promise keeping', and 'Lying is bad' is equivalent to 'Boo to lying', and the question of the truth or falsity of the utterances does not arise. Hence the labelling of the theory as the 'Boo–Hurrah theory'. Purported propositions of religion, aesthetics and morality all come under this classification.

It would be quite mistaken to believe, in the light of this analysis, that morality was simply a subjective and hopelessly relative business. We can get clearer about the nature of moral reasoning and moral judgement by asking what kind of response we make when we are challenged to justify a particular moral judgement or when we seek to evaluate an action. We never, in fact, respond by saying that we have somehow observed the property of goodness in the action. Rather we proceed to give reasons for our judgement or apply criteria of evaluation to the action. For example, we will be concerned to discover whether the action judged promotes well-being or causes harm, or maybe whether there is a balance of harm or benefit produced. On the other hand we might be concerned to discover whether the action was one that was expected of the person concerned or whether it was something over and above the call of duty. Or perhaps we shall note that the motive for the action was suspect, or admirable. We might look to see whether it was self-seeking or altruistic, premeditated or impulsive, generous or mean, honest or devious, and so on. All these considerations and more are involved in the making of moral judgements; they mark the limits of what counts as moral judgement – limits which are not fixed by the whim of individuals but by public rules of language.[20] Someone careless of making some or many of these distinctions we might call morally insensitive whether in commission of their own acts or in the face of the actions of others. Someone who deliberately flouts the standards embodied in them we would call immoral or even evil. But their lack is not one of ignorance for, apart from the psychopath, they will know perfectly well what such distinctions come to.

However, the activity of moral evaluation is even more complex than the foregoing description suggests for there might be considerable disagreement in the application of the criteria, or in the manner in which tensions between these criteria are handled. It is here that profound disagreements can arise which might still give the impression that the whole business is irredeemably subjective. Such an impression would, however, be wrongheaded. Let us take the application of the criteria as an example. We noted that the question of the harmfulness of an action was morally significant. But to decide whether an action is harmful or not is more difficult than to decide whether a given banana is yellow or green. There might be disagreement as to what constitutes a harm. This difficulty arises commonly in cases which are part of the subject matter of medical ethics.

The celebrated topic of abortion offers us an ideal case as this is a candidate for providing the most polarised views on the rights and wrongs of clinical intervention. The pole positions are generally occupied by, on the one hand, those who are concerned to represent the interests of the unborn child and, on the other, those who are keen to protect the freedom of women to choose what shall happen to their bodies. How can we go about reconciling such disparate views as those which regard abortion as an act of murder and those which regard it, in extreme cases, as the removal of offending biological tissue? We should first note that that latter description would indeed be an extreme and unrepresentative description of abortion for most pro-abortionists who recognise that, because of the special nature of the tissue involved, termination of pregnancy for most women is a far more traumatic issue than the removal of an inflamed appendix. Nevertheless it is a possible view espoused by some.

At the heart of the dispute is the question of the status of the human embryo or foetus. Is the embryo or foetus a human being, is it a child as yet unborn or is it something else? Science is unable to provide an answer to this question and its inability to do so has nothing to do with lack of information. If we take the case of the pre-embryo (a human embryo before the fourteenth day of gestation when individuation occurs) we will see that the leap forward in information about its biological nature has not reduced moral disagreement about use of abortifacients to prevent implantation of the embryo. While science can now tell us that the pre-embryo is an aggregate of un-differentiated cells which has the potential of developing naturally into two embryos, or artificially into a number considerably greater than two, this does not settle the issue of whether the pre-embryo is a human being. For some, as we shall see later in the book, this information has made a difference to the way they view the early human embryo but for others it has made no difference – and there is no logical inconsistency in this despite appearances to the contrary.[21] Logic does not demand that the biological facts commit us to seeing that the pre-embryo is not a human being. What the pre-embryo really is is determined by more than its biology. Indeed there is a good case for saying that far from the facts determining our moral views about such matters our moral beliefs determine the facts. For example, if one espouses the view that human life is a gift from God and that any human interference in its development constitutes an affront to human dignity and borders on the sacrilegious, one will tend to see the pre-embryo as a human soul. Others have argued, similarly, that our account of human nature and human needs is determined by our moral views rather than the reverse.[22] But this is not to make morality a purely subjective matter for, as each of the authors referred to are at pains to point out, how any individual sees the world is necessarily related to a public context such as that embodied in the religious belief detailed in the example.

The innocence of medical language

We have already noted that the consequences of succumbing to the temptation to provide a universal answer to our question – 'What are we really doing to patients?' – are far more serious than those which have followed the attempts of philosophers to provide a universal and authoritative account of meaning or significance. It is therefore of extreme importance to note both that the temptation does express itself in medicine and that, while it is philosophical in character, the practical results of succumbing to its charms can be extremely serious for patients and for those committed to care for them. Recognition of the lost innocence of medical language is a necessary stage in the protection of patients in that it will bring the patient perspective into view and thus curb the *hubris* to which modern medicine is prone.

Let us consider three illustrative areas in clinical intervention and health care provision generally where this temptation expresses itself. We shall do this with a view to clarifying both the claim that the temptation exists in Medicine and the serious consequences of providing the kinds of answers it demands. Later in the book we shall consider each of these problem areas in more detail.

Identifying treatments

We have noted that the provision of termination of pregnancy might be variously perceived by prospective patients. However, given the emotive nature of much of the discussion surrounding such cases and its rather high-profile exposure in the media we would be well advised to seek a more mundane example of clinical intervention to illustrate the pervasiveness, subtlety and import of the temptation in the treatment of patients.

Let us consider the example of hysterectomy as investigated in a research paper by Drellich and Beiber.[23] The authors of the paper interviewed 23 patients who had undergone a hysterectomy for both benign and malignant disease of the reproductive tract. They discovered that these patients held a variety of beliefs about the nature and function of the uterus and that these beliefs profoundly affected their perceptions of the nature of the clinical intervention which they had experienced. We might wish to ask whether these beliefs were true or false, whether the resulting perceptions of the patients were rational or irrational, whether they were partly formative of outcomes and in that sense inextricably bound up with the reality of the patient's state whether true or false in themselves, and finally whether they made any difference to the identity of the clinical intervention undergone.

The dominant beliefs held by the patients about the nature of the uterus were six in all, viz. that it was a:

(i)   childbearing organ;
(ii)   excretory organ;
(iii) regulator and controller of bodily processes;
(iv)   sexual organ;
(v)   reservoir of strength and vitality;
(vi)   maintainer of youth and attractiveness.

It is pretty clear what numbers of these come to. The ability to bear children is clearly sacrificed when the uterus is removed (i) and further it is commonly accepted that hormonal changes produced by the removal of the uterus accelerate changes which are associated with ageing (vi). Not only are these beliefs readily understandable but they would also be thought of as accurate or true by informed clinicians. Given the intimate relationship between sexual activity and the reproductive process it is not surprising that the organ is associated with the former. Whether the physiological changes involved in the removal of the organ causally affect sexual desire and drive (iii) might not be established to everyone's satisfaction, nevertheless it is a natural source of anxiety in the prospective patient, and the belief – even if not founded on physiological fact – might turn out to be self-fulfilling despite reassurances which might be given to the patient to the contrary. Similar considerations apply to (ii), (iii) and (v). Women reported that they believed periods cleaned them out and that, connectedly, the inability to get rid of waste might have deleterious effects upon them (ii); surges of energy corresponded with stages of the menstrual cycle facilitating extremely productive periods of work (v) and finally that the uterus provided a centrally important control in the regulation of bodily processes (iii). How much truth each of these contains in terms of physiological and affective processes of the human body as such is a matter of debate. Yet, even if such beliefs are thought of as far-fetched or unlikely, the fact that they are entertained by the patient can have definite effects upon recovery and self-image. Thus we need to ask whether what it is that is really done to the patient can be determined in isolation from individual consideration of the role which each believes the uterus plays in her life.

We do have an agreed clinical description of the surgical procedure each of these patients had undergone – each had had her uterus removed. It is also important that their treatment is capable of a general description of this kind. Without such general descriptions it would be impossible to initiate surgeons into the diagnostic and therapeutic techniques based upon physiological understandings of the working of the human body as such. Here we owe much to the advances of scientific knowledge and to the refined techniques of abdominal surgery which are based on generalisable propositions about human biology irrespective of whose body we happen to be operating upon. The growth of knowledge in medicine has been closely related to the increased emphasis upon general descriptions of this sort. The increased contribution of science to medical practice since Harvey's functional account of the heart and circulation marked a move away from the traditional way of viewing disease. From the time of the Greeks disease was seen as an aspect of the health of the whole person and was visualised in terms of harmony and equilibrium. Disease consisted in a disturbance of the harmony of the whole man and not as being located in some specific part of man. With the Enlightenment came the birth of modern science and a very different view of disease took root. We have already referred to the work of Harvey, an early example of the new science in medicine, in which the body was seen largely in terms of function, or rather the functioning of sub-systems of the organism as a whole. The body now began to be viewed as a complex machine in which component parts played their part in a series of separate systems and organs. As a result of this change disease was now thought to be located in parts of the body and a subject of empirical observation, its nature being capable of generalisations in the forms of laws. Under this model of disease the independent objective observer replaced the patient as the expert on the patient's condition and the consensus of the medical experts replaced the importance of the patient's experience and interpretation of his illness. The doctor became the expert understanding better than the patient the disease processes in the patient – processes now seen as being both objective in that they could be described in value-neutral terms and determinate in that their presence could be demonstrated by empirical tests. In all this change the sense of the purpose of the whole organism disappeared and the divide between the body and personhood developed.[24]

But it is as dangerous to overestimate the contribution of science to medicine as it is to underestimate it. While modern medicine is greatly indebted to sophisticated sciences such as anatomy and physiology they do not make the practice of medicine a science. Indeed these are not in themselves medical but part of the science of biology, which is interested in man as no more than one in an indefinite number of animal species and whose truths are expressed in law-like generalisations. But the age-old practical – as opposed to scientific – task of medicine has not changed with the advent of the new scientific approach. It is to take care of the health of patients with the mandate of society and insofar as the sciences assist in this they are welcome allies. But the practice of medicine remains a social practice, a practice older than the new science, performed for centuries without the aid of science as we know it. The doctor works with individual patients armed with the abstract and universal knowledge of the natural order of the human body but in the context of personal and individual circumstances where her work is more akin to an art than to a science. She ignores the patient's narrative at her peril for it is the patient for whom she has to care and not simply his body. The significance of the clinical phenomena is cashed properly only in the context of the life of the patient.[25]

Thus with our hysterectomy cases we have to ask what it was which the surgeon did to each of the patients. If we rely on the mechanical scientific model we have to say that he did the same thing to each of the patients, whereas the findings of the researchers were quite removed from this. Herein lies the danger of succumbing to the temptation of elevating one description to the status of the authoritative account of what was really happening in the lives of these patients. The common physiological feature of the events they endured is factual but the fact that it is common to them all does not make it the defining feature of their experience. For some they had lost their youthfulness, for others their attractiveness as lovers, and so on. Thus the procedure to which they consented was importantly a different procedure for some than it was for others. Maybe they would all have chosen to go the way of the surgery given their lives over again but the price each paid, the significance of the surgical act, the reality with which they had to come to terms was not the same in each case. To ignore these matters in the approach to treatment and simply to concentrate on the physiological facts would be to run the risk of leaving untouched vital constituents of the clinical cases and in so doing jeopardising the best interests of the prospective patients.

Identifying treatment outcomes

In these times of economic stringency and soaring demand in health care provision we have come to hear a great deal about efficiency in the use of resources. Health Care Economics has burgeoned as a sub-discipline and we have seen the vigorous application of cost-effective and cost–benefit analysis in the field. There can be no justification for leaving some patients untreated because resources have been squandered in the treatment of others due to inefficiencies in either the design or the execution of programmes of care. Where aimed-for outcomes are agreed then it is thus right to employ cost-effective analysis to seek the most efficient means of achieving those outcomes where those means have been subjected to adequate ethical scrutiny. For example, where two chemotherapy regimes are thought to produce equally good long-term outcomes but one is vastly more expensive than the other it would be unacceptable to opt for the expensive regime, other things being equal. However, other things might not be equal in that the short-term side-effects of the cheaper regime might be so horrendous that a sensitive clinician would object to subjecting her patients to the rigours of the treatment. Here we would run up against an ethical objection to the most efficient use of resources in terms of achieving the long-term benefits.

However, cost–benefit analysis creates much greater problems for here the identification of the aimed-for outcome is itself part of the procedure. The analysis is designed to enable the health care manager to deploy his resources in such a way as to maximise the benefit that is produced. Thus the ends of the treatment regimes are themselves the subject of measurement, enabling comparisons. There are considerable philosophical problems encountered in such measurement and comparison which have been long debated, especially since the utilitarian theories of Bentham and Mill appeared on the scene.[26] Notable among them is the impossibility of weighing incommensurables: how, for example, can we rank the undesirability of blindness with that of intense pain, or with the threat of a foreshortened life, or with severe disfigurement, or with immobility or childlessness? These problems are intensified when we try to compare the childlessness of one person with the immobility of another and that in turn with the pain of another, and so on. We shall later ask whether attempts to provide common measures of these kinds of suffering, such as are found in health economics theories, are doomed to failure.[27]

The problem we shall address here, however, concerns the connected and difficult question of the identification of outcomes. What shall we regard as the successful outcome of a clinical intervention and who shall define it? Until we have satisfactorily identified what constitutes a successful outcome then we shall not even be able to begin the difficult task of choosing between them. There is a danger, once again, that the manager will be tempted to opt for the straightforwardly measurable outcome and that this will coincide with the allegedly definitive description of the physiological, biochemical, or some other functional account of bodily systems.

Consider an interesting piece of research on outcome measurement which perfectly illustrates the problem.[28] Seventy-five consecutive patients from one group practice whose mild hypertension was well controlled by means of a variety of hypotensive drugs were asked to complete a quality-of-life questionnaire. The treating doctors and the close companions of the patients were also asked to complete the questionnaire. The overall results divided the responses into three classifications of assessment: (i) improved quality of life; (ii) worse quality of life; and (iii) no change in quality of life. The results are reproduced in Table 1.1 below.

The clinicians' estimates of the success of their interventions in improving the quality of life of their patients are startlingly out of line with the assessments of the patients and frighteningly out of line with the assessments of those closest to the patients. For example, less than half the patients (48%) felt that there had been any improvement though 100% of the clinicians believed an improvement had been achieved. The comparison with the relatives' assessments is little short of incredible in that only one relative believed an improvement had been secured (1.3%). One might understandably ask why such discrepancies occurred. The answer in part is plain to see. The gap between the clinicians' judgements on the one hand and that of the patients and relatives on the other can be attributed to the simple fact that the clinicians had one measurable feature of their patients' condition in mind, viz., bringing the diastolic blood pressure below 100mmHg. None of the patients

Table 1.1 Results of Quality of Life Responses

	Improved			No change			Worse		
	Doctor	Patient	Relative	Doctor	Patient	Relative	Doctor	Patient	Relative
Male	34	10	1	0	20	0	0	4	33
Female	41	26	0	0	12	0	0	3	41
Total	75	36	1	0	32	0	0	7	74

Adapted from Jachuck et al., 'The effect of hypotensive drugs on the quality of life', Journal of the Royal College of General Practitioners 32 (1982), 103–5.

had complained about their treatment and thus no adverse events were recorded. We must remember that the doctors' judgement was a quality-of-life judgement. Yet no account was taken of the context of these reduced readings in the lives of the patients.

Once the latter move was made, three classifications of changes in quality of life emerged: mild, moderate and severe. The 74 relatives' ratings of impairment of various parameters of the patients' experience came out as shown in Table 1.2 below.

That almost one half of the patients were perceived by those close to them to have a moderately impaired quality of life and almost one third a severely impaired quality of life is worrying, given the total ignorance of the treating clinician of any impairment whatsoever.

The impairment of sexual activity was not measurable across the whole spectrum of patients as numbers of the closest relatives (25) were not in a position to assess it. Nevertheless of the 50 who were able to assess this feature of impairment of quality of life due to the treatment, 64% claimed that current sexual interest in the patient was either nil or was very much reduced, there being no discernible difference between male and female patients in this respect.

The conclusion of the researchers in this study is worthy of note:

> The deteriorations in the faculties of life observed in this study do not leave any clinical signs for the doctor to detect during clinical assessment, but they certainly affect the quality of life and create problems in social, marital and occupational readjustment.[29]

The lesson is clear. If we succumb to the temptation to elevate the medical description of the outcome to a position of definitive importance then we shall miss crucial elements of the significance of the intervention in the

Table 1.2 Impairments of Quality of Life Responses

Overall impairment group on rating scale (n = number, ( ) = per cent)

	Mild (n = 19)	Moderate (n = 33)	Severe (n = 22)
Memory	–	11 (33)	13 (59)
Worry	–	9 (27)	13 (59)
Irritability	3 (16)	13 (39)	17 (77)
Mood	–	13 (39)	21 (96)
Interest	–	3 (9)	15 (68)
Energy	13 (68)	26 (79)	22 (100)
Activity	2 (11)	14 (42)	18 (62)
Hypochondria	2 (11)	21 (64)	18 (82)

Adapted from Jachuck *et al.*, 'The effect of hypotensive drugs on the quality of life', *Journal of the Royal College of General Practitioners* 32 (1982), 103–5.

patients' lives and fail to recognise what it is that we are really doing to them. In so doing we shall be likely to misread what counts as a benefit simply because of our preoccupation with what is objectively measurable.

Identifying health needs

It might be thought that we could avoid many of the ethical problems in the management of health care resources if we were willing to move away from the maximisation of utility theories, which tend to dominate the agenda today, and concentrate rather on prioritising health care services according to the relative needs of patients. Certainly a concentration on the needs of patients would seem to offer protection of the interests of individuals and minorities whose interests might well be sacrificed when the greatest good of the greatest number of patients is the guiding light of resource allocation policies. However, even here the central temptation with which we have been grappling throughout this chapter rears its ugly head for we have to determine precisely how we can go about safely identifying health needs. Once again we can be caught in the trap of elevating medical considerations above their proper level of importance and consequently limiting the range of need with which the health care manager ought to be concerned.

Let us consider briefly an example which is exercising numbers of purchasers of health services throughout the developed world at present, viz. the provision of assisted procreation services.[30] Infertility is a strange candidate for the status of health need in a number of ways. For example, it is a state which is in fact thought desirable by many and is an outcome in which, furthermore, most purchasers of health care invest resources to achieve for many patients. Both male and female sterilisation and contraception have been part of the armoury of clinical interventions to preserve the health of patients for longer than assisted procreation techniques have been available. Yet those interventions are successful insofar as they achieve a biological harm in the patient – i.e. they produce a biological dysfunction. Additionally unexplained infertility is a condition which sometimes attaches to couples when it attaches to neither member of the couple individually. It is almost a novel idea to regard groups of patients as opposed to individual patients as having a health care need when no individual in that group can be said to suffer it, though the advent of genetics and the possibility of potential parents each with a recessive gene having a potential problem together, which the individuals cannot be said to have, and the advent of family therapy offer us some other rare examples.

This biological dysfunction in a couple or in an individual patient is often not regarded as being worthy of the investment of health resources and sometimes this is because it is not regarded as a proper object of clinical intervention, given that it does not fit into accepted nosologies. If the infertility is explicable in terms of some disease condition then it is often possible to access medical services to attend to the problem. Consider the example of purchasing patterns in the United Kingdom National Health Service. According to officially produced reports from the Human Fertilisation and Embryology Authority, couples with unexplained infertility in the UK have a 40% chance of achieving a live birth over three treatment cycles in 12 months.[31] Yet in 1994 almost a quarter of Health Authorities refused to purchase *in vitro* fertilisation services and over one third refused to purchase intrafallopian transfer services.[32] In the same year almost 94% of Health Authorities purchased tubal surgery services despite the fact that it is one of the most expensive and least effective means of assisted conception.[33] How can we explain this extraordinary state of affairs?

We are helped to understand the pattern by a research study on purchasing patterns of infertility treatments carried out in the UK in 1993.[34] In that study the reasons given by a number of Authorities which purchased assisted procreation services were compared with the reasons given by an equal number of Authorities who refused to purchase such services. Predominant among the reasons for not purchasing was the assertion that those with unexplained infertility were not ill, their infertility was not a disease. Even some who did purchase the service did so on the basis that it was a prophylactic intervention to stave off stress and mental illness. It was also the case that many regarded childlessness – the real condition attended to in assisted procreation – as a social rather than a clinical need. Apart from the inconsistency involved in this attempted justification of purchasing habits – for resources are committed by those Authorities to treat other biological dysfunctions, such as deafness, which are socially debilitating even though those dysfunctions are not in themselves disease conditions – the narrowness of the role in which health needs are cast is unacceptable. If all socially constructed need is eliminated from the remit of medicine and health care then health carers will be left with relatively little to do, for longevity, lack of blemishes, and even relief of pain might be said to derive their significance from social contexts. To ignore the social significance of childlessness removes infertility from the list of clinical needs even though it is amenable to clinical intervention and touches something at the heart of most people's well-being – namely, living in and rearing families.[35,36] We shall see later that a strong case can be made for saying that since unexplained infertility can be addressed by the new technologies it has been transformed into a clinical need. The temptation to appeal to traditional medical nosology in the absence of the context of this condition in the lives of sufferers in order to deny it the status of a health need is a further example of making a narrow range of biological conditions definitive of the realities which patients face.

Conclusion

We have seen that in the three areas of identification of treatments, identification of outcomes and identification of health needs the relation between biological conditions and facts about peoples' lives as a whole is bound up with the social and personal context in which the biological features are construed. The facts on this account are not value free but are imbued with value in that they provide reasons for valuing or disvaluing both the conditions and proposed interventions to deal with those conditions. Practitioner and patient might indeed be said to see different worlds where any dissonance occurs. To elevate the biological description to a position of paradigm importance by asserting that it is really what constitutes the health need, the successful outcome or the procedure to which the patient consents is to betray a susceptibility to the temptation felt by philosophers seeking a once-and-for-all account of meaning and significance. As we have seen, the misguided attempt to satisfy this temptation might have far more serious repercussions in medicine and health care than in Moral Philosophy, for example, where it has merely spawned multitudes of rival accounts of what constitutes a proper method of solving moral problems – solutions which in their application, mercifully, have rarely had far-reaching sinister consequences.

John Wisdom, the celebrated Cambridge philosopher, once referred to the expertise of Mr Flood, a keeper of lions at Dublin Zoo. He had never lost a cub and was regarded as a world authority on breeding lions in captivity. When asked for the secret of his success he replied 'Every lion is different'. There was no universal answer to the question of what any particular lion really needed. The expert, as Wisdom pointed out, brought his experience with many lions to bear on his understanding of any particular lion but always remained free to see that lion for itself.[37] It is to the task of caring for patients that clinicians are called, not merely to treating their various conditions. To discover what it is that they are really doing to patients they will, in the end, have to eschew universal answers and focus on the individuals into whose lives and private space they are privileged to enter. This is something to be remembered by all involved in health care provision, from policy makers and managers through to hands-on carers. It is not a lack of goodwill which most inhibits this but rather the impressive achievements of science in tandem with the age-old longing for security and authority in knowledge. Clinicians, together with philosophers, will find the recurring temptation to generalise and ignore the particular a hard one to resist, but resist it they must if patients are to receive proper care.

Notes

1 J.A. Davis, 'Whose life is it anyway?' *British Medical Journal* 292 (1986), 1128.
2 L. Wittgenstein, *Tractatus Logico Philosophicus*, London: Routledge & Kegan Paul, 1961.

3 L. Wittgenstein, *Philosophical Investigations*, Oxford: Basil Blackwell, 1953.

4 For a fuller discussion of these criticisms see D.M. Evans, 'Photographs and primitive signs', *Proceedings of the Aristotelian Society* LXXIX (1978), 213–38.

5 See, for example, S. Kripke, 'Naming and necessity', in G. Harman and D. Davidson (eds.), *Semantics of Natural Language*, Dordrecht: Reidel, 1972, pp. 253–355.

6 L. Wittgenstein, *Philosophical Investigations*, Oxford: Basil Blackwell, 1963, 21e.

7 L. Wittgenstein, *Tractatus Logico Philosophicus*, 3.26.

8 K. Hokusai, *One Hundred Views of Mount Fuji*, G. Braziller (ed.), London: Thames & Hudson, 1988, pp. 176–7 and 197.

9 T.R. Harrison, *Harrison's Principles of Internal Medicine*, 9th edn, K.J. Isselbacher, R.D. Adams, E. Braunwald, R.G. Petersdorf and J.D. Wilson (eds.), New York: McGraw-Hill, 1980, p. 1002.

10 I am indebted to Nelson Goodman for this comparison. See N. Goodman, *Languages of Art*, New York: Bobbs-Merrill, 1968, p. 229.

11 L. Wittgenstein, *Philosophical Grammar*, R. Rhees (ed.), Oxford: Basil Blackwell, 1974, p. 213.

12 F. Talbot, *The Pencil of Nature*; cited in A. Scharf, *Art and Photography*, Baltimore: Penguin, 1974, p. 187.

13 R. Barthes, 'Rhetoric of the image', *Working Papers in Cultural Studies* (Spring 1971), 49.

14 For a balanced discussion of the use of high tech interventions in the intensive care unit see: B. Jennett, *High Technology Medicine: Benefits and Burdens*, Oxford: Oxford University Press, 1986, pp. 76–93.

15 G.E. Moore, *Principia Ethica*, Cambridge: Cambridge University Press, 1962, 6–7.

16 S. Toulmin, *The Place of Reason in Ethics*, Cambridge: Cambridge University Press, 1950.

17 D. Hume, *A Treatise of Human Nature*, L.A. Selby-Bigge (ed.), Oxford: Oxford University Press, 1888.

18 See: C.L. Stevenson, *Ethics and Language*, New Haven: Yale University Press, 1944; R.M. Hare, *Freedom and Reason*, Oxford: Oxford University Press, 1963; and R.M. Hare, *The Language of Morals*, Oxford: Oxford University Press, 1960.

19 A.J. Ayer, *Language, Truth and Logic*, London: Victor Gollancz, 1948.

20 See especially: P. Foot, 'When is a principle a moral principle?', *Proceedings of the Aristotelian Society* Supplementary Volume 28 (1954), 95–110; P. Foot, 'Moral arguments', *Mind* 67 (1958), 502–13; and P. Foot, 'Moral beliefs' *Proceedings of the Aristotelian Society* 59 (1959), 83–104.

21 For a fuller discussion see D.M. Evans, 'Pro-attitudes to pre-embryos', in D.M. Evans (ed.), *Conceiving the Embryo*, Dordrecht: Martinus Nijhoff, 1995, pp. 27–46.

22 See: P. Winch, *Ethics and Action*, London: Routledge & Kegan Paul, 1972, pp. 75 & 84; and A. MacIntyre, *A Short History of Ethics*, New York: Macmillan, 1966, p. 148.

23 M.G. Drellich and I. Beiber, 'The psychologic importance of the uterus and its functions: some psychoanalytic implications of hysterectomy', *Journal of Nervous and Mental Disease* 126 (1958), 322–36. I am indebted to Louise DeRaeve for bringing this study to my attention and to her sensitive discussion of it in an unpublished paper 'Serious physical illness' written for a European Commission research project on Decision Making and Impaired Capacity, 1997.

24 I am indebted to David Greaves' analysis of the history of Medicine in: D. Greaves, *Mystery in Western Medicine*, Aldershot: Avebury, 1996, pp. 19–37; and D. Greaves 'The historical conceptualisation of impaired capacity and some

ethical implications', an unpublished paper written as part of the European Commission research project on Decision Making and Impaired Capacity, 1997.

25 Diego Gracia makes this point in 'The evaluation of incapacity: a practical judgement or an epistemological problem', an unpublished paper written as part of the European Commission research project Decision Making and Impaired Capacity, 1997.

26 D.M. Evans, 'The limits of health care', D. Greaves and H. Upton (eds.), *Philosophical Problems in Health Care*, Aldershot: Avebury, 1996, pp. 159–73.

27 D.M. Evans, 'Limits to care', in Z. Szawarski and D.M. Evans (eds.), *Solidarity, Justice and Health Care Priorities*, Health Service Studies 8, Linkoping: Linkoping University Press, 1993, pp. 28–41.

28 S.J. Jachuck, H. Brierly, S. Jachuck and P.M. Willcox, 'The effect of hypotensive drugs on the quality of life', *Journal of the Royal College of General Practitioners* 32 (1982), 103–5.

29 Ibid., p. 105.

30 D.M. Evans, 'Infertility and the NHS', *British Medical Journal*, 311 (1995), 1586–7; and D.M. Evans 'The clinical classification of infertility', in D.M. Evans (ed.), *Creating the Child*, Dordrecht: Martinus Nijhoff, 1995, pp. 47–64.

31 Human Fertilisation and Embryology Authority, *Fourth Annual Report*, London: HFEA, 1995, p. 29.

32 R. Wiles and H. Patel, *Report of the Third National Survey of NHS Funding of Infertility Services*. London: College of Health, 1995.

33 A. Lower and M. Setchell, 'Should the NHS fund infertility services?', *British Journal of Hospital Medicine* 50 (1993), 509–12.

34 S. Redmayne and R. Klein, 'Rationing in practice: the case of in vitro fertilisation', *British Medical Journal* 306 (1993), 1521–4.

35 Ibid., note xxv.

36 J. Emery, 'Silent Suffering', *British Medical Journal* 311 (1995), 1647.

37 J. Wisdom, *Paradox and Discovery*, Oxford: Blackwell, 1965, pp. 137–8.

Chapter 2

Radical disagreement and cultural dissonance

Radical disagreements

In Chapter 1 we noted two unacceptable views of moral judgements which contend, on the one hand, that because they do not correspond with the character of empirical judgements then they are not subject to rational evaluation and are meaningless or, on the other hand, that as reasonableness is demanded of all judgements then ethical judgements must be like empirical judgements and, as a result, cannot be the subject of any disagreement which will defy resolution by rational people, given adequate information, time and patience. The two views are related insofar as they each assume a uniform view of factuality. A radical disagreement is one which cannot be resolved by an appeal to reason or evidence. The possibility of such disagreements in morality marks off moral discourse from standard empirical discourse. That is, while many moral disagreements might be resolved by appeal to reason and evidence neither of these sources can guarantee that reasonable people will agree.

We have already noted that the richness of facts with which doctors have often to deal produce rival conclusions about what patients really need, what are successful outcomes of medical interventions and what is the nature of clinical interventions. These separately or together provide different answers to the question of what should be done to patients. But these crucial differences are not due to the lack of reasonableness on the part of the various patients and practitioners. Rather they are due to the fact that the people involved see different worlds. These are not worlds which are impenetrable to others but neither are they worlds which those others inhabit insofar as they cannot come to see or construe relevant situations similarly. For example, what more widely differing notions of reality could there be than that which, on the one hand, construes the destruction of early embryos in stem cell research as murder and disrespectful of human life and, on the other hand, that which sees this respect as demanding such research in order to alleviate the suffering of humanity. That reason cannot eliminate such a disparity of views does not make the dispute between the parties unreal or insignificant.

Indeed each protagonist might feel that their view is worth making great sacrifices for in order to overcome the other.

Before moving on let us examine a number of specific arguments which have been made against the possibility of radical disagreement in ethics. We shall subsequently explore what the role of reason might be in the face of some apparent radical disagreements produced by cultural dissonance, a growing area of difficulty in health care delivery.

Defences against radical disagreement

A cluster of counter-arguments to the possibility of radical disagreement in ethics, which represent strands of thinking about ethical disagreement, have been usefully brought together by Carl Wellman.[1] In the following discussion they are titled in such a way as to draw out their central features.

The unlimited discussion defence

This defence claims that it is misleading to assert that after full discussion two perfectly rational men may fail to agree on moral matters because there is no such thing as a complete discussion.

The process of rational criticism has no limit: it is an open-ended process of discussion and reflection.[2]

Thus, in the case cited above, it follows that if agreement is not actually reached by two rational people as a result of exchange of views today, matters should not be allowed to rest there. It cannot be ruled out that further features might be canvassed tomorrow as the process of discussion and reflection is open-ended. That further discussion might well lead to a resolution of the dispute, hence ruling out the possibility of radical disagreement.

There are two important criticisms to be made of this defence of the unlimited powers of reason to resolve ethical disputes. First, if it is true that the process of rational criticism is open-ended then just as it is possible for two rational men not to have come to agreement after an incomplete discussion today, it is equally possible for them never to come to agreement, as nothing can count as a complete discussion. This supports the view that radical disagreement is a distinct possibility. Second, the status of agreements also have to be tentative as actual agreement at any point is not a good reason for concluding the discussion; the matter must always be left open. Indeed the discoveries of the nature of early pre-embryos as a result of their availability to researchers courtesy of *in vitro* fertilisation have caused people who previously agreed about the moral status of embryos to disagree. Some have been persuaded that these entities are not human lives as such at this stage whereas others have been unmoved by the discoveries that each of the embryonic cells at the 2-cell stage are totipotential and by the fact that up until the laying down of the primitive streak at fourteen days the possibility of division into monozygotic twins is possible. We shall return to this dispute later in the book. For the present, however, it is a nice example of a case where leaving matters open to future discussion allows the possibility of disagreement to dispel agreement whereas Wellman's thesis is that continued discussion rules out the possibility of radical disagreement.

Second, the premise that all rational criticism is open-ended is false. If nothing counted as a complete discussion then discussion would be meaningless. That is, to claim that rational discussion is open-ended is an invitation to scepticism and not a defence against it; for if nothing counted as a sufficient or conclusive reason for something then we could not properly be said to know anything. But this observation does not rule out the possibility of radical disagreement in ethics. Such conclusive arguments always concern situations where there is no dispute about the facts. But radical disagreements in ethics arise precisely at this level of dispute. Whether the pre-embryo is or is not a human being is not is not an empirical question in the ordinary sense. Indeed it is, to use an unfortunate term in the circumstances, a conceptual dispute. Reflections on the matter are not empirical in character but philosophical as they have to do with what it makes sense to say about the pre-embryo. To insist on further discussion beyond certain points in argument is not to display rational caution but to betray a lack of grasp of the logic of the area of discourse in question. In all fields of knowledge discussion must come to an end somewhere in the sense that no further reasons can be given. Asking for further reasons in these situations undermines the conditions of sense of the discourse involved.

The general moral principle defence

This defence consists of a critique of the following case for radical moral disagreement: it may be thought that moral reasoning is always conducted by means of the practical syllogism. But, if this is so, then where there is disagreement over the major premises, the general moral principles, then agreed conclusions cannot be reached. Wellman rightly concludes that the possibility of radical disagreement is not thus established but he does so for the wrong reasons.

Let us assume, with Wellman, that all moral reasoning is conducted by means of the syllogistic model such as in the following argument: to engage in destructive experiments using early human embryos is wrong, embryonic stem cell research involves the destruction of human embryos, therefore embryonic stem cell research is wrong. The major premise might be the conclusion of a more general syllogism such as: killing human beings is wrong, conducting destructive experiments on early human embryos involves killing human beings, therefore conducting destructive experiments on early human embryos is wrong. There comes a point, and maybe we have already reached it in this case, where we cannot move to a more general premise as the starting point of our argument. Thus the most general premise is not formed by reason. This is true of the premise that human pre-embryos are human beings in that there is no crucial piece of empirical evidence which guarantees its truth. It constitutes a stopping point of discussion for many engaged in the dispute.

Wellman notes that general principles form the logical, not temporal, starting point of arguments and that occasionally, disagreement about such premises may be resolved in the course of an argument. But what of the ultimate propositions which are not derivable from reason such as the one cited above? These, he thinks, may be gained from experience:

> Moreover as we live our lives we acquire new beliefs and attitudes, including general beliefs and attitudes, as well. These may function as first premises in our reasoning.[3]

Thus, he asserts, disagreement on first premises is not an inevitable prologue to radical disagreement, for agreement on the same may be reached in the course of discussion and not necessarily as a result of reasoning. However, this defence against the possibility of radical disagreement is not strong enough. While it is true that disagreement on general premises does not inevitably lead to radical disagreement, neither does it rule out the possibility that it may so do. It allows for possible agreement in the face of initial differences on general principles but at the price of removing those principles from the scrutiny of reason. Is not their objectivity thus undermined? Not quite, for he suggests that they may assume the status of empirical hypotheses as testable as those of empirical science. Sadly, no examples are forthcoming. We are not told what kind of evidence would be presented to resolve, for example, the differences between the protagonists in the embryonic stem cell debate who disagree about their starting points in the discussion – one asserting that human pre-embryos are human beings and the other asserting that they are not. What set of facts would be conclusive in showing the one to be correct and the other mistaken vis-à-vis these general premises? As we saw in countering his first defence the moral status of the pre-embryo is not an hypothesis to be confirmed or disconfirmed by appeal to evidence.

The factual content defence

This defence contends that many judgements of value or obligation are inferred from purely factual premises. Consequently, the claim to objective truth in ethics can be sacrificed only at the price of denying the possibility of objective truth in factual statements. As the latter is incoherent, then objective truth in ethics is guaranteed.

Wellman asserts that the valid movement from facts to judgements of obligation is not deductive. Rather it is conductive. That is, it consists in 'the drawing together' of several independent facts. However, no account is given of what distinguishes valid from invalid moves. Clearly not just any facts drawn together will lead to judgements of obligation. Indeed some collections of facts could not do so, such as the following list: this object is in the laboratory; the laboratory is situated in the hospital research wing; the object is not visible to the naked eye. Only when another fact, such as that the object is a human pre-embryo, is added could an inference of obligation follow such as: 'Care ought to be taken to make the laboratory secure.' But what is it that marks off the extra fact from the rest? It invokes a whole custom of custodianship, responsibility to patients in that the progenitors of the embryo have consented to its being stored there for specific purposes, and so on. In other words, though it is a fact that the object is a pre-embryo it derives its meaning from the moral context in which it is placed. It would be mistaken therefore to call it a pure fact if by that is meant one which is understood without reference to any moral practice.

The success of Wellman's third defence depends on the status of facts which are drawn together. If they are purely factual, or as some philosophers have labelled them, brute facts[4] then his defence stands, that is if they are facts without moral import. But they clearly are not all facts of this kind, and indeed cannot be so if a moral conclusion is to emerge from their being drawn together.

Of course the moral conclusion might not always follow. For example, it might be that the pre-embryo was produced by researchers without the consent of its progenitors, or that it was being stored for a purpose other than that for which they had consented to its production. The reaction to these additional facts might vary from one moral judge to another. Some will still believe that the intrinsic value of the pre-embryo demands its protection. Others will not feel this way and believe that it would be better if the researchers were denied the opportunity to use it for their purposes, simply because of their lack of proper procedures. However, the additional facts should make no difference whatsoever if, as Wellman suggests, the original facts cited are together sufficient condition for the conclusion to be drawn. The point is that they may make a difference for some and may not for others.

Further, one could imagine a society where there was no practice of custodianship of human parts or of anything else. There the additional facts would place the hearer under no obligation whatsoever. Thus only if the additional facts are made other than they really are, viz. drained of all moral significance, can the factual content defence be mounted. But then it cannot succeed.

The human psychology defence

This defence trades upon the notion of normality in human experience and thought. Wellman believes that individuals differ in both these respects due to cultural gaps. However, within a society individuals' drives, impulses, and so on vary and this affects their thinking. But such differences are not incompatible with the existence of a normal way of experiencing and thinking, for the norm need not be thought to be universal. If a median can be found around which individual differences cluster, then a statistical norm is established. But, of course, the existence of such a norm has not been established. However, the very existence of public language presupposes psychological similarity between men. Given such a norm, then, if critical discussion is carried on far enough, agreement on the objective truth of moral conclusions will emerge.

Leaving aside difficulties about the character of such a norm, there is a serious flaw in what is thought to be a good reason for its existence. Wittgenstein has shown that it is true that concept formation depends upon certain general facts of human nature, viz. what he calls agreement in primitive reactions (see, for example, his remarks on the concept of time in *On Certainty*[5]). His crucial observation is worked out in detail in the *Philosophical Investigations*[6] where he shows that, as a matter of fact, given a certain training, people do cotton on to following a rule, grasp the meaning of 'and so on', react in a common way. This is a fact of human psychology without which communication would be impossible. However, he is at pains to distinguish this agreement from agreement in particular opinions:

> It is what human beings say that is true or false: and they agree in the *language* they use. That is not agreement in opinions but in form of life. (Emphasis in original text.)[7]

Cottoning on in this way is what makes it possible for people to have language and thus opinions, which in turn may be justified or otherwise. This agreement in psychology is the precondition of both agreement and disagreement in opinions, if only because without it the very questions about which people agree or disagree could not be asked. For example, a simple dispute as to what is the correct time cannot occur without the sharing of a common concept, which in turn is dependent upon agreement in primitive reactions as mentioned earlier. Of course, such a dispute is, in most instances, settleable beyond question.

However, if we are to take seriously the social nature of human beings then we cannot disregard the institutions, or what have been called the activities,[8] within society which help identify people, their feelings and their perceptions of the world. To envisage a common psychology totally independent of these backgrounds is to misconstrue human psychology. These institutions have a longer history than the individual and cannot be explained in terms of the psychology of the individual. Rather the reverse is the case. It is for this reason that Anderson asserts that it is only when we identify the activities which pass *through* (*sic*) an individual that we can understand the activities which go on in that individual. As surely as a sinking feeling in one's stomach can be identified only by means of the context in which it occurs – either sadness at saying farewell to a loved one, or disappointment on receipt of a poor examination result, or fear at the receipt of a poor prognosis, or just a sinking feeling *simpliciter* at the sudden descent of an elevator – so more general societal features such as rival conceptions of the nature of family will facilitate a possible range of moral feelings of obligation, care, and so on. In other words the social context identifies the feeling but is not explained by it.

Similarly, perceptions of the nature of health care interventions are determined by the context in which they occur, as we saw in Chapter 1. These contexts may be specifically culturally differentiated and this calls for culturally sensitive approaches to patients on the part of health care professionals if best practice is to be achieved.

We shall consider this matter in more detail in response to Wellman's final defence against the possibility of radical disagreement in ethics.

Even if these logical considerations are waived, the human psychology defence is not entirely satisfactory, for if the assimilation occurs in other ways than by rational discussion then it has no bearing upon the logic of moral discourse. It may well be that through some catastrophe only one society, whatever that is, would survive and radical disagreement from this source would disappear. But this would not alter the fact that such differences are imaginable; which alone is sufficient to show that moral discourse is distinct from, for example, discourse about material objects.

The mode of thought defence

This defence employs the notion of the difference between normal and abnormal thinkers. By abnormal thinkers Wellman has in mind those affected by brainwashing, drugs, brain surgery, and so on. Such people may think consistently in a way contrary to the rational community. For example, they may totally lack sympathy and consequently view moral matters differently. Thus our embryonic stem cell researchers might believe that they could be rid of the moral hang-ups which obstruct their research by opting for some kind of intervention, like brain surgery, which would render them less sensitive to the needs and interests of others. The question then raised is: what justification do they have for thinking in the way they currently do when they have the choice of thinking in these other ways? If they cannot offer a justification, then it seems that the notion of 'objective truth' cannot find a foothold in ethics. Consequently Wellman endeavours to provide one.

He is correct when he says:

> All reasoning and all justifying rises from the rock of actual human thinking but this rock itself stands in need of no rational justification.[9]

However, he thinks that this rules out only the question: what rational justification can rationality be given? It is not thought to rule out the question: what rational justification can I have for continuing to reason as I do when I have the choice to change, e.g. by subjecting myself to brain surgery? He fails to see that a response to this latter question can serve as the defence he requires only if it is confused with the former. A man may intelligibly be able to give reasons for adopting some other mode of thinking. They may be pragmatic. For example, in the case cited, the researcher might justify submission to brain surgery in order to become less sensitive to the needs and interests of others by means of the gains achieved, viz. freeing him up to get on with his research. Reasons against such a change may also be given, e.g. the Hobbesian reason that social cohesion would be sacrificed if all men so changed.

However, the example does not rationally establish any mode of thinking *per se* in that the researcher appeals to values embodied in his present mode of thought in making the decision. Only if it is thought to achieve as much can it act as the defence Wellman hopes for. But he himself says, as we have seen, that such a justification is unintelligible. In fact, his example shows the opposite to what he has in mind. There are people who, not out of choice, are less sympathetic than others; situations strike them differently in that they do not call for action from them when they may do from others. Though we may morally judge such people, there is no common framework within which one can guarantee to be able to show that they are mistaken. What is required in them is not a correction of mistakes in reasoning, but a change of heart which suggests that radical disagreement is a real possibility in ethics.

The cultural assimilation defence

This defence refers to what is by far the most obvious possible source of radical disagreement in ethics. It is the one on which we shall concentrate in the remainder of this chapter. It is often argued that radical moral disagreement arises out of cultural differences between peoples. How one perceives the world and how one reasons about it depends on the concepts and customs of one's society. Consequently as there are cultural differences there will be radical moral disagreement. But this assumes that cultural differences are insurmountable. This is false, however, for anthropology has shown that such differences can be overcome and furthermore they may be overcome by rational discussion. Thus radical moral disagreement from this source may be ruled out.

There is truth and error in this defence. It is true, as pointed out in the response to the previous defence, that our ways of experiencing and thinking about the world are facilitated by the concepts and customs of our society. However, while it is true that we may learn new concepts and old ones may fall into disuse for us, as often happens when cultures interact, it is senseless to talk of our concepts being true or false, rationally justified or otherwise, correct or incorrect. They are part of language and language is not true or false. Rather it is what is said in language that is true or false. If concepts of different societies are modified by interaction between those societies, what judgements are now made, what things are now said will have no rational bearing upon things said previously. They are neither more nor less rational judgements because of such change, they are simply different. Conceptual agreement, that is agreement in the language we use, is a precondition of both agreement and disagreement in judgements. Thus cultural differences in concepts are not settleable by rational discussion as Wellman suggests they are.

Of course, cultural assimilation is an established fact. It may well occur, and often does, through conflict where one institution is overthrown by another. A new institution will win the allegiance of an individual and an old one lose its grip upon him. This may arise out of new aspirations and aims of the individual. These changes have been observed by the author in the experience of African young men from rural backgrounds who remove to town to find work. The institution of the extended family, so much a part of the fabric of society of the bush people, often loses its hold upon these young men. They begin to live for things, status symbols of a success quite foreign to their relations back home. With such change often go changes in ideas of responsibility. No longer are those whom Europeans would call nephews regarded as brothers for whose education and welfare the man in town is responsible. His concept of the family is now more nuclear due to European influence. Thus the question: who is my brother? is often the focal point of moral dilemmas. To think that it is a question amenable to an answer with which it would be impossible to rationally disagree, is to fail to see that what counts as a good reason depends on the moral outlook in question. The bushman's idea of the good or successful life is far removed from his relation's new view of the matter. Thus they have no common rationale to which to appeal in settling their disagreements. So, as a guarantee of eradicating radical disagreement in ethics, the Cultural Assimilation Defence will not do.

However, it is important to ask how far reason can take us in the face of apparent radical disagreements arising from this source as the phenomenon of cultural dissonance is something which presents considerable problems in health care delivery. Many societies are now multicultural and it is dangerous to assume that all their citizens have a common view of the world of medicine and its interventions. Consider a specific example to illustrate the importance of not coming to precipitate conclusions about classifying disagreements as radical. It concerns the application of new genetic technologies in New Zealand. The material presented in the description of the case derives from a study of Maori perceptions of emerging genetic biotechnologies based on a series of interviews with Maori respondents.[10]

Identifying a cultural perspective

It is clear from the results of these investigations that the search for a defini-tive Maori view of these matters is a vain pursuit. A number of ethical positions were taken on various matters by various respondents some of which were incompatible with each other. In some cases individual respond-ents expressed views which were in tension with each other, sometimes self-consciously and other times not. These disagreements were the result of a number of factors which will be discussed below. Suffice for now to note the awareness of many of the participants of the difficulty of trying to establish the Maori ethical viewpoint on the genetic manipulation of plants.

I think that you're using the term Maori and you're thinking everyone has the same viewpoint but that isn't correct, Maoris are like any other race, they have people that have viewpoints that are different so you can't just say Maori and think you will get one viewpoint. That is incorrect. (Interview V3)

Key Interviewee T3 (KIT3) responded to the following question: 'I want to ask you, because you've said it a few times, which I think is really important, what is the disadvantage of using the word Maori?'

It's good because there's an immediate understanding that it's a non-pakeha [non-Maori or European] way of looking at things or a more indigenous way of looking at things, however it's not rigorous in its application. A Maori viewpoint, as with many Maori things, gets put across everybody without looking at different iwi [tribe] or tribal tradi-tions that may or may not be relevant to these kinds of things. Definitely we have people who were expert in definite areas and who would never call those things, teachings out of the whare whananga [fellow travellers], you never say that it was Maori or they do Maori schools of learning, it's so little for what it actually is so it's a convenience label in some instances but doesn't pick up the whole realm of thinking around things . . . I could say this and this could be what I've learned from my Mum . . . maybe totally different from another iwi, or you know across the stream from us, because they are my whanau [family] experiences and I don't think it's a very rigorous way of thinking because there are definite differences in the way that we think. You need to point out those kind of differences. It's an inconvenient way because you slip into it quite quickly.

In a similar vein Key Interviewee T4 (KIT4) responded to the question: 'I just want to pick up on something you mentioned before about your Maori view and it not really being the only view, in your opinion what is a better way of representing the views of Maori?'

> Maori are so diverse, I mean short of going and consulting every Maori, I don't know. Maybe these key informant interviews with people who come and sit across that Maori continuum might be the best way of doing it. Maori who are steeped in their tradition, what are their viewpoints: and from the other fold, those who are far removed from it as can be imaginable, Maori who live in a mainstream non-Maori lifestyle; they have no knowledge of Te Reo [Maori language] or their iwi or nor do they want to, so far removed from any sense of a Maori world and yet are Maori. Try and get their . . . try and get as many people across that continuum as you can.

This response invites us to accept that views grounded in Maori traditions and those sincerely held by Maori distanced from those traditions are properly regarded as Maori views. This is so despite the fact that a Maori lifestyle is characterised as one where those traditions play a significant role. But this descriptive account of Maori views is not accepted by KIT3 who rather provided a normative account of the matter as an answer to the question: 'Does it make a difference to you if there are Maori scientists doing the genetic work?'

> Its about cultural connectedness which is an awful way to say it because there is no way I am going to say 'Well you're not concerned enough' because I think there are all different journeys that we have to take in terms of knowing who we are as Maori. 'Maori scientist' doesn't give me a label of capability and capacity when it comes to things Maori. Are they ethnically identified as Maori so they are a Maori person who is practicing science in whatever form or are they practicing science from a Maori point of view, two hugely different ways . . . Connectiveness does come from people who whakapapa [culturally identify] to that way of thinking and being, so Maori scientists, who identify as Maori, if they could not stand up to the same rigour around things Maori I wouldn't be any happier, in fact I'd be more shocked that they were participating in these things; without the kind of rigour they wouldn't

be with the tautoko of their iwi ... they don't have those kind of connections with their own whanau so if something goes badly wrong that they have that protection, that ropu tautoko [societal support] at a fundamental cultural level then you question what they're doing or are they just a Maori person doing a pakeha thing.

While such connections allow for different viewpoints those viewpoints are, according to the KIT3, limited. This approach is particularly sensitive when we are discussing ethical points of view. While the call for logical limits to what counts as a Maori view is convincing, the translation of these into ethical limits is dangerous. That is, ruling out certain moral viewpoints on the grounds of their falling outside a cultural orthodoxy calls for careful examination. Who are to be the guardians of the line dividing the morally acceptable from the morally unacceptable on the grounds of what is and what is not cultural orthodoxy? Who is to decide what is and what is not a proper extension of a cultural viewpoint? And in whose interests are those limits drawn? We shall see that this is a continuing source of puzzlement as we explore the gathered data on the genetic manipulation of plants. It is, however, important to characterise this problem a little more fully before we proceed with our analysis of Maori perceptions.

Perhaps it would be helpful to consider an analogy. In the Roman Catholic tradition, a social institution with an even longer history than the New Zealand Maori tradition, there has been much discussion about emerging biotechnologies. Perhaps the most celebrated has been the discussions surrounding the status of the human embryo in IVF and human embryonic stem cell research. This institution does have a history of procedures to distinguish the orthodox from the unorthodox. Unorthodox Catholic views range from the philosophically conceivable extensions of orthodox views to the heretical. In the last analysis Papal authority can determine what lies within and without the orbit of Catholic teaching. In the case of the status of the embryo, official teaching that a human life begins at the moment of conception only began with the *Apostolicae Sedis* of Pius IX in 1869. Prior to that date, in line with Aristotle and Aquinas, the notion of ensoulment was important. That is, some time after the vegetative soul came at fertilisation the rational soul came to be, constituting a true human individual.[11] Ford, himself a Roman Catholic priest, argues that the church's teaching is that a human life is brought into being at fertilisation but that whether it is yet ensouled, that is, whether it is yet a person is a matter on which the church is uncertain, and is a matter for philosophers to determine.[12] He is persuaded that this status is not attained for at least the first fourteen days of embryonic development, that is until the primitive streak is laid down. It is possible, of course, that the church could firm up its views on this, as many believe it to have done, in which case

Ford's view would lie outside the Catholic teaching and would not be a Catholic view, even though it was held by a Catholic – except on the pains of his excommunication from the church for holding an heretical belief. At present, however, on his account, there is room for disagreement on the personhood status of the embryo as there is, as yet, no authoritative ruling that the notion of delayed ensoulment, which reaches far back into the tradition, is false.

What can we learn from this analogy? We must first notice that there is no parallel in Maori society, or indeed in any society as such, to Papal authority. We must also note that even in the relatively tight confines of the Roman Catholic tradition there can be varied views related to historic strands of that tradition. These might be seen as more or less important depending on one's views of the evolution of the tradition. For some Catholics reference back to Aquinas's view would appear to be irrelevant as the tradition has developed beyond it, whereas for others, like Ford, some conceptual connections are still seen to be important. Nothing short of an *ex cathedra* pronouncement from the Pope could resolve the question of the orthodoxy or otherwise of the competing views. On Ford's account the church is extremely wary about taking this decisive step.

But there is no such possible appeal open to Maori to determine what is and what is not an orthodox view of matters surrounding the new bio-technologies. Clearly, to be a Maori perception any view has to be related to Maori tradition and custom or, at the very least, the Maori identity of the viewer. But this is not to rule out evolution of Maori culture about which there might be considerable disagreement. Nor is it to rule out varied interpretations of that culture. Each of these possibilities are represented in respondents' comments.

First, with respect to the evolution of Maori culture, respondent P6 contemplated in an interesting way the manipulation of plants by the insertion of animal genes and even human genes to produce more nutritious foods or medicines.

> I don't like the idea of genetically engineered food. If my profession is about getting the DNA of an animal or a human in order to make the plant flourish better before it's even used, before anything like that would even (be) introduced to the plant I would not even think about it at some point . . . I know my tipuna were cannibals before even any of this has happened but I think that we've become civilised enough to think, it's just a thought that knowing that that food you're eating can be from another human source even another animal. I don't really mind so much about the animals.

P6 was grappling with the objection which some people make to the insertion of human genes into plants, viz. that it would result in our eating people. This is not an idea which is entirely foreign to the long traditions of some Maori but it does seem to the respondent that Maori society has moved beyond that, 'has become civilised enough' in her words, to give pause for thought before proceeding with such activities. Such changes often come about in societies as a result of contact with other societies but who is to determine which changes constitute the process of 'civilisation' and which constitute the decline of a culture?

Could this link with distant traditions even provide some justification for proceeding with the insertion of human genes into plants to produce medicines? Might not this be a means of showing respect for other humans in the way that cannibalism denoted respect for the mana [authority] of slain enemies insofar as the victors were thought to thus take on the strength of the slain? Such a view was expressed by a contributor to the Bioethics Council Gisborne hui [meeting] on xenotransplantation.

> What is being discussed here was practiced many years ago by our tipuna [ancestor]. She was attacked so that they may eat her heart to take her mana. It was done to take her mana. The cannibalism wasn't just for the sake of the meal, and now we are moving genes into other organisms. It's just the same.[13]

While this might be considered by some to be an extreme example, it does illustrate the difficulties facing those who claim to be able to pronounce on what is or is not a view which can properly belong to a culture.

Second, there is the question of the interpretation of the features of a culture. A number of respondents referred to the creation stories found among Maori. For some they underpinned resistance to any interference with nature. For example, when asked about cultural issues surrounding the alteration of plants for producing food, P8 observed:

> It is unethical isn't it? They're playing around with nature, what nature gave us, so it is unethical . . . would Tane Mahuta [the god of the forests] like his children mucked around with, I don't think so.

On the other hand it is clear that a different view of the creation myth is possible. One Maori respondent asked the question: 'In the search for the uha [female] in Maori cosmology, could this be the first form of GM?' This is an approach which was developed in a sophisticated way by Maori

Interested Party witnesses to the Royal Commission on Genetic Modification.[14] They went so far as to suggest that the activities of Tane can be perpetuated by the new science as a model for improving life forms. Far from prohibiting genetic modification by appeal to respect for the whakapapa which Maori are thought to have with all animate and inanimate objects and to the givenness of species, they considered that there is a Maori framework which permits us to adapt and develop the environment, including the mixing of species.

> Maori already have a history of undertaking practices that involve blending life forms and mixing tapu [sacred, forbidden] across species . . . The story of creation has been told, and will be told again, many thousands of times. At one level it is a convenient explanation of how the world around us came to be, however at another level the story is also an important metaphor for development. It is a lesson about the need for Tane and his descendants to sometimes take control of the world around them for the betterment of people . . . in a sense it is also the first significant genetic modification as Te Rangikaheke [celebrated Maori tribal leader] says there was originally only one ancestor who was the joined together Ranginui [the Sky Father] and Papatuanuku [the Earth Mother]. Tane and his brothers, after much deliberation, took it upon themselves to separate this one body into two for the betterment of the people.

Other features of the creation story are open to similar interpretation, on their account. They claim that resistance to genetic manipulation of the environment on the basis of an appeal to a Maori world view are 'at best the result of a romantic analysis of Maori customs . . . At worst it is a simplistic corruption of Maori philosophy'.[15]

We cannot attempt to adjudicate on these matters here but rather to note that radically different, and incompatible, views of the genetic manipulation of plants is possible within the context of Maori scholarship. It is therefore important to keep this in mind when one world view is used as a guillotine in the discussion of ethical possibilities with respect to the genetic manipulation of plants, animals or even humans.

The stability of cultural perceptions

It is interesting to note the differing degrees of security with which respondents expressed their views of the genetic manipulation of plants. It became clear that numbers of those interviewed were prepared to change their views in the process of the interviews. Where change occurred it was always in the direction of a move towards a more liberal view of the technology in the face of initial outright rejection of it, or, in some cases, in the face of profound doubts about it. Two stimuli to changes of view were identified in the research. Each of these led to a process of reflection on the part of the respondents. The first was the provision of further information about the technology and the second was concerned with tests of expressed views by appeal to critical situations.

The role of information

It had been noted in a baseline questionnaire study of Maori perceptions that large numbers of respondents had said little or nothing about their views on bioscience or biotechnology. Those who were asked for an explanation professed that they knew insufficient about these things to have views about them. This was also true of the research interview participants.

In the interview-led research some respondents expressed their need for more knowledge before coming to final conclusions. For example, VD3 said:

> My knowledge on the whole subject is actually quite small, minute actually and my thoughts and views are naïve on the fact that I don't have a lot of knowledge myself but more than anything my views are driven by the fact of a fear of introducing things into the food chain that sustains our lives is very concerning and until I know more that's the view I have at this stage and it's actually up to me to know more and to do something about knowing more because no one is going to give me that information.

Others who were prepared to express strong negative views about genetic technology identified the sources of their information. In numbers of these cases the sources were unreliable and, consequently, people's views were coloured by misinformation. For example, some who took a very conservative line because they believed that tampering with nature was very dangerous imagined that the technology was either aimed at, or at least capable of, producing macabre results. Respondent V1 expressed some scepticism about beneficial outcomes from genetic manipulation of seeds and quoted the *Rocky Horror Show* as the source of information about plants that evolved into man-eating things. V2 was ambivalent about the use of modified plants to provide treatments for serious diseases due to unreal fears about possible consequences.

Well I think the thing is that a lot of people don't know and they need to be educated on it and I don't know much about plants myself . . . I support for medicinal, beneficial and scientific purposes, mainly to see if it, I was to die of cancer, I was diagnosed with and they had a cure for me and it had come from a plant seed or animal seed, anything, I would take it. I would straight up say yes because life's too important and on the negative side, things might go bad and could find someone walking down the street with two heads because things got mixed up.

A similar phenomenon occurred at the New Zealand Bioethics Council.[16] One contributor observed that:

There was a mokupuna [grandchild] at the hui for the Royal Commission on Genetic Modification who spoke about not wanting to walk past a paddock and hear a singing sheep. I am totally opposed.

and another asserted that:

It means our kids are going to look like Ken and Barbie because they want to form and manipulate the look of our children.

We have all seen and heard this kind of negative propaganda about genetic modification in the media. For many citizens it is the only kind of information which they have been able to access. Nevertheless, it does not follow that all the negative attitudes towards the genetic manipulation of plants expressed in the interviews were based on this kind of distortion of what is being done in the name of biotechnology purportedly to improve the quality and the supply of food and to provide new medicines. Many people gave serious reasons for their opposition to such activities without resorting to such outlandish risk scenarios.

The interviewers were able to provide certain levels of information about genetic biotechnology to their research participants and to pursue fruitful discussions on that basis. In some cases this made a considerable difference to the views expressed. For example, H1 ended the interview with the following comment:

> Yes, this interview process has been good for me because I never thought about GE with regard to medicinal purposes so it's actually changed my whakaro [thinking] for that reason and it's something I would never have thought about before, so thank you.

Some people changed their views in the process of these discussions in line with the conviction that the Maori community generally faces a major challenge of lack of information in this area[17] but that more sophisticated discussion is evolving. The activities of Environmental Risk Management Authority's (ERMA) 'Kaihatu' group [Nga Kaihauttu, Maori Advisory Committee to the Environmental Risk Management Authority] are illustrative of this, though it does not follow that Maori support for ERMA proposals is more easily obtained.

Critical incident tests

In some of the interviews respondents got around to talking about how they would react if some of these biotechnological developments offered help to them or their family in situations of serious, and possibly life-threatening illness. One described the difference such an experience had actually had on her views. These situations we could call critical incident tests. That is, they offer the respondent a chance to reflect on how deeply held their stated ethical perceptions go with them in three ways. First, there is the challenge of temptation to behave in a way that ignores ethical views. Second, there is the realisation that the stated ethical views do not continue to grip them when really put to the test and that some other ethical commitments trump them. Third, there is the most interesting possibility of the critical situation producing a gestalt change in them. This involves a new understanding of various features of their culture hitherto construed in ways which are now supplanted by richer views. There were hints of each of these possibilities in answers given in the interviews.

In one case the respondent Vicki5 was not quite sure how to characterise her reaction to the critical incident, running together all three of these possibilities in her response to questions about mixing animal and human DNA with plants. In a moving dialogue with her interviewer she grappled with conflicting reactions to an unfolding scenario which teaches us much about the nature of absolute moral values.

She was asked the question: 'Do you agree with mixing a plant seed with an animal seed?' Her reply was:

No, more so than just mixing plant with DNA. It's just not natural, it's not right. I think who are we as human beings to tamper with nature for our own selfish reasons, playing God. I don't think we have the right. I mean where does it end?

And what about (mixing) a plant with a human seed?

Absolutely not. No . . . Like again, belief in trying to preserve nature, I think that we've gone too far now and the world's gone crazy I think. I mean the last generation things were kept sacred and kept natural and whole without being tampered with and I mean I think once you believe that, you know, that you can tamper with nature and things you are on a bit of an ego trip and you feel sort of self destructive.

We are then, thus far, faced with an unequivocal and absolute objection to interfering with species identities. But when faced with the possibility of saving lives by these means her view changes. At first she admits that she would not be bound by this view, and that her departure from it would be a form of yielding to temptation:

I think it depends. If it's going to be lifesaving I would probably go back on my word and say for that purpose of lifesaving, yes. Do it. If it was me or one of my children, my mum, do anything you can, I don't care what it is, all morals out the window as long as that tampered DNA is segregated and we are informed. Absolutely.

But on further reflection about other possible uses, such as commercial gain, which would call for the same reaction, a different account begins to emerge:

No again I think that is tampering with nature for selfish reasons, commercial, monetary gain and what have you. But I think absolutely yes for medicinal lifesaving type scenarios. How could you not?

It emerged that this lady had been placed in such a situation with a very premature child and was grateful for the advances of science which had occurred through procedures which would have been ruled out by previous generations as absolutely out of the question.

> We have accepted what they wouldn't have fifty years ago. That's what I was saying, it's so borderline and then what is not acceptable today with mixing a human gene for example, today I am saying no, no, no whereas in fifty years time it will probably be normal, in hospitals, who knows?

How, indeed, could you not err on the side of life? To be placed in such dire circumstances can have the effect of testing just how deep previously held beliefs really go. We can, all of us, passionately hold views which have never been tested or subjected to serious scrutiny. We might well be surprised with our reaction to situations which do force us to so reflect and measure our convictions. Such circumstances might serve to strengthen our resolve to hold fast whatever the cost. On the other hand they might bring us to see those convictions for what they are, shallow and theoretical strictures which must give way to values of far greater moment. So, in this specific case our respondent was led to assert that, faced with the death of her child but for the provision of a procedure previously thought to be culturally unacceptable she would opt for it:

> Absolutely, I mean for my cultural, spiritual beliefs about not tampering with nature that all goes out of the window, I mean if it's going to save a life too bad about your high horse and your morals and ego.

While she is still tempted to think that opting for her child's life involves turning her back on morals, it is far more plausible to construe her concern for her child's life as placing an absolute requirement on her – and what is this if it is not a moral reaction?

But why should we conclude that such a choice would place her somehow outside the mores of her culture? Might it not be, rather, that some of the values of that culture have been seen to yield to others, and in such a way as to loosen the grip which those other values have had on her?

Yet the change might be more profound than this for the critical incident might serve to open the eyes of the sufferer to an understanding of her culture which goes deeper than that she had previously achieved. Cultures develop in this way. Pakeha culture, if there is any such thing, has certainly gone this way in light of numerous developments in medical science over the centuries. Even during the past forty years the advent of organ transplantation and *in vitro* fertilisation have each produced profound moral disquiet at first but now, for the vast majority of people, have been absorbed as proper advances in our care for each other. In our respondent's case the apparent challenge to the values which have hitherto informed her life, her cultural identity, has now provided a richer appreciation of that culture, one of which is able to make sense of and invest significance in events which would previously have been personally and socially destructive for her. As such the event has facilitated a cultural development. As she herself put it when asked whether any cases of plant modification could be seen to be absolutely wrong from a cultural standpoint:

> Culturally I don't think it should, I don't think most Maori will agree especially old people. I think culturally it is wrong in the first place but then again putting it in different contexts and scenarios you sort of tend to sway your cultural beliefs.

This informative and honest reflection on the part of a respondent who worried that she had 'contradicted herself about four times' in the interview gives us good reason to question whether anyone is entitled to speak for all Maori, whatever their life experiences and personal narratives, in terms of what is an acceptable Maori ethical view of genetic technologies involving plants. It also suggests both that we should not be at all surprised at radical disagreements arising over these issues between Maori, producing moral conflict nor assume the impossibility of ethical agreements across cultures as to what should be done in health care interventions.

Conclusion

There are occasions when disagreements about what should be done cannot be resolved by reason. This might not always be due to stubbornness, ignorance, lack of patience or time, or failures in logic. Rather they might be due to rival views of the world which grip the disputants. These views are rooted in the social contexts and the narratives of the rival parties. They are not simply rival views about what should be done but are contrasting descriptions of the facts employed in deliberations about what should be done. These might be descriptions about what is harmful or beneficial, what is a person, what is the proper weight to give to an agreed fact in a discussion, who is my brother, and so on. It is out of disagreements at this level that radical disagreements in ethics arise.

Appeals to a common rationality which will prevail given sufficient openness in discussion are vain in that they tackle the possibility of radical disagreement at the wrong level. The process of discussion cannot proceed until the relevant facts to be discussed are agreed. But the roots of radical disagreement in morality lie at this level. Neither can the possibility of radical disagreement be eradicated by an appeal to agreement about the general premises which underlie all moral discussion as those premises might themselves be subject to disagreement. The appeal to the paradigm of objective truth in empirical discourse similarly fails to rule out the possibility of radical disagreement in ethics as it assumes that all facts are of a similar kind. But some facts have moral import while others do not. Moral conclusions cannot be drawn from collections of facts with no moral import but neither can agreed conclusions be guaranteed from discussions involving facts with moral import as their import might be different given the different contexts and experience of the discussants. Appeals to a common psychology among people based on the fact of the existence of public language are similarly destined to fail as defences against the possibility of radical disagreement in ethics. This is because even though certain fundamental agreements in reactions are necessary to facilitate the development of public language they thereby facilitate the possibility of both agreement and disagreement in opinions. An appeal to normal modes of thought to eliminate radical disagreement fails too. This is due both to the fact that establishing the norm might itself be a matter of dispute and to the fact that justifications of any given norm are not independent of the mode of thought in which they are justified. Finally the observation that apparent radical disagreements which arise out of cultural dissonance are sometimes overcome does not undermine the possibility of radical disagreement. This is because when such agreement is reached it is not by some process of reason or judgement but rather by a war of attrition between rival perceptions which result in a change of heart rather than a change of mind in either one or both of the disputants.

The final defence is particularly significant in health care contexts where cultural plurality is an increasingly important factor. The dangers of cultural imperialism have to be guarded against in clinical practice. This is especially important with respect to clinical judgements. The patient's perspective cannot be ignored in good practice but preserving respect for cultural differences is demanding. For example, it is important to recognise that rival agendas might be at work in making appeals to cultural differences. Nevertheless such differences should not be written off because there are those who might seek to exploit them in unjustifiable ways. But neither should disputants cut short efforts to come to mutual understandings. However, where efforts to achieve such understanding between doctor and patient result in agreement about what should be done in situations of this sort, the agreement is best seen as a development of the moral views of either or both of the parties involved than as one which should be binding in all other cases for it is not a change which occurs as a result of the discovery of mistakes in the original view of either party but one which goes much deeper. It will be a change which will affect the view of many other features of the doctor's or patient's world. Such changes are rather like the dawning of an aspect when one sees the face of an animal in a puzzle picture. It is to acknowledge a difference in sense or significance in features of the case rather than to arrive at a different opinion based on further consideration of what remain the same perceived data.

Notes

1 C. Wellman, 'Ethical disagreement and objective truth', *American Philosophical Quarterly* 12 (1975), 211–21.
2 Ibid.
3 Ibid.
4 E. Anscombe, 'On brute facts', *Analysis* 18 (1958), 69–72.
5 L. Wittgenstein, *On Certainty*, G.E.M. Anscombe and G.H. von Wright (eds.), Oxford: Basil Blackwell, 1969.
6 L. Wittgenstein, *Philosophical Investigations*, Oxford: Basil Blackwell, 1953.
7 Ibid., p. 88e.
8 J. Anderson, *Studies in Empirical Philosophy*, Sydney: Angus and Robertson, 1962, p. 341.
9 C. Wellman, 'Ethical disagreement and objective truth'.
10 The project is funded by the New Zealand Foundation for Research, Science and Technology. In order to conduct a comparison of Maori ethical perceptions of emerging biotechnologies with other views extant in New Zealand society, a series of 67 interviews were conducted by Maori researchers with a cross-section of Maori respondents. They comprised members of the following groups: rangatahi (young people), middle-aged people, kaumatua (elders) and Maori key personnel with special interests, including scientists. The data discussed in this chapter were concerned with Maori perceptions of biotechnologies involving plants. While these data were collected by Maori researchers, the subject matter of the interviews was informed by discussions between them and a group of bioethicists, made up of philosophers, clinicians and a research scientist. The interviewers were thus apprised of the kind of interest which ethicists have in these matters but were given a free hand in conducting their inquiries, employing this advice as they saw fit. Verbatim content of these interviews is produced in italics throughout this chapter.
11 N.M. Ford, *When did I begin?* Cambridge: Cambridge University Press, 1988, p. 41.
12 Ibid., p. 64.
13 Bioethics Council, *Gisborne – Te Turanga-nui-a-kiwa*. Wellington, New Zealand, 13 March 2004.
14 Ibid.
15 Royal Commission on Genetic Modification Witness Brief of Paora Ammunsen and Tamati Cairns on behalf of Life Sciences Network (Inc), 2001.
16 Bioethics Council, *Gisborne – Te Turanga-nui-a-kiwa*.
17 B. Tipene-Matua, 'A Maori response to the biogenetic age', in R. Prebble (ed.) *Designer Genes*, Wellington: Dark Horse Publishers, 1999, pp. 97–109.

Chapter 3

Mystery in surgery

We noted in Chapter 1 that claims to objectivity have characterised medicine more and more since the Enlightenment when empirical science began to play an increasingly dominant role in clinical practice. This process accelerated beyond recognition during the second half of the twentieth century and with the advent of evidence-based medicine it would seem that we have almost arrived at a place where the knowledge and expertise of the practitioner has displaced the narrative of the patient at the heart of clinical practice. The doctor as expert on the patient's condition exercises skill and clinical practice has become a series of techniques applied to the dysfunctional body to restore it to functional normality. David Greaves refers to this historical shift as a disappearance of mystery in medicine and infers that, despite the advances which science has afforded clinical practice, something very important has been lost in the process.[1] This would seem to be true above all in the practice of surgery where technique clearly plays a more prominent role than elsewhere in medicine. If ever the human condition is transparent to a practitioner, it would seem, it is surely to the surgeon who uncovers the problematic features of the body and deals with them before his very eyes. Mystery, it would seem, is never further away in clinical practice than at the operating table.

> The wounded surgeon plies the steel
> That questions the distempered part;
> Beneath the bleeding hands we feel
> The sharp compassion of the healer's art
> Resolving the enigma of the fever chart.[2]

But where has the mystery gone? Did it consist simply in our ignorance of the functioning of the macro-organism now laid bare before our eyes? Or does the disappearance of mystery really mean that we have, in the march of progress, lost sight of something important which once was evident but has now become obscured? A further examination of the preoccupation with objectivity in surgical practice will facilitate an awareness of the ethical dimension of that practice.

Surgery as a skill

If we try to provide a respectable answer to the question 'What is good surgical practice?' we shall, of necessity, have to look at the skills employed in practice.

Given the choice between, on the one hand, sensitive and empathetic Mr A, a surgeon with high rates of morbidity and mortality and, on the other, officious and uncaring Mr B, a surgeon of great expertise with high rates of outstanding outcomes in his practice, it should not surprise us that patients would opt for Mr B. The inculcation of sophisticated skills is part of the training of surgeons and lack of requisite skill marks out the practitioner as deficient. But what is a skill? On analysis skills are seen to involve means–ends relationships. Goals are set, means are designed and executed to attain them. Maximising the ends and minimising the means to achieve them marks the practitioner out as efficient. There are ethical dimensions which attach to this element of the surgeon's practice. For example, lack of efficiency cannot be condoned where scarce resources wasted on one patient are thereby denied to another; nor when patients are subjected to unnecessary risks such as prolonged periods of anaesthesia. Thus for a surgeon's practice to be described as good it needs to be skilful.

But what of setting the goals to be aimed for? Here we are confronted with an element of practice which simply cannot be reduced to a matter of skill, for the worthiness of such goals might be inescapably contestable, whereas their modes of realisation will be subject to evidence-based evaluation. Here the subject matter of the surgeon's art, persons, marks off his practice from that of the engineer and the tailor. It calls for a different kind of appreciation for his is a feeling, suffering, perceiving, hoping, fearing, thinking subject. The good surgeon needs an insight into the experience or narrative of this subject before he can hope to set a worthwhile objective for an intervention. The engineer can identify a malfunction and know that its correction will restore the machine to a state of well-being – the functional state for which it was created. But what counts as well-being for a patient might not be related straightforwardly to issues of function. Herein is located the mystery in medicine alluded to earlier, its identity as an art rather than a skill. Its focus is the subject matter of practice, understanding and caring for people. Treating people properly is an ethical responsibility for all, not only surgeons, a responsibility which is coextensive with human life both within and without the context of clinical practice. Once we remember this we invoke a set of values over and above the value of efficiency.

These are the values which inform our relationships with other human beings and they lie at the heart of the emerging sub-discipline of Medical Ethics. They can be found in any textbook on the subject and their identity is not a source of dispute as we have all employed them in evaluating human behaviour since we learned to talk. Respect for them is constitutive of good

behaviour and thus of good practice too. They are often identified as autonomy, beneficence, non-maleficence, truthfulness, dignity and justice.[3] Such a
list might not be exhaustive but these values certainly figure prominently in
moral discourse generally. However, they have been cast in an unhelpful light
when they have been identified as moral principles. As such they appear to be
rules for resolving problems and in surgery their application might be
regarded as simply an elaboration of the techniques already cited. This is a
major mistake and is another route to the denial of mystery in the human
encounter. As such it dilutes and distorts human relationships and in the case
of surgery it can vitiate good practice. In the remainder of this chapter I shall
try to illustrate the proper role some of these ethical ideas might play in
orthopaedic surgery and so restore the element of mystery with the aim of
approaching an answer to our question: 'What is good surgical practice?'

Tensions between values

Let us first consider some examples in practice where such values are challenged. Contrast the temptation to perform an unnecessary surgery upon a
patient because it offers us a handsome fee with the case of Patient C, where
the difficulty was to decide whether to amputate a gangrenous limb in order
to save his life when he refused to consent to the procedure.[4] In the former
case we have only one ethical feature at stake, respect for the value of non-
maleficence which is countered by our own ulterior non-ethical designs,
whereas in the latter case we are called upon to satisfy simultaneously respect
for beneficence – the well-being of the patient – and respect for the patient's
autonomy. It seems that we cannot fulfil both duties. But this is not because
of any weakness on our part; it is a logical impossibility.

In the first challenge we might be under pressure not to choose to take the
ethical path because of a rival motivation, the promise of financial reward.
However, where we so struggle to do the ethical thing we do not have a moral
problem, though we might have a problem with our own morality. We are
simply dealing with good old-fashioned temptation in such cases. However,
the second challenge is significantly different. Here we find a tension set up
between the ethical values we have identified. In this case any attempt to
preserve respect for one value – the autonomy of the patient – seems to bar us
from the possibility of showing respect for another value – the concern for the
patient's well-being or beneficence. In such situations there is at least a prima
facie case for thinking that whichever way one decides to go then it is undesirable ethically and to be condemned. Things might not be quite so desperate
as this for there are two possible levels of tension. The one produces what
we might call moral problems whereas the other is productive of moral
dilemmas.

At the very least we have a moral problem on our hands. Indeed this is how
moral problems originate. But for the call for respect of a plurality of values

we would have no moral problems for we would always know what it is ethical to do. We have a moral problem when we have difficulty in deciding what it is right to do because we have rival ethical demands made on us. But such problems might be resolvable in a number of ways.

We might, on reflection, discover other features of the situation which release us from one of the obligations. For example, we might discover that the patient is not in a state of mind whereby we could consider him competent to make a decision about his treatment. If such is the case then his autonomy is already compromised and our acting without his consent would not manifest disrespect. The autonomy claim would be shown to be a prima facie claim only and could be laid aside as we do what is now clearly demanded of us ethically. Where there is no doubt that the patient is competent the clinician, in New Zealand, is legally obliged to desist from amputation, even against his judgement that it is in the best interests of the patient to be treated, as such patients have the right in law to refuse treatment.[5] Once again there is no problem about what must be done though the surgeon might feel obliged morally to lobby for a change in the law if such abstention is abhorrent to him.

On the other hand, laying aside consent issues, we might recognise that there is a tension between our concern to aid the wellbeing of the patient and our concern not to harm him – values which are clearly related in a number of ways. Clinical judgement might clearly advocate intervention in that it could be reasonably expected that net benefit would ensue from the intervention which is, admittedly, harmful as few would deny that it is a harm to lose a leg. Once again the ethical problem is resolved.

However, occasionally the clinician will not be so fortunate. There will be situations where, no matter how much we reflect we shall be left with our impossible choice such that whichever way we jump we shall do what we shall always regret. In such cases we have a moral dilemma. Many clinicians have found themselves in such a bind and have been obliged to act to the best of their ability, yet they have carried the baggage of such choices for many years. It is important for them to recognise that morality is not a tidy business. Sometimes life backs us into corners from which there is no ethically clean escape. Given one's life over again one might still proceed in the same manner and still carry a sense of guilt about it. Such is the nature of moral dilemmas.

Application of values

It would be mistaken to conclude from the preceding observation that it does not matter how one proceeds in practice, that the ethical dimension is a matter of little import given the possibility of such intractable difficulties. The temptation here might be to opt for apparent solutions too readily. Consider further the details of Patient C. He was a chronic paranoid schizophrenic transferred to Broadmoor Special Hospital from Brixton prison following diagnosis. After thirty years there he developed gangrene in a foot which was clinically diagnosed as imminently life-threatening, his estimated survival chances without amputation assessed as no better than 15%. Mr C refused to consider the treatment. Hospital authorities thought at first that they could proceed without the patient's consent. At best the tension between autonomy and beneficence in this case seemed to be apparent only. After all Mr C was mentally ill and had been for a very long time. Surely if a best interests judgement was ever called for it was here. The reasonable medical personnel had concluded that the right way to go was to amputate. It seemed that the patient's refusal evidenced his lack of reasonableness and a compromised competence to make important decisions about his future.

If on this basis, the use of choice of reasonable outcome as a criterion of competence, the clinicians are given the edge in such cases then the whole process of patient consent becomes an idle wheel. That is, the patient finds himself in a *Catch 22* situation. If he consents to the procedure then it will be carried out. If he refuses to consent then it will still be carried out because his refusal will be read as a demonstration of his lack of competence to decide, given that it does not accord with the reasonable judgement of the clinician. But the criterion is one which looks unobjectionable. Though we do not rule out the possibility that competent people might make foolish choices, or take wild risks or bet on extremely long odds, we assume that they do so with their eyes open. But in the case of Patient C some of the clinicians were not persuaded that he was capable of seeing the risks which his refusal involved. The forensic psychiatrist applied pressure to obtain a consent in the light of the prospect of C's imminent and unnecessary death but her efforts were unsuccessful. It seemed to her that C was not gambling on a favourable outcome but rather failing to comprehend the situation in which he found himself.

The court disagreed and concluded that C's grandiose delusions did not relate to his refusal to consent. What was not brought out in the judgement, however, was the underlying cause of the dispute between C and his carers. It was assumed that though he understood the information given him about his condition he did not really believe it. As it turned out he would have been correct to be sceptical as conservative treatment averted the threat of death. But the challenge of the case lies elsewhere than in this uncertainty of prognosis. The variability in application of the value of autonomy in deciding the issue arose from a more fundamental source, viz. rival understandings, rather than rival forecasts, of what was in the best interests of the patient. This is another level of the reasonableness of outcome criterion of competence in applying the value of autonomy. It is also the source of variability in the application of other values, such as beneficence and non-maleficence, and therefore calls for closer attention.

Specificity of values

In medicine it is tempting to assume that when one carries out a procedure, such as the amputation of a limb below the knee, one is doing the same thing to all patients for whom it is indicated. We saw in Chapter 1 that this is an unwarranted assumption. There we considered the procedure of removal of the uterus and noted the variability in perceptions of the role of the uterus among the patients involved in a study. These perceptions played a formative role in their description of the procedure as it was applied to them. Those who thought that the organ was the source of their sexual attractiveness consented to something different from those who saw it as a cleansing organ in the body, and different again from those who saw it fundamentally as the organ facilitating pregnancy. Some thus gave the surgeon permission to do to them something quite different from what others consented to. They perceived different worlds. As we are reminded that in surgery we are caring for people rather than bodies these patient narratives become extremely significant. They often embody world views different from those of the treating clinician. It is here that the most fundamental variations in application of the values cited earlier arise.

So it was with Patient C who did more than simply refuse amputation. He gave reasons for so doing in that he declared that he would rather die with two feet than live with one.[6] It might be that he thought that being crippled or one-legged would constitute an unacceptable assault on his dignity. He certainly did not regard survival as an unmitigated good as did his carers, though he did regard the loss of his limb as an unmitigated evil. The quality of the life saved counted for something and in his estimation it would be intolerable. We thus have rival views here of what could count as a benefit. We do not have to disagree that aiming for benefit or health gain is an integral part of surgical practice to account for the disagreement between C and his surgeon. Rather we need to recognise that it is what counts as harm or benefit that is at issue. For C the loss of the limb would be a fate worse than death whereas for others such a loss would not. The amputee from World War I so vividly described by Siegfried Sassoon is a case in point. Sassoon writes sympathetically of the man though he himself refused to be invalided out of action and the risk of death. For the poem's hero loss of his limb is his salvation but it also guarantees the preservation of his dignity:

> Safe with his wound, a citizen of life,
> He hobbled blithely through the garden gate,
> And thought: 'Thank God they had to amputate!'[7]

To claim that amputation would have amounted to the same thing for each of these men would be to fly in the face of the facts as the facts are constituted by the perceptions of the patients in question. If we are tempted to see C's refusal to lose his limb as placing mistaken importance on being two-legged, we will have to come to terms with the consequences of our judgement in other difficult cases where the narrative of the patient might be even more difficult for us to access.

Consider the recently publicised cases of BDD (Body Dysmorphic Disorder).[8] Kevin Wright, father of a young family, wished to have his healthy left leg amputated above the knee and approached orthopaedic surgeons to perform the operation. This desire had dominated his life from the age of eight years. Should the surgeons have complied? The vast majority refused to become involved though the procedure would not have been illegal. Most were convinced that the problem was psychological and that non-surgical interventions were the proper avenues to be explored. All of these were unsuccessful. Robert Smith, a Scottish surgeon, was approached. He took Wright's story seriously, controversial though he knew such an intervention would be. He read the psychiatric and psychological reports. He researched the phenomenon of BDD and assessed the case over a long period. He concluded that some expressions of the condition were beyond the limits of proper surgical practice and that the concept of BDD was too diffuse, embracing self-mutilation for personal gratification, a craving for dependence on others and sexual fetishism. Wright's case, he believed, was different from all these. For him fixation on the one limb for a very long period made his life impossible and, moreover, it was not susceptible to non-surgical treatment. Some years have passed since the surgery and Wright is delighted with the outcome, describing the intervention thus: 'By taking my leg away the surgeon has made me complete. It just didn't feel like part of me.' The surgeon reports that he has no regrets about it.

Ranking ethical values

One promising route to resolving some of the moral problems facing orthopaedic surgeons would seem to be to secure a ranking of ethical values. For example, in the case of Kevin Wright, if autonomy is seen always as a trump card then the possibility of disrespecting non-maleficence and causing the patient undue harm would not count against the decision to proceed. This solution is clearly unsatisfactory as it implies that there are no limits to what clinicians should be allowed or expected to do according to the wishes of the patient. Such a consequence would make it impossible to discriminate between the various kinds of BDD as Mr Smith did. No clinician should be obliged to engage in interventions which, in his professional judgement, result in net harm to the patient. However, this is not to say that the right of a patient to refuse treatment should not trump the clinician's desire to be beneficent, for such a right is embodied in the Health and Disability Commissioner Act 1994 as previously cited.

If there is one value in the list provided earlier which might be the trump card in the Ethics pack it must be justice or equity, for of any decision based on applications of the other values we might yet ask: 'But is it fair?' Efforts are being made currently in orthopaedic surgical practice and other specialties in New Zealand to inject greater equity into the health care system given the inevitability of rationing scarce resources. This enterprise has highlighted the problems in producing objective, and consequently general, standards for assessing patient states and proper treatment decisions. The production of Clinical Priority Assessment Criteria (CPACs) in order to rank patients for elective procedures has presented challenges which illustrate some of the foregoing complexities of engaging in the art of clinical practice. Given such complexity it might be tempting to turn away from the task and find refuge in some arbitrary general measures of patient need based purely on the physiological condition of the patient. But, as we have noted, this would undermine the quality of surgical practice. What practitioners are obliged to do, in the name of their art, is face the complexities head on and do their best to approach decisions with sensitivity and courage. Two major problems need to be addressed. The first is the external pressure to maximise benefit, the second is the identification of health need.[9]

When the National Waiting Time Project was being developed in New Zealand, a two-fold criterion of access to services was envisaged, viz. degree of need and capacity to benefit. Tools were to be designed to incorporate each facet of this prioritisation criterion. There is, of course, a logical relation between the two. If a patient cannot possibly benefit from a proposed intervention then she cannot be said to need it. For surgery to be indicated it is necessary for the patient to attain a score which crosses the clinically acceptable threshold (CAT), thus such a score is dependent on the patient's capacity to benefit from the procedure. In this regard the capacity to benefit is a threshold concept. If the answer to the question 'Is this surgery indicated for this patient?' is yes then the patient is scored above the CAT. There is thus far no threat to equity as equity demands that no resources be wasted on unnecessary interventions which would deny treatment to those in need. The danger is that capacity to benefit might be treated otherwise than as a threshold qualification. This occurs where the degree to which a patient will benefit is employed as a discriminator between patients. Where this occurs equity is threatened for now maximising benefit, which would seem to be demanded by respect for beneficence, might militate against the interests of certain groups of patients such as the old, the chronically ill and the mentally ill. It follows that the question 'Is it fair to discriminate in this way?' would invite a negative answer. If the enterprise is to treat patients according to their degree of need – the most needy first – then so long as the treatment is indicated, by which we mean that it is likely to be beneficial, it should not be denied to the most needy on the grounds that the less needy would benefit more from it. It would therefore be a mistake to allocate varied scores to patients on the basis of the degree to which they are likely to benefit once the treatment is indicated for them. The degree to which they are likely to benefit is not a reliable indicator of their degree of need and should not figure in the CPACs. Insofar as this is true, equity is seen as trumping beneficence.

However, this observation does not exhaust the complexities of the scoring system. The greatest challenge comes in assessing the degree of need. On what basis is this to be done? Given what has been said above, the surgeon cannot ignore the narrative of the patient in his assessment. This will result in taking into account more than physiological criteria. Sound clinical judgement in assessing a patient's condition has always involved more than a physical examination. Patient information plays a crucial role. But here we move away from secure ground as subjective criteria come into play. Such criteria are not unimportant simply because they are subjective. They should not thereby be ignored, but they might present peculiar challenges in assessment. Among these will be pain reports and accounts of the social implications of the condition. We have already noted in Chapter 1 that until a physical condition is cast in the context of the life of the person suffering it we cannot assess that person's health need.[10] Thus the same physical condition found in two patients might constitute a health need in the one while it might not in the other. Similarly the degree of need might vary according to the social significance of the patient's condition. For example, an elderly patient whose independent life is threatened by her arthritic hip might be said to have a greater health need than her neighbour with an identical condition who lives happily in the home of her extended family. Making such judgements will present the clinician with difficult calls and it will not always be possible to be secure in such judgements. They will often call for an imaginative access to patients' narratives such as that of Mr Smith in the case of Kevin Wright. There will not always be unanimity and such efforts might challenge the clinician's views of what is desirable. Nevertheless, though mistakes might be made and some decisions become more difficult, refusal to take on such a task would be likely to produce far more injustices, and would challenge the increased equity which the booking system was envisaged to ensure. We shall go into more detail about the Waiting Times Project in Chapter 4.

Conclusion

Surgery is probably the area of clinical practice in which it is most tempting to adopt the medical model which makes the surgeon, the direct observer of the patient's physiological condition, the authority on what the patient needs. Discovering the patient's needs seems rather like discovering a seam of coal which simply lies out of sight waiting to be uncovered. Patient perceptions play little or no part in this process of discovery though they might have provided clues as to the whereabouts of the problem. The discovery itself is a matter of straightforward, though expert, observation achieved by the application of evidentially based techniques.

But this is an illusion. Though the expert application of established techniques is an indispensable part of the clinical activity it does not constitute a complete description of it. The surgeon is charged with providing clinical care to patients, those whose bodies are the subjects of the techniques, and these are embodiments of whole ranges of emotions, hopes and fears, preferences, values and outlooks on their worlds. As clinicians are privileged to enter those worlds, they have to take the treated person as a whole into account. But this removes surgical activity from the realm of straightforward empirical observation and scientific certainties. Surgeons cannot themselves know what it is that they do to their patients nor know what their patients need without knowing much more than what bodily observations permit. It is at this level that patient values define their clinical situations. As these will vary from patient to patient, subtle but crucial uncertainties are introduced to the surgical scene. These demand a different quality of attention from the practitioner than the careful application of technical skills which are so prominent and integral to good surgical practice.

Insofar as these observations are true then it might be said that there is an element of mystery in surgery. But there is more to the element of mystery than this in that, in addition to the variations in what patients see as their needs and as desirable treatments or outcomes, there are the challenges of moral deliberation with which the surgeon has to cope. Knowing what to do in individual cases is not achieved by the application of techniques of thought which will also remove uncertainties on every occasion. It will be tempting once again to generalise and seek to resolve some of the tensions between ethical values which individual cases will produce by applying techniques such as a prioritised and delimited set of values. But this will blind the surgeon to important possibilities and result in unethical practice.

Pointing out these uncertainties which inevitably characterise good surgical practice might make that practice more difficult and demanding. However, if it is in the nature of surgery to be more than the application of a series of skills then embracing mystery in surgery will produce a heightened awareness of those uncertainties and both protect and improve the quality of practice.

Notes

1 D. Greaves, *Mystery in Western Medicine*, Aldershot: Avebury, 1996, pp. 19–37.
2 T.S. Eliot, 'Four quartets: East Coker' in *The Complete Poems and Plays of T.S. Eliot*, London: Faber and Faber, 1969, p. 181.
3 Following the influential book of Beauchamp and Childress: T.L. Beauchamp and J.F. Childress, *Principles of Biomedical Ethics*, 5th edn, New York: Oxford University Press, 2001.
4 *Re C (Adult : refusal of treatment)*, 1 Weekly Law Reports, 1994, 290–6.
5 New Zealand Health and Disability Commissioner Act 1994. Section 74(1) Appendix B, Right 7.7.
6 *Re C (Adult : refusal of treatment)*, 1 Weekly Law Reports, 1994, 291.

7 S. Sassoon, 'The one-legged man', in *Collected Poems (1908–1956)*, London: Faber and Faber, 1961, p. 26.

8 P. Taylor, 'My left foot was not part of me', *The Observer*, Manchester: Guardian News and Media Limited, 6 February 2000, 14.

9 For a fuller discussion see D.M. Evans and N. Price, *Ethical Dimensions of the National Waiting Time Project*, New Zealand: Health Funding Authority, 1999.

10 See p. 23.

Chapter 4

Equitable health care

Towards the end of Chapter 3 we considered that the best candidate for the number one position in any ranking of ethical values must be justice or equity in that whenever any decision is made for whatever reason one might always ask whether it is fair. Nowhere is this more plausible than in the management of health care resources as the conceptual limits to good health care explored up to this point pose considerable challenges for those who have to manage health care services and allocate scarce health care resources. Here there is an understandable temptation to seek for definitive management solutions in the application of models which assume general and objectively verifiable answers to rationing problems.

There is much to be said for the application of transparent systems of rationing valuable resources when they are in short supply. Such is the case with health care resources everywhere. However, rationing models are usually based on a utilitarian theoretical base and seek to maximise the health benefits which accrue from the investment of health dollars. While equity is a major problem for such models, there are other serious obstacles to their implementation. These are related to the calculations demanded by such theoretical approaches which often involve assumptions about the nature of people's health and their needs consonant with the temptation to abstract them from patient narratives. This chapter seeks to explore these various threats to good health care provision and to consider one recent effort to address them.

Where there is a shortage of supply and apparently endless calls for goods, some of the latter will inevitably remain unmet. It would appear that this is most painfully true in the area of health care provision. It is often expressed as a practical problem in the form that limited resources cannot meet unlimited demand. Whether this is a genuine problem in health care provision is something we should ask. We shall see that even if the answer is yes then the problem of limits to care in allocating resources is vastly more complex than one which is open to any straightforward practical resolution. Some of the apparently practical problems in health care provision find their origin in other kinds of limits than mere shortfalls in resources. For example, they have to do with conceptual limits connected with the enterprise of identifying and aggregating goods in health care provision. Such limits are centre stage in all maximisation theories of resource allocation in health care, the theoretical approach most favoured and that with which we shall be largely concerned in this chapter. Beyond and beneath both these kinds of limits we can identify moral limits to the provision of health care which might impose either further restrictions on what may be offered to sufferers or, in other contexts, impose different patterns and methods of distribution on the resources allocated. Once such limits are recognised then we are faced with the problem of deciding who gets what, which calls should be heeded and which ignored.

The problem of shortfalls

Is either side of the expression of the problem of the need for rationing in health care provision accurate? Is there really a shortage of resources? Is there really unlimited demand? The two notions are in one sense inseparable. Unless there is unmet demand, or at least unmet need which may be quite a different matter, there cannot be a shortage of resources. Whether the resources thrown at a problem are adequate necessarily depends on the nature of the problem. If no health care needs remain unmet then it would be difficult to justify increased expenditure on Health Services except in relation to correcting injustices of remuneration to health service employees or maintaining and improving hospital and other hardware provision in order to guarantee a continued adequate service. Though these additional issues have figured in discussions of the under-resourcing of the Health Service in the United Kingdom, for example, they are not the focus of the debate about rationing. It is the claim that the demands made on the service are unlimited which figures most prominently together with the obviously true claim that resources are not infinite. Even if the figure of 5.8% of the Gross National Product (GNP) spent on health care provision in the United Kingdom in 1991 (4.1% in 1950, 5.5% in 1976, 6.1% in 1983)[1] was extended to the 14% of GNP spent on health care provision in the United States, this would not guarantee that there would be no shortfall between resource and demand. Indeed the fact that there is such a glaring shortfall of this kind in the United States suggests the likelihood that the same would occur elsewhere, especially with the decline of automatic welfare state provision which is occurring in developed countries.

It would be false to imagine that the shortfall in the United Kingdom is a recent development. It has been convincingly argued that it is at least as old as the National Health Service itself,[2] prior to which the provision of health care to large proportions of the population was admittedly inadequate, many of the population not having the wherewithal to purchase the quality of health care which they required, which is a different version of the limited resources and unmet need equation. The ghost of inefficiency stalks the corridors of the National Health Service in the UK, whose reforms have suggested that the problem has been one of inefficient use of the resources available. This has been strongly disputed, it being claimed contrarily that the quality and comprehensiveness of the health care purchased in the United Kingdom on around 6% only of GNP in 1991 was remarkably good value for money.[3] It rather looks like being the case that the shortfall between resource and demand or need is caused by the very success of the delivery of health care. The Beveridge Report in the United Kingdom led politicians to expect that when the National Health Service was set up and resources were thrown at the health problems of the nation those problems would be met, the health status of the population improved and the levels of demand decrease.[4] However, no such outcome occurred. Though spending has increased, the calls upon the Health Service have increased far more quickly. This should really surprise nobody for a moment's reflection on just one health care intervention will illustrate the nature of the problem.

Consider the treatment of renal failure by dialysis. Only a few decades ago someone suffering renal failure would make immediate but brief demands on health care resources. Given the hopeless prognosis of the condition the terminal care of the patient would constitute the total demands that patient would make on the service. With the advent of renal dialysis, a medical success story, such lives can be saved and considerably extended even without the benefits of transplantation surgery. However, far from making a dent in the demands or needs knocking at the door of the health budget, so reducing costs, the very success of the therapy guarantees the production of an acute need for the rest of the patient's life – which may be many years. The cost of the dialysis fluids alone will commit the caring authorities to the expense of at least £10,000 per annum to which must be added the cost of maintaining surveillance and monitoring of the patient, dealing with infections, and so on. The cost of success is therefore very high in that the meeting of one short-term, albeit fundamentally acute, need creates a further acute long-term need which commits considerable sums from the budget to a patient who, without treatment, would long since have made no demands whatsoever on health resources. The same is true of many other areas of medical intervention. Indeed every life-saving intervention commits health authorities to the cost of continued care of the life saved. In the case of pre-term babies the initial heavy investment of resources guarantees a full lifetime of demands, in many cases of extraordinary demands. At the other end of life the success of the Health Service in improving the health status of the UK population has resulted in very large numbers of people living very much longer than they would otherwise have done, thus presenting the most serious drain of resources by any group of patients. It is this level of efficient delivery of health care which has done the opposite to what the Beveridge Report expected. Each successful intervention, each new life-saving or life-enhancing technology has created new demands. Thus by its very nature health care provision is subject to unlimited demand; the more we have of it the more we shall expect and demand of it.

But given that a shortfall between resource and demand is inevitable in the nature of the case, how shall we make decisions about what ought or ought not to be provided, which demands ought or ought not to be met? Two approaches stand out as the main theoretical options. The first is the maximisation of benefit approach and the second, which may on occasion be a variant on the first, the prioritising of need approach. Let us consider them in turn.

The maximisation of benefit

This is by far the most popular approach recommended and practised in health care economics. This is well expressed by the health economist Gavin Mooney as follows:

> What I would want to emphasise is that I see the issue here as being one of efficiency – essentially, maximising the benefit (however defined) to society at large from the resources available (however constrained).[5]

This enterprise seems at first blush to be ethically unobjectionable or even admirable. In times of scarcity those resources used inefficiently on one patient are resources denied to another patient who stands in need of them. Economists refer to this phenomenon in terms of opportunity costs. It is impossible to justify wasting valuable commodities. The only problem seems to be a practical one of determining what counts as the maximum benefit to be produced from a given unit of resource. If this was only a matter of complexity due to the intricate character of the calculations involved then resource allocation in health care would be no more than a tricky but morally non-threatening activity. However, there is far more to it than there appears to be. For a start it is blandly assumed in what has gone before that if maximum benefit is not achieved (given that such can be identified) then resources have been wasted. But is this true? Something less than maximum benefit may nevertheless be morally worthwhile and achievable only at the price of marginal inefficiency. The saving of a life only to lose it within hours when the risks of such an outcome were high may signal the importance of other values than maximally efficient use of resources in our assessments of what is morally justifiable and what is not. Indeed that resource allocation problems normally apply only at the margins of health care provision and not at its heart, for example in many acute interventions, denotes this.

But the problems with maximisation theories of resource allocation go deeper than this. They attach in part to conceptual limits to care, that is to limiting features of the concept of maximal benefit and of benefit *per se* and additionally to moral limits of care, that is to relations that providers of care have with individual sufferers and their respective perceptions of their suffering.

The theoretical stable of ethical theory out of which this model of resource allocation comes is that of consequentialism. It is exemplified in the utilitarianism of Jeremy Bentham and John Stuart Mill[6] but is in fact a more general position of which there have been many variants produced even up until the present.[7] The position holds that in order to determine the right course of action in any given situation one should attend only to the consequences of the action. In attending to these one should endeavour to calculate the greatest net balance of benefit over harm. Whichever action produces, or is likely to produce, the greatest good for the greatest number is the action which can be morally justified. It is clear that such a theoretical stance is attractive to planners of health care who have the responsibility, on behalf of the public, to best provide for the health needs of whole populations. Here attention to individual needs should, it would appear, not distort the overall allocation policy and, in the name of justice, each individual should count for one and no more than one. There are traditional problems associated with such a model which plague its application in the area of health care resource allocation. Much of what follows in this chapter is an effort to begin to identify and work out some of those difficulties.

Cost-effectiveness analysis

Two of the major problems which traditionally threaten consequentialist theories of ethics are the identification and the aggregation of goods. It will be interesting to enquire whether and to what degree these problems prove troublesome in the application of the two models of analysis employed in health economics which embody the maximisation principle as their *raison d'être* – cost-effectiveness analysis and cost–benefit analysis. On the face of it the former, cost-effectiveness analysis, is the more ethically innocent of the two as it appears to avoid the problem of identification of goods *ex hypothesi* given that the good aimed for has to be written into the model before it can be applied. However, the problem of aggregation of goods still arises in the application of the model, despite the apparently singular interest of the model in the selection of the good aimed for. In attending to this difficulty we might well discover that there is reason to doubt the absence of the problem of identification of goods in the model.

This tool of economic appraisal does not involve the setting of objectives or goals. It first demands that those planning health care provision present their chosen goals for analysis. The analyst then attends to the various means available to achieve those ends and endeavours to identify which are the most economical. Roughly speaking if the goals can be maximised and the means minimised then maximal effectiveness will be achieved. However, there almost always have to be trade-offs between these measures. Consider a hypothetical case. It may be that the application of a given screening regime for detecting genetic risk in potential parents would pick out 100 cases per 1,000 screened if only families known to be at risk are entered into the programme. The cost per detected case will then be only 1% of the budget allocated to the procedure. However, by restricting the programme to known 'at risk' couples many other cases will necessarily go undetected. The programme could be extended in various ways. Maybe, for the sake of argument, there is some evidence of unequal demographic distribution of the conditions in question. It will then appear to make sense to widen the pool of candidates for screening to include all potential parents in those areas under suspicion. The result will most likely be, even if there are special local causal agents present, that smaller numbers of cases will be detected in a greatly increased number of screenings. Let us imagine that they will amount to 10 further cases out of an extra 10,000 people screened. For each of this group of 10 the costs will be, all other things being equal, 10% of a vastly greater budget. For each extension based upon more tenuous links between the selected groups and the condition to be detected, the cost per detected case will increase at alarming rates. We are thus faced with a situation of diminishing returns. It is clear that vast sums of money will be required to detect each single extra case beyond a given point. The aim of maximising the goal will soon have to be abandoned because of its cost implications.

The balancing act between cost and benefit is even more demanding than this. It also involves the problems of aggregating goods despite the apparently singular good presented for analysis. Imagine a case where an apparently singular objective is set and cost-effectiveness analysis applied. For example, if by adopting a regime of day surgery 50 hernia operations can be performed for the cost of 20 by means of hospitalised care then, all other things being equal, this would be the most cost-effective and therefore the right form of management to adopt, given that the maximal use of resources is the ideal goal for which to aim. The catch, even here, where like is being compared with like, is that all other things are rarely equal. It may be argued that all sorts of disagreements about what constitutes a successful outcome, what constitutes good care, and so on might still arise. The emotional cost of anxiety caused to the patient by discharge to home so soon after surgery, the possibility of readmission for complications, the burden on informal carers, possible prolongation in recovery time, and so on cloud the issue. That a precise number of hernia surgeries are performed is but part of the story. These other considerations, the avoidance of which might go towards constituting a successful outcome, present additional objectives to be weighed against the set objective of performing the greater number of operations. Once this is recognised then cost-effectiveness analysis ceases to be useful for all the objectives call for weighting and this is a task the analysis cannot perform. Health economists recognise this limitation of cost-effectiveness analysis:

Strictly, cost-effectiveness analysis can only cope with a programme in which there is a single output. This is because it cannot deal with different weights to be attached to multiple outputs.[8]

So even in cost-effectiveness analysis both the problems of identifying goods and aggregating them occur, despite initial appearances. These problems are, however, up front in cost–benefit analysis.

Cost–benefit analysis

This economists' tool sets out to answer a different kind of question from the question of which means is the most effective to produce a given health care outcome. It endeavours rather to determine which health policies ought to be pursued by asking which outcomes are to be preferred in relation to the cost of achieving them. Before any calculation of the balance of goods can be attempted, goods must first be identified and weighted. But this is by no means a straightforward matter as we have already begun to see. Not only are there problems in achieving universal agreement about what constitutes a good in the health care setting but there are also additional problems in ranking those goods which are identified. For example, does the condition of sterility constitute a good or harm? A little reflection will show that it is possible for people to disagree about this. For some people the inability to procreate is a blessing – indeed we have provided a facility in health care to achieve such a condition in both men and women by deliberately doing them a biological harm producing the condition which is a biological dysfunction. Though in some cases such procedures are designed to resolve or avoid other biological harms, in many cases the reason for the procedure is social or personal. Elsewhere in the health service we invest considerable sums of money to rectify such a dysfunction or, in some cases, to circumvent it by means of assisted conception procedures. These are not available to large numbers of people because, as we saw in Chapter 1, purchasing authorities do not regard them as legitimate solutions to medical problems or, in other words, do not regard the outcome of such procedures as health goods. This is a topic we shall consider in more detail in the next chapter. In the meantime we must ask how cost–benefit analysis can offer the planner any assistance?

Many other examples could be cited. Perhaps the most dramatic cases are those where certain physiological conditions are recognised as calling for treatment in one place whereas they are thought to constitute no claim on treatment services in others, for example, the condition of low blood pressure for which thousands of people are treated in Germany but for which no one is treated in the United Kingdom. Or again cases such as the control of diabetes by means of porcine insulin, the transfusing of blood, and the practice of so-called therapeutic abortion where a given therapy may possibly be regarded by some patients as harmful by definition whatever the outcome for them.

There will be reason to think about such cases when we consider the identity of health needs as variously identified by the social context of the physiological conditions rather than by the biological facts themselves. The facts of benefit are socially constructed and are not simply givens about which there can be no dispute.

Yet cost–benefit analysis boldly claims to be able to help us in the area of identification of benefits while wearing its maximisation-of-benefits heart on its sleeve.

> Ideally, if cost-benefit analysis were widely applied in health care, those policies that show the greatest benefit per £ of resources used should be given the greatest priority. Cost-benefit analysis thus has all the virtues and requirements of cost-effectiveness analysis plus the capacity to assist in decisions about worthwhileness.[9]

How then can such a tool enable us to tackle the problems of the identification and aggregation of benefits? It usually does so by producing a measure of benefit which can be universally applied to all health outcomes, i.e. it assumes that all benefits are, in the last analysis, reducible to one kind of thing. This technique is a straight replication of that employed by John Stuart Mill in his utilitarian theory. For him all goods were cashable in terms of happiness:

> The utilitarian doctrine is, that happiness is desirable, and the only thing desirable, as an end; all other things being desirable as means to that end.[10]

Mill himself recognised problems with the employment of a single measure of what could be regarded as a good and was eager to distinguish various kinds of happiness, some weighing far more than others. The higher pleasures, including intellectual pleasures, he regarded as being more important or considerable than lower animal pleasures. Hence the dictum 'It is better to be a human being dissatisfied than a pig satisfied; better to be Socrates dissatisfied than a fool satisfied'.[11] Arguments about both the identity and application of this measure have been waged for many years without any consensus being reached. One problem, for example, may be said to concern whether the measure involves what people do regard as happiness or rather what they ought to regard as happiness, for there are many who would quarrel with Mill's ordering of intellectual and animal pleasures. Mill leaves this task to a group of experts who are, in a sense, representing the view from nowhere in that they are simply picked out as suitable judges given their experiences of all the pleasures and pains in question. Furthermore they are to deal particularly with the tricky business of assessing the quality and quantity of goods.

According to the Greatest Happiness Principle . . . the ultimate end, with reference to and for the sake of which all other things are desirable (whether we are considering our own good or that of other people), is an existence exempt as far as possible from pain, and as rich as possible in enjoyments, both in point of quantity and quality; the test of quality, and the rule for measuring it against quantity, being the preference felt by those who in their opportunities of experience, to which must be added their habits of self-consciousness and self-observation, are best furnished with the means of comparison.[12]

Of particular interest in its application to resource allocation in health care he asks:

What is there to decide whether a particular pleasure is worth purchasing at the cost of a particular pain, except the feelings and judgement of the experienced?[13]

As he anticipates, in the health care setting we are immediately presented with precisely the same difficulties when devising and applying a singular measure of benefit. Who shall decide what that measure shall be based upon and whose weightings of various outcomes shall count in its creation? It is one thing to propose an abstract unitary theoretical measure which threatens no one but the philosophically sensitive soul and quite another to produce an applied tool which must, to be applied at all, be invested with valuations of various outcomes. The moral attractiveness of the abstract measure, which as we have seen declares war on wasted resources, becomes morally threatening once it betrays a commitment to a particular set of valued outcomes.

Let us look at some examples to illustrate the point. The Welsh Office of the UK Government produced a measure in 1992 which it called *health gain*. This is but one of a number of health status indices which have been produced by health economists. It is, like happiness, on the face of it a fine concept because health gain for the patient is what every health care intervention aims for. For practitioners to desire deterioration in the health status of their patients would be as perverse and as counter-intuitive as someone wanting to be unhappy. But, like happiness, health gain is an elusive entity to track down and measure.

Producing health gain is described as a two-pronged activity – viz. adding years to life and adding life to years, precisely imaging Mill's references to quantity and quality. In combining these elements it also resembles in many ways the QALY produced by Alan Williams who describes the measure as follows:

The essence of a QALY is that it takes a whole year of life expectancy to be worth 1, but regards a year of unhealthy life expectancy as worth less than 1. Its precise value is lower the worse the quality of life of the unhealthy person (which is what the 'quality adjusted bit' is all about). If being dead is worth zero, it is, in principle, possible for a QALY to be negative, i.e. for the quality of someone's life to be judged worse than being dead.[14]

Thus each of these indices is faced with the difficulties of identifying and measuring the added life produced by health care interventions. The quantity element of the measures is pretty crudely measured in terms of improvement in life expectancy and the mortality figures give some guide to us in this respect. However, there is no consensus on what constitutes added quality in every respect nor how balances of added quality are to be calculated. For a start the kinds of goods to be weighed in the common balance of health gain, or QALYs, are simply incommensurable. We would each have difficulty ranking pains, immobility, the delivery of healthy neonates, enhanced life expectancy, disfigurement, mental deterioration, and so on as being more or less desirable than each other in our own experience. Presumably if we could rank them at all they would be ranked differently in different phases of our lives depending on our circumstances. Determining how much of one would be tradeable for how much of another is a further intellectual and emotional challenge. No doubt there would be very considerable ranges of disagreement between individuals if such ranking were attempted. How much more difficult it is when we pretend to be able to determine how one person's pain weighs against another's or how the moderate pain of one hundred sufferers weighs against the excruciating pain of one, or how the pain of one person is to be weighed against the immobility of another, and against the foreshortened life-expectancy of another, and against the safe delivery of another's child. We have then to add the challenge of the cases referred to earlier where conditions some regard as constituting health problems are not so identified by others. Neither of the theoretical backgrounds of the indices mentioned put tools into our hands to determine these imponderables. Some QALY theoreticians have employed an empirical model which seeks to determine a ranking by means of questioning a sample of the public as to their preferences. The sample was extremely small and unrepresentative. In any case such a method of fixing the measure leaves out the crucial question of whether conditions devalued by minorities of people would thus be ruled out as possible candidates for health care interventions. We shall attend in more detail to this question of rival assessments of what are the important features of health status later when we consider the question of health care needs.

The problem of justice

We have so far been concerned to examine two major problems with maximisation of benefit modes of health care resource allocation, viz. the identification and aggregation of goods. It would be mistaken to imagine that the ethical challenges faced by the maximisation of benefit are exhausted by these problems as we have so far examined them. Nevertheless we shall see that they continue to pose difficulties even when we face wider ethical challenges to the maximisation approach.

Consequentialism has numerous rivals in the field of ethical theory. Rights, duty and virtue theories immediately spring to mind. For example, it has been well argued that gross injustices could result from pursuing a maximisation of benefit approach by using the QALY measure. The group inevitably discriminated against in the use of such a measure, it is claimed, is the aged. Where both quantity and quality of added life are incorporated into the measure of health outcome, those least likely to score well on the quantity side are those who are advanced in years and those who are suffering terminal illness. They will be discriminated against. This may be said to constitute an inequity in access to treatment and be unfair, or it may be said to breach the rights such persons may have to access treatment services, for example by virtue of their lifelong payments to health insurance funds or by their low rate of demand on health services hitherto, or both. Similarly those least likely to score well on the quality of life side of the equation, such as the terminally ill and the chronically sick, may be discriminated against as only marginal improvements in their condition can be achieved. Thus in addition to the burden of the debilitating condition they suffer they may face the further burden of losing the little improvement in health they could enjoy to others who suffer less and who, by means of the same resource, enjoy the possibility of a far greater improvement in health.[15]

It is the issue of justice which is the most prominent ethical challenge to maximisation theories. This should come as no surprise as it was the problem of justice which threatened to shipwreck John Stuart Mill's utilitarianism. Indeed he recognised this himself though he was never able to resolve the threat adequately.

> In all ages of speculation, one of the strongest obstacles to the reception of the doctrine that Utility of Happiness is the criterion of right and wrong, has been drawn from the idea of justice.[16]

Those who follow in his footsteps often make the same acknowledgement. For example one leading health economist writes:

> Whatever the financing mechanism, the question of justice and equity in health care seems important. Whatever else people dispute in health service policy, there is general agreement that fairness should be a part of health care.[17]

Mooney goes on to show that preserving a place for efficiency while having regard for equity presents profound problems for health economists. One of the most obvious ways to attempt this is to measure efficiency of health care provision in terms of its success in meeting health care need as opposed simply to meeting health care demand. This involves identifying and ranking needs to enable maximisation of benefit calculations to proceed again. However, we then come up against our old problems of identification and aggregation of goods in another guise. To examine this claim let us consider an example of consequentialist resource allocation theory which makes justice or fairness a central consideration.[18]

The prioritisation of need

Daniels's theory effectively recasts what we have been considering as benefits, or aimed-for outcomes of health service provision, in terms of responses to negative states which constitute needs. Thus, for example, the goal of amelioration of pain would be transposed into meeting a need for the relief of pain, increasing mobility would be transposed into meeting a need for relief of restriction of movement, and so on. Thus we are enabled to introduce a rule of distributive justice into the scheme of maximisation. If we invest our resources in meeting needs then we will have ruled out the provision of unnecessary goods – non-essential demands. If, furthermore, we are committed to meeting the greatest need surely all will be well on the justice front. All that we shall now require is a criterion for identifying health needs which will also, if possible, be amenable to quantification. This will facilitate the ranking of outcomes and allow us to proceed with their aggregation, providing us with an equitable maximisation of benefit model. The proposed criterion is spelled out in terms of what Daniels labels the *normal range of opportunity*. Health care needs impose limitations on how people are able to live their lives as they restrict the range of opportunity of those who suffer them. According to the degree in which a health care intervention restores a normal range of opportunity, it ought, more or less, to be pursued.

Does this gesture towards fairness succeed in overcoming the major inadequacy of the maximising of benefit approach to health resource allocation? If it does then, it has to be said, it does so simply insofar as it gives us a possible means of distinguishing needs from demands to which a bare maximisation of benefit theory would be indifferent. But much more than that it cannot offer us because it runs into precisely the same problems in identifying health needs as we found earlier in identifying benefits. Further to this it also inherits the problems of incommensurability of needs. Moreover, despite appearances to the contrary, it too may be indifferent to degrees of need where they occur in certain groups or are of certain kinds. Let us briefly review some of these problem areas.

In recognising that questions of ultimate ends were not amenable to direct proof Mill used the example of health as an illustration.

Whatever can be proved to be good, must be so by being shown to be a means to something admitted to be good without proof. The medical art is proved to be good by its conducing to health; but how is it possible to prove that health is good?[19]

But we must ask whether what he claims to be true of health itself is not also true of particular health states. Because of the manner in which these individually inform the life of the person in question we may wish to consider them as goods in themselves. Daniels does attend to this question in his treatment of health needs. He borrows a distinction to make his point, viz. that between course-of-life needs and adventitious needs.[20] The former are needs which are basic to life whereas the latter are needs created by virtue of the adoption of various enterprises or ends. The former would be needs which men have *qua* men whereas the latter would be optional, in a sense. If, for example, a boxer chooses to build up body weight in order to compete as a heavyweight rather than a middleweight then he will need additional supplies of red meat. Red meat is an adventitious need. However, to survive at all he needs food in the natural course of things. It is a course-of-life need.

Do all needs fall into such comfortable categories? The answer must be no for there are some features of a person's life without which their whole life will be rendered pointless which in another person's life may count for little. This may depend primarily on the social context of the condition or, as we have seen, on the variety of social movements which pass through individuals in a pluralistic society. Infertility, as we have noted, is a prime example. It is not simply that someone needs to be fertile when they decide on the project of having children, though sometimes having a family may be no more than one project among others. For some women the inability to have children is a fundamental dysfunction which renders their whole life meaningless. That this might not be so with everyone or even a majority of people is beside the point. In the life in question it is regarded as a course-of-life need. It is the social setting of such features of life that determines the category into which they fall.[21] We shall pursue this topic further in Chapter 5. Other examples could easily be cited such as longevity, physical grace, intelligence and even, in some cases, the amelioration of pain. While not all societies would set great store on one or all of these, others would and certainly individuals in various societies will vary in their assessment of the importance of them as features of a healthy life. Daniels himself acknowledges that the notion of normal opportunity range is too general to be straightforwardly applied because of limits placed upon it by such societal considerations, by age and other limiting factors.[22] However, he fails to see that the discriminator dies the death of a thousand qualifications as an attempt to find a common measure of human need.

What then shall we say of maximisation theories of health resource allocation? We cannot quarrel with the attempt to eradicate wastage of scarce resources. Inefficiency is not a virtue. Indeed as a rule of thumb general maximisation techniques may offer us useful guides in planning health policies where there is a broad level of consensus on what constitutes health. However, the application of such theories calls for modesty and sensitivity lest the interests of minorities be threatened and the preferences of self-appointed experts win the day in determining what health care provision people shall receive in ignorance of or in indifference to peoples' perceptions of their own lives and interests.

It might appear from what has been said above that we are in a hopeless situation when we are called upon to ration health services on the basis of need. However, we should not be deceived by appearances. Though it is true that there is no prospect of finding a rigorous framework to calculate definitive apportionments at the macro-allocation level because of the impossibility of devising a common measure which is applicable to all health conditions, at the micro-level prioritisation of need is possible. Indeed it is an ethical imperative.

Such prioritisation has been attempted of late with respect to access to elective surgery. Two such systems were mentioned in Chapter 2 and earlier in this chapter. One has been designed and employed in New Zealand and the other has been designed by the Western Provinces of Canada though the latter has not been implemented as yet. Each of them involves the attempt to inject equity into the waiting times for elective surgery. The former seeks merely to prioritise patients to ensure that those with the greatest need, rather than those capable of benefiting most, are given preference of access to treatment. The latter is more ambitious in that it seeks not only to prioritise but also to determine maximum waiting times for elective patients.

It has been noted that the systems consist in the development of measures of need within services. No attempt is made to apply these measures across services. That is, we might say that horizontal equity is not aimed for. This respects the conceptual objection about incommensurability of goods canvassed earlier. However, within a service vertical equity is a goal. Consider the example of cataract surgery. It is possible to compare the severity of this condition by means of objective measures insofar as acuity and so on can be determined conclusively. However, the measure developed in the scheme also endeavours to build in social and emotional implications of the condition. This respects the earlier observation about the nature of health needs, i.e. that they constitute more than medical descriptions in that such conditions have to be cast in the context of the life of the sufferers in order to constitute health needs. The measures are developed by specialist clinicians in the relevant services. In one sense this is no more than a refinement of the comparisons that have been made traditionally in medicine which enable clinicians to distinguish acute from non-acute cases. That is not to say that formulating tools for such comparisons is easy. It has been an arduous business but it has proved to be possible. Thus, for example, a patient with a slightly worse acuity test result than another but whose life is more significantly affected by the condition could score more highly.

The scheme involves the development of clinical priority assessment criteria (CPAC). They are developed by clinicians to reflect the standards of best clinical practice. Their role is to score patients according to a number of different features. Overall they enable ranking of patients in terms of their degree of need for the treatment in question. Those who need it most are prioritised to be treated first. The score range is 0 to 100, and the score which marks out the point at which surgery is indicated for patients becomes the Clinically Acceptable Threshold (CAT). Achieving this score makes a patient a candidate for surgery but does not guarantee access to surgery. Everybody below the clinical threshold is considered to be best treated conservatively. Patients are treated from the most needy to the less needy down the priority rankings until resources are exhausted. That point marks out the Financially Sustainable Threshold (FST). Thus a visible group of patients remain who need the surgery, but cannot access it. They are carefully managed and if their score increases sufficiently they access surgery. If further resources are provided they might access treatment as a result of a lower FST.

Numbers of those patients below the clinical threshold have in the past been treated in the private sector. Such intervention is unethical as it is not in the best interests of those patients. Here the waiting-time project has helped to curtail such practice because numbers of surgeons will not now operate, however much patients are prepared to pay or insist, if their score comes below the clinical threshold.

In the early stages of the scheme one of the tools employed in the clinical priority assessment system was designed to score the need for a joint replacement procedure. It illustrates some of the tensions experienced in designing the allocation tools. First of all, the history of the condition was required, followed by an assessment of the degree of pain, function limitation and social limitations imposed by the condition. Some of these assessments are difficult. People say that they are subjective; and indeed they are. However, this should not be seen as a lack in the system. Medicine isn't a science as we have seen and scientific precision cannot apply to all features of the human experience. The degree of need for a hip replacement can only be determined when the condition is cast in the context of the patient's experience. Thus attempts have to be made to build in the social dimension to the scoring system. Each of these assessments attracts a proportion of the 100 available points in the final score.

However, another assessment was included at first which constituted the sting in the tail in the development of this musculoskeletal tool. Some clinicians insisted on building into it the capacity to benefit from surgery as part of the measurement of the degree of need of the patient. This was problematic as it endeavoured to build a maximisation element into an equity tool. This element served to confound the measurement of the need of the patient as some patients who were less needy than others would be able to reap greater benefits from surgery. This is why the capacity to benefit must play the role of a threshold concept only. The prioritisation scheme is designed to choose between such candidates in terms of their degree of need, not in terms of how much benefit will accrue from their treatment.

The ethical case for the system

So where have waiting lists gone? They have disappeared, though this is a paper clearance only. Patients who come above the FST are booked in for surgery. Thus, strictly speaking, there is no waiting list of people to be offered surgery. This can be seen as an ethical gain as the waiting list system was open to a variety of abuses.

Visibility

First people on long waiting lists were easily forgotten. It is well known that in developed countries waiting lists in public health services often contain large numbers of deceased patients, or patients who have purchased the treatment from private facilities. Often little or no organised surveillance of the patients has occurred as they have waited patiently, and in sublime ignorance of their slim chances of ever being called for surgery. One doctor has described the process as 'telling patients that they were on the waiting list and jollying them along until death'. In the prioritisation system we are considering patients cannot disappear from view in this way. Indeed the group caught between the CAP and the FST become highly visible.

Equity

The second major ethical gain is the very object of the scheme, viz. equity of access at the point of need. Under the waiting list scheme people moved up the list for all kinds of reasons, many of which were totally unrelated to their health needs. Research has shown, for example, that patients of some primary physicians endured average waiting times three times greater than those of other primary carers. On examination it was discovered that the deciding factor was whether the primary physician and surgeon were at the same medical school. Other social relations irrelevant to health need and special pleading also accelerated many less needy patients towards the operating theatre. This was not a fair way of dealing with people's health needs. Both the patient and primary care physician need confidence that the system within which they collaborate is fair.

Transparency

The third gain is transparency. The kind of leapfrogging described above happened, by and large, without those who were left behind knowing what had happened. The natural assumption that at the end of a year or two years of waiting for a procedure a name would be nearer to the top of the list was not a safe one. In the prioritisation system patients know why it is that they are not booked in for surgery. They know that there are others whose need is greater. Though such knowledge will be disappointing for them it does not strike them as being unjust and prejudicial. Neither do they feel abandoned as a programme of continued surveillance and care is put in place.

Certainty

A fourth claim to ethical gain in the scheme is that it affords certainty to patients, either that they are or are not going to have surgery. The former is clearly reassuring news. The latter might not appear to be a gain. However, it is to be preferred to living in forlorn hope, which is a recipe for disappointment and can interfere drastically with the ordering of one's affairs. Patients know that certain deteriorations in their condition will afford them access to the surgery which they need.

Criticisms of the scheme

The scheme is not perfect. Given the nature of the problems in identifying and aggregating health needs it would be foolish to think that any rationing scheme was immune to ethical criticism. However, many of the criticisms made of the scheme are not justifiable.

Sub-optimal health care

Let us first consider the claim that the scheme cannot provide the most effective health care. This is an important observation. The scheme commits carers to waiting until disease conditions progress to a relatively advanced state before surgical intervention occurs as patients have to wait until they are among the most unhealthy patients before they are booked for theatre. But, it is argued, it is generally true that the earlier the intervention the better the health outcome. Indeed this is the principle embodied in the distinction between acute and elective procedures. Acute cases are those where either death or irrecoverable deterioration and damage might occur if treatment is delayed. What can we say to this accusation? There is certainly an important element of truth in it. While many deteriorations in elective cases are recoverable others are not and better outcomes would be achieved for the latter group of people if earlier treatment was available. But, given the resource restraints with which the health services are faced, what would the cost be of treating these patients first? It would be to turn our backs on those in greater need and with predictable and dreadful prospects. The distinction between acute and elective patients is underpinned by the presumption that we cannot prefer to leave the very sick untreated where the choice is between them and others. That there is a moral cost to the prioritisation of the most needy cannot be denied but it is necessarily less than the cost of abandoning the most needy to treat others optimally.

But how far should we take this? What of the cases where the gain is marginal and the expense is immense? If we say that people with the greatest need should be treated first, aren't we committed to treat in cases where the need is immense, but the gain minimal? Clearly there are such cases. For example, should we spend large amounts of health resources providing joint replacements for incredibly sick people, with numerous co-morbidities and maybe advanced secondary malignancies when there is an almost negligible chance of improvement in their quality of life? If our rule is to treat the patient with greatest need then it seems that we are committed to this path. But this would constitute a major problem for the management of health care. How can we deal with it?

We will have to invoke what could be called a more liberal concept of futility here. Of course it would be wrong to offer surgery to somebody for whom it is not indicated. It would be a futile intervention, and a waste of resource, as well as harmful to the patient. But this is the conservative notion of futility with which we are all familiar. A more liberal view of futility could apply to cases where the possible health gain is so small as to be not worthwhile. We have to tread very carefully here lest we set dangerous precedents which would cause us to slide back into maximisation of benefit models of resource allocation. However, we can all imagine examples of cases where we would want to regard the intervention as being as near as makes no difference to being futile. Consider the extreme case where a large investment of theatre time and skills could only secure a very brief extension of life of the very poorest quality – like a few days of semi-conscious life on sophisticated life support apparatus with no possibility of interpersonal relationships or decision-making capabilities. If extension of life in itself is to be regarded as a gain then we do not have a conservatively futile intervention here. But very few would regard the outcome as a worthwhile gain in such circumstances. It is not possible to say where the line should be drawn precisely marking off the first group of futile interventions from these others. But we can all see the difference between the kind of case outlined here and cases where, even if the extension of life is brief, meaningful contacts with people and meaningful decisions would be possible for the patient. The former we might not regard as worthwhile whereas we could regard the latter as such.

Unreliability

The second criticism has some moral force. It is that the system cannot be trusted because of the unreliability of the scoring tools it employs. At first the unreliability of the scoring tools was worrying. There was considerable inter-rater variability in scoring patients. There was also some intra-rater variability, where on different days, the same scorer scored the same patient differently. However, the provision of training and regular review of the tools has gone a long way to resolving these difficulties. These tools are the key to the whole procedure of prioritisation and their proper formulation demands a great deal of expert clinicians' time.

However, even when the tools are well formulated concerns still arise about the reliability of their application, for instance those cases where marginal decisions to treat or not to treat occur. Consider a case where one patient's score is 55, and another's is 54? What should be done? Can clinicians be secure in their judgement that the former patient has a greater need than the latter? It is fairly clear that we cannot be absolutely confident about the matter. So what is the alternative? Well, one might suggest tossing a coin as there appears to be next to nothing which separates the claims to treatment. No great injustice could be done in such cases. However, there is an obvious difference between the scores of 75 and 35 which cannot be challenged. It would be unwise to discard the scheme in the face of marginal cases as in the vast majority of cases secure judgements of relative need are feasible. The problem remains about what to do in the marginal cases. The sensible way forward would appear to be to go along with the scores as they represent the best comparison we can hope for and the resulting decision is likely to be fairer than one reached by ignoring those scores.

Threshold clustering

Another problem with the scheme is the tendency of clinicians to employ the tools in good faith but to do so under pressure to do their best for their patient in line with their obligation to provide the best standards of care possible. Thus the following phenomenon sometimes occurs. Peaks in the distribution curve of scores arise around the clinical threshold. When applying the scoring tools doctors know that the patients before them will not receive surgery unless they hover somewhere around or above that threshold. The result is that the assessment results get sucked into this vortex; there is an upward thrust produced by the doctors' concern to treat.

However, this is a matter which can be managed in the system. Given the transparency of the scheme it is possible to compare the scoring practices of clinicians in various centres. In one such comparison all the patients of one team were scored above the CAT whereas in all the others normal distributions occurred. Monitoring practice in this way enables managers to identify outliers and to investigate their cause. Of course it might turn out that in a given area all the patients presenting with a problem such as arthritic hip indicating joint replacement are uniformly severe cases. It is very unlikely to be the case and further training on the application of the scoring tools would be indicated by the eccentric pattern of assessments.

Gaming the system

The previous criticism of the scheme under discussion concerned doctors acting in good faith in using scoring tools. However, it is possible to act in bad faith in employing them, in other words, to game the system. A given scorer could deliberately score all patients as urgent. Similarly patients might employ various techniques to exaggerate the severity of their condition. However, this does not disqualify the system. Any system can be subject to this threat. The scoring system is, however, much more difficult to game than the system it has replaced or any other which has yet been devised. Insofar as this is the case then it remains the best we can do at the moment.

Clinical autonomy

It has been claimed by some practitioners that the prioritisation scheme imposes restrictions on professional clinical autonomy. This is a valid criticism but it is important to ask how much weight it should carry. The claim that the scheme restricts good clinical judgement is false. The tools are supposed to reflect the best standards of clinical judgement. But the scheme does provide a mechanism which obliges practitioners to refuse to treat some patients. The surgeon can no longer treat whom he or she likes, for whatever reason he or she might have. That is a restriction of autonomy. But it is an ethically justified restriction. Furthermore it is, in one sense, an unreal restriction. The scheme is neutral as to how many patients shall be treated but it is not neutral about which of the candidates for treatment should receive it. Thus the number of patients the doctor is obliged to refuse to treat is not increased by the scheme. The ethical gain of the scheme is that those who are selected for treatment are the right group of patients. It would be an injustice for any of these to be refused treatment in deference to others lower on the prioritisation list.

Atomising care

It is important to recognise the tendency which a prioritisation scheme of allocation has to atomise patient care. Consider two kinds of problem cases which might arise.

First, patients who need a particular service are scored for their degree of need in that service. However, they may have other needs in other services, where they will be scored quite separately and discreetly. The result might be that we are presented with patients who do not score enough in either service to access treatment for either condition, though their co-morbidities might have a devastating effect on their quality of life. That is, their compounded health need is very serious. If the scheme is to succeed in determining who should be treated in order of their degree of need then such patients must not fall through the scoring net if equitable care is to be provided.

A second kind of case has occurred in the application of the scheme. A patient scored highly enough to access hip replacement surgery. When her anaesthetist was asked to look at her on admission he became aware that she had quite serious coronary artery problems. He estimated that there was a more than 20% chance that he would kill her by administering the anaesthetic. He refused to take this risk. The solution seemed to be to resolve the coronary problems in order to provide the care she qualified for. But this entailed accessing another service, viz. for coronary artery bypass surgery, when other patients with that condition had higher scores.

What can be done to maintain equity in the distribution of health resources in cases of this kind? The system needs to make room for clinician discretion in these cases in order to maintain equity. In each of these cases a holistic view of the needs of the patient is called for. A judgement has to be made about the weight of the composite need which requires access to a service which is unattainable when restricted needs alone are taken into account. It will be difficult to provide any quantitative framework to achieve this as the variety of cases is potentially large. However, the solution arrived at in the second case might serve as a pointer to the kind of compassionate and commonsense approach which is called for. The coronary bypass surgery was offered to the patient in order to make the orthopaedic surgery possible. Thus the very serious need was met together with a serious need. The moral cost of this was to prolong the waiting of another candidate with a serious need for a coronary bypass graft by one place. The moral cost of not proceeding in this way would have been to fail to meet both a very serious and a serious need of the patient who was treated. However, we have yet to tackle the difficult issue of the identification of a health need. This will be pursued in the next chapter.

Clinician integrity

The final criticism made of the scheme to prioritise health needs is that it erodes clinician integrity. This is related to the phenomenon of threshold clustering mentioned earlier. Doctors are committed to provide the best possible standards of care to their patients. Refusal to treat patients who need treatment does not seem to fit comfortably with this general obligation. Therefore the scheme is contrary to good clinical practice.

There is a good rebuttal of this criticism available. The motivation of the scheme is to produce equity in health service allocations. This aim is adopted in the face of the inescapable fact that there are not sufficient resources for everyone's health needs to be met. Given that this is the case it is impossible for doctors to fulfil the obligation to provide the best standard of treatment to everybody in need of treatment. For patients to be said to have a right to the best treatment of all their health problems seems to commit us to saying that some claim rights cannot, by the very nature of things, be claimed. But this would be confused. All schemes of rationing health care are based on the assumption or understanding that there are not sufficient resources to enable doctors to offer all treatments to all patients as needed. It follows that it is impossible for all doctors to fulfil the obligation to treat all patients with the best possible treatments. Thus they cannot have such an obligation. The obligation they have is to provide the best standard of treatment possible in the circumstances in which they find themselves. If resources simply are not available to treat some patients then doctors cannot be blamed for that.

However, the prioritisation scheme offers to doctors a better prospect of providing good standard health care to their patients than the old waiting list system it replaced. We have noted that in this scheme patients who fall between the CAT and the FST become highly visible. This offers their carers great assistance in advocating for their needs. In one case the progress of a group of patients needing coronary artery bypass grafts were monitored over a two-year period. Once the number of deaths and serious events suffered by the group were reported to government, extra funds were provided to lower the FST. Insofar as the scheme facilitates this kind of informed advocacy it enables the clinician to provide a higher standard of care to patients than was previously possible.

Conclusion

While the promotion of justice or equity to the head of the list of ethical values which feature in health care provision is most plausibly justified in resource allocation it does not facilitate the making of incontestable rationing decisions. This is partly because establishing both the identity and degree of health needs in patients and comparing them cannot be an exact science. Nevertheless needs-based systems of allocation offer the best opportunity for achieving equitable care as they avoid the injustices which characterise maximisation of benefit models of allocation which are so popular in contemporary health care planning.

Within limits set by the possibility of comparison of health needs methods of allocation can be devised which inject greater equity into health care provision. These involve prioritisation of cases within services which provide for identifiable needs by means of grading the cases according to the degree in which those needs are suffered by patients. Decision making of this sort is possible in elective surgery, for example, whereas, by definition, it is not possible in acute care.

The application of such schemes in elective surgery has shown that it is possible to build the narrative of patients into the prioritisation process. It has also demonstrated clear ethical advantages when compared to standard waiting list procedures.

While there are some weaknesses intrinsic to such schemes, such as the moral cost of providing sub-optimal care to waiting patients, the alternatives are inevitably less fair. Ours is not a perfect world and scarcity of health resources is inescapable. Hence not all who need treatment will be enabled to receive it promptly and many will not be able to receive some needed treatments at all. The determination of who will receive treatment and when, therefore seeks to avoid the maximisation of benefit for the maximisation of fairness by selecting the most needy patients first. Like any other system of allocation it is open to manipulation by practitioners but it is more difficult to game than the standard waiting list method, is transparent and preserves clinical integrity. The constant refinement of such schemes in the light of unforeseen consequences of its application, such as the temptation to atomise care, is necessary to ensure that equity remains its focus and that mechanical applications of it are avoided.

Notes

1 J. Appleby, *Financing Health Care in the 1990s*, Buckingham: Open University Press, 1992.
2 See: M.F. Drummond, *Principles of Economic Appraisal in Health Care*, Oxford: Oxford University Press, 1980, p. 2.
3 See: D.W. Light, 'Observations on the NHS reforms: an American perspective', *British Medical Journal* 303 (1991), 568–70.
4 See: A.J. Culyer, *Needs and the National Health Service*, London: Martin Robertson & Co., 1976.
5 G.H. Mooney, *Economics, Medicine and Health Care*, Brighton: Wheatsheaf Books Ltd, 1986, p. 91.
6 J.S. Mill, *Utilitarianism*, London: Longmans, Green, Reader, and Dyer, 1874.
7 For example see: J. Griffin, *Well-being: Its Meaning, Measurement and Moral Importance*, Oxford: Clarendon Press, 1986.
8 G.H. Mooney, E.M. Russell, and R.D. Weir, *Choices for Health Care*, 2nd edn, London: Macmillan, 1986, p. 42.
9 Ibid., p. 49.
10 J.S. Mill, *Utilitarianism*, p. 32.
11 J.S. Mill, *Utilitarianism*, p. 9.
12 J.S. Mill, *Utilitarianism*, p. 11.
13 J.S. Mill, *Utilitarianism*, p. 10.
14 A. Williams, 'The value of QALYs', *Health and Social Service Journal* Supplement (1985), 3.
15 John Harris has noted these two weaknesses in the application of the QALY measure in: J. Harris 'QALYfying the value of life', *Journal of Medical Ethics* 13 (1987), 117–23.

16 J.S. Mill, *Utilitarianism*, p. 38.
17 G.H. Mooney, E.M. Russell, and R.D. Weir, *Choices for Health Care*, p. 107.
18 I have in mind the theory of Norman Daniels as set out in N. Daniels, *Just Health Care*, Cambridge: Cambridge University Press, 1985. For a more detailed critique of this theory see D.M. Evans, 'Limits to care', in D.M. Evans and Z. Szawarski (eds.), *Solidarity, Justice and Health Care Priorities*, Health Service Studies 8, Linkoping: Linkoping University Press, 1993, pp. 28–41.
19 J.S. Mill, *Utilitarianism*, p. 4.
20 See: D. Braybrooke, 'Let needs diminish that preferences may prosper', *Studies in Moral Philosophy*, Oxford: Blackwell, 1968.
21 For a fuller discussion of this example see: D.M. Evans, 'The clinical classification of infertility', in D.M. Evans (ed.), *Creating the Child*, The Hague: Martinus Nijhoff, 1996, pp. 47–63.
22 N. Daniels, *Just Health Care*, pp. 33–5 and 88.

Chapter 5

Is infertility a health need?

Dealing with the prioritisation of health needs is dependent on the more fundamental activity of the determination of health needs. Challenges in this activity were alluded to in Chapter 1 where infertility was considered as a possible candidate. Let us now take up this interesting example in more detail in order to throw further light on the conceptual (*sic*) issues which have to be faced by resource allocation policy makers.

The dangers of generalising

Chapter 1 concluded with a reference to the words of Mr Flood, the lion breeder at Dublin zoo. 'Every lion is different', he said when asked to account for his secret of success, which he had summed up in two words only: 'understanding lions'. One might venture to suggest that those asked to provide assisted conception services to people would do well to remember his words, for what is perhaps surprisingly true of lions is more manifestly true of persons.

John Wisdom has used the example of Mr Flood to illustrate the way in which philosophical activity can turn out to restrict understanding:

> The trouble is that the concepts, without which we do not connect one thing with another, are apt to become a network which confines our minds. We need to be at once like someone who has seen much and forgotten nothing, and also like one who is seeing everything for the first time.[1]

So, he points out, the Dublin zoo-keeper brought his great experience with many lions to bear on his understanding of any particular lion but always remained free to see that lion for itself.

With respect to the philosophical literature devoted to a clarification of the concept of human need it is most certainly true that comparisons made between one thing and another have led many writers to talk in general terms about what it is that people as people need. Insofar as this is true one might contend that understanding health care needs may well be restricted by such considerations. Infertility in particular may be a condition which either ranks low on lists of health care needs or even drops off such lists altogether where such philosophical analysis informs resource allocation models. In posing the question: 'Is infertility a health need?' we might seek further clarification. Without ignoring general accounts of human need that have been promulgated we can still emphasise the dangers of seeking an answer to the question in a general theory and preserve a respect for particulars.

Of course, the generality of the question invites a general answer. Moreover, the pressures on health care providers to prioritise services encourage blanket-type responses to such queries. How much more attractive to managers is an ostensibly objective matrix in which conditions can be categorised, ranked and evaluated, than an untidy and apparently ad hoc approach to determining what shall or shall not be offered to individual patients. However, the uncritical deployment of general theoretical models of allocation does violence to the needs of patients and is morally questionable.

The peculiar candidature of infertility

Before proceeding to the question posed, it is worth pointing out that there are some peculiarities attaching to the condition of infertility as a candidate for treatment as a health need. For example, together with a limited range of recognised health needs, the majority of treatments offered for the condition do not in fact treat the condition at all but rather circumvent it. The infertile person is enabled biologically to parent a child but remains as infertile after the procedure as before. For example, though tubal surgery may resolve a woman's infertility, in that she will be enabled to conceive naturally thereafter, the procedure of IVF does nothing to alter the ability of the woman to conceive naturally. For the vast majority of women treated this is not a very important consideration as their concern in seeking treatment is usually to be enabled to bear a child rather than to restore normal reproductive functioning. It would be rare indeed for a woman simply to wish to become fertile and not wish to conceive a child, though one can imagine situations where this would be so. Then again methods of resolving infertility or sub-fertility in men would also rarely be designed to restore fertility. Indeed most procedures which fall under the umbrella of infertility therapies are designed to resolve the problem of childlessness rather than infertility. This has extremely important implications which we shall examine later.

Further, in the case of infertility we are faced with a unique possibility.[2] Neither partner of a given relationship may be technically infertile. Yet together they may be incapable of achieving a pregnancy. In other words, while neither can be said to 'suffer' from the condition, neither is biologically dysfunctional in this sense, taken together they are reproductively dysfunctional. Thus they may be said to have a fertility problem though neither, individually, can be said to have the problem. While one can think of possible scenarios in psychological therapy where such paradoxes arise, it is difficult to think of any other candidates. This kind of case highlights the issue of consent of both partners in a relationship to seek therapy though that issue might, of course, also be very important in the execution of assisted conception procedures in cases where one partner's infertility hinders the achievement of a pregnancy.

A further related oddity in infertility treatments is found where the alleged treatments involve the use of donor gametes. The biological problems of the couple are circumvented by compromising the biological contribution of one, or both, of the partners. In the case of uses of donor oocytes the mother's biological role is reduced. In the case of use of donor sperm the 'father's' biological role is dispensed with. It is rather odd then to regard such treatments as treatments of his infertility.

We may make one final observation about the oddity of infertility as a candidate for health need status. While for many the condition is a source of much grief and is properly said to be suffered, for others it is a blessing. Indeed fertility is regarded as a health problem by many. This is generally recognised in health services throughout the world where sterilisation procedures are commonly offered. It is not easy to think of other biological conditions which are open to such rival perceptions. Some, like sickle cell anaemia, which may be advantageous, on balance, in some geographical settings while simply a disadvantage in others, may bear some resemblance. However, there are crucial differences which we shall see are important. In short, in the case of fertility and infertility there is no common measure which can help us determine when it is proper to regard one or other condition as an advantage or a disadvantage.

Theories of human need

Let us now turn to the question of whether or not infertility should be classified as a health need. The character of attention we pay to other human beings is a matter of moral import. This attention is manifested in the kinds of judgements we make of them and in our responses to them. It is not something which we may ever make explicit to ourselves but it is, nonetheless, something for which we are morally responsible.

Such attitudes may surface in philosophical theorising even when we are ostensibly seeking or promulgating a neutral account of human nature. They most certainly appear in health planning policies which embody assessments of peoples' needs. Perhaps the most general features of such accounts are the most difficult to acknowledge as betraying moral views and as undermining their purported claim to neutrality. The most ubiquitous feature of all is the generality of such accounts. Theories or allocation models which talk of people as people show a disrespect for the particularity of persons which tends to do violence to the assessment of needs of those who fall within their scope. Some writers of this kind wear their hearts on their sleeves – perhaps none more so than Jacques Maritain who writes:

> I am taking it for granted that you admit that there is a human nature, and that this human nature is the same in all men. I am taking it for granted that you also admit that man is a being gifted with intelligence, and who, as such, acts with understanding of what he is doing, and therefore with the power to determine for himself the ends which he pursues. On the other hand, possessed of a nature, being constituted in a given, determinate fashion, man obviously possesses ends which correspond to his natural constitution and which are the same for all – as all pianos, for instance, whatever their particular type and in whatever spot they may be, have as their end the production of certain attuned sounds. If they do not produce these sounds they must be tuned, or discarded as worthless.[3]

But who is to determine what is or is not the function or end of people? And who could claim plausibly that such a determination is value neutral? A brief reflection will show that the analogy he employs is morally offensive to many, if not most. An artifact made to fulfil an identifiable function is judged according to its effectiveness. A piano which cannot be tuned cannot fulfil its function. It is not a good piano unless the fault can be rectified. Of course it may not be discarded because other functions are found for it, or because it is aesthetically pleasing as a visual object, or it is of historical or sentimental value, and so on. But as a piano it is no good and merits no consideration. The space it occupies, the expense it may incur, the worries it may bring cannot be justified. It is fit for the breaker's yard. From time to time people have been similarly assessed but such episodes of our history are not sources of pride or even matters of mere note. The employment of such an analogy as a means of identifying the needs people have is clearly not morally indifferent.

We find the temptation to generalise in this way in theories of ethics, some of which have been influential in the formulation of resource allocation policy. They have been neatly described as theories which assert that our moral views and judgements are of types rather than of particulars.[4] Diamond emphasises the importance of the imaginative life in making moral judgements which involves an openness of response to the human world:

> Moral judgements are not here seen as abstractly true or false, true or false out of connection with their life on their occasions of use, their rootedness then in the heart, the imaginative life, of the person who thinks the thought or makes the moral judgement.[5]

She illustrates such imaginative activity by reference to Wordsworth's description of the tender scene in which he saw a labourer cradle his sickly child in his brawny arms:

> He held the child, and, bending over it
> As if he were afraid both of the sun
> And of the air which he had come to seek,
> He eyed it with unutterable love.

Experiences of this sort, not the framing of general rules, in other words the moral psychology of the perceivers, is bound up with their conception of the dignity and fullness of human life. What the framing of general rules tends to do is blunt the edge of moral sensitivity; it presses the particular into the general mould and blinds us to important possibilities. This is certainly true of utilitarian views, which have probably been most influential as an intellectual background to current resource allocation theories. We might best recognise the importance of sensitivity to the individual life in the making of moral judgements by means of a final reference to Diamond's paper, which links with Wisdom's observation with which I began.[6] She quotes the poem of Walter de la Mare entitled 'Ducks'. Having delineated various types of duck such as the Tufted, the Labrador and the Goldeneye, he writes:

> All these are kinds. But every Duck
> Himself is, and himself alone:
> Fleetwing, arched neck, webbed foot, round eye,
> And marvellous cage of bone.
> Clad in this beauty a creature dwells
> Of sovran instinct, sense and skill;
> Yet secret as the hidden wells
> Whence Life itself doth rill.

The child, for whom the poem is written, is taught to respond to an individual life – the particular duck which is himself. This is very different from a response to a type of creature, and more demanding of the perceiver. How much more demanding are such responses to individual human lives, the kind of response we have to people we know, our lovers, our children, our friends. Yet, Diamond points out, it is such response to particularity which informs the urgency we see in the rescue of a stranger:

> The urgency we see in the rescue may be tied to a sense of each person being who he is, with his one life. There are situations in which we keep from ourselves this awareness of the individual life of people whom we do not know, precisely because of the kind of difficulties such realization can create for us, for example in official roles.[7]

How revealing this is in the context of health policies where decision making is moved away from the clinician to the manager, a move from the particular to the abstract, from knowledge of the patient as a person to the processing of the patient as a type. In identifying human needs philosophers have succumbed to just this temptation and this has shaped proposals of how priorities should be set in health care. This, as we shall see, has an important bearing on how infertility is regarded. As we have already noted, in Maritain's assertion, one way of identifying the needs of something is to identify a function that something has. A knife will need to be sharp if it is to cut well; a motor will need fuel if it is to drive a machine, and so on. One short route then, it may be thought, to identifying human need would be to elicit some end of people as people.

A biological model

Nowhere in the context of the philosophy of medicine has the identification of a goal of people as people been attempted more heroically than by Christopher Boorse.[8] His position promises to tell us much about a possible answer to our question regarding the status of infertility. He argues that health is not an evaluative notion and that a value-free science of health is possible. In the course of his thesis he conceives of man, fundamentally, as a biological organism. The goals of any organism are not difficult to identify from its biological design. Indeed the higher-level goals of survival and reproduction turn out to be those goals in terms of which the functioning of each component part of the organism is assessed. These he calls the apical goals of an organism. Theoretical health, therefore, becomes functional normality which is 'strictly analogous to the mechanical condition of an artifact'.[9] Disease then is an objective biological term with no ethical import constituted by an unnatural deficiency in the functional efficiency of the body. Illnesses, on the other hand, are a sub-class of diseases having normative features – they are conditions devalued by the sufferer and thus the term illness is inapplicable to non-humans. Importantly, then, both the theoretical and the practical concepts of health are disease orientated and are rooted in the nature of the species – in the nature of people as people.

However, Boorse is reluctant to talk of health needs. In fact the assertion that his concept of health is value free prevents us reading any implication of need into disease conditions, for it prevents us assuming that health is desirable *per se*. The value of health is nothing but the conformity to an excellent species design, and biological normality is, for Boorse, an instrumental rather than an intrinsic good.[10] Thus it is only in the context of the desires of individuals that their needs can be determined – they do not, after all, belong to people as people. Thus, despite its promise for those who wish to regard infertility as a health need, Boorse's account of human nature establishes no such thing. Yet even he acknowledges that mankind is a social being. 'It must be conceded that *Homo Sapiens* is a social species', he writes.[11] He does not attempt a universal account of human nature in these terms but where he wisely demurs others have been more ambitious. They have attempted to identify certain basic needs which are contrasted with needs created by the adoption of certain ends. This distinction between basic and instrumental needs is supposed to make the important separation between needs and demands or desires on the one hand, and also between objective and subjective needs – whatever that distinction is supposed to come to – on the other. Let us look at some examples and see whether this quest for the holy grail of basic needs holds out any promise of an acceptable universal account of human nature in terms of which we can categorise the condition of infertility.

Human good and harm

Phillipa Foot has attempted to underpin the whole of morality by an account of human needs, that is, by an account of what all people want, which in turn depends on what they need.[12] She has performed a valuable service to moral philosophy by showing that there are logical limits to what can be regarded as a moral principle or a moral concern. As there are internal relations between an emotion like pride and possible objects of that emotion, between descriptions like dangerous and possible subjects of such descriptions, so there is an internal relation between moral commendation and its objects. Unless a principle is somehow related to a family of concepts, including concepts such as honesty, murder, stealing, ostentation and treachery, then we are justified in asking why such a principle is to be regarded as a moral principle at all. Similarly if we are interested in whether something is a legitimate object of moral concern and we cannot relate it in any way to the concepts of human good and harm, we can make no sense of it as a moral concern. The concept of need is clearly a matter of moral concern as it can be so related without difficulty. Thus it might be sufficient justification of my action towards others to point out that they needed the assistance I rendered to them.

All of this is very helpful as it rules out the possibility of principles being adopted, or objects or states being desired, as a matter of whim standing as candidates for moral status. There are limits to what it makes sense to say in morality and they are objective insofar as they reside not in the individual but in the form of life, the social environment of the persons concerned. Thus Foot asserts:

> It is surely clear that moral virtues must be connected with human good and harm, and that it is quite impossible to call anything you like good or harm. . . . It would be . . . odd if someone were supposed to say that harm had been done to him because the hairs of his head had been reduced to an even number.[13]

Clearly then, on her account, no one could claim plausibly that he has a need to have an even number of hairs upon his head. And surely she is right.

However, Foot is concerned to do more than point out the general limits of moral discourse. She wishes to harden them into a positive theory of ethics and tries to do so by positing a positive theory of human nature. Might not there be features of our experience which carry the same inescapable significance for us all? Might there not be needs which we all share by virtue of our being human? Her answer to these questions is a firm yes. The fact of human nature she develops most interestingly, from our point of view, is the need to avoid injury.[14] What counts as physical injury is clear to everyone who uses the word. It involves the impairment of some or other function. So there are pretty narrow limits to the notion of injury which enable us to empirically identify cases without dispute. Further, injury is necessarily a bad thing, and this can be shown by reference to what all men want which, in turn, can be shown by reference to what all men need. Thus to show that some course of action will lead to injury is necessarily to give a reason for not pursuing such a course. Freedom from injury is part of what constitutes human good and harm. If the whole body of elements making up such features of human life was formulated it would show us what all people *qua* people really needed.

Such an enterprise is destined to fail. As far as injury always counting as a reason against an action goes, it has been shown that this thesis is false.[15] There may be cases where considerations of injury may be thought to be quite irrelevant to whether or not one should pursue a course of action. Maybe the action is far too important for such considerations to come into play. Here we are not simply considering situations where there is an incidental gain derived out of injury. Rather they are cases where the business of injury carries absolutely no weight whatever in the deliberations. It does not constitute a negative element to be weighed against advantages produced by the action. This suggests that there are rival notions of human good and harm and that far from its being true that human good and harm, determined by what all people need, determine what moral beliefs they will espouse, it is rather the case that what moral beliefs men espouse determine what they regard as really good and really harmful, and thus what they really need.[16]

The concept of factuality then is more complex than Foot allows. Various data may be given various weightings by observers according to what they think is important. This will have the result of producing different descriptions of situations, including descriptions of need. These are not factual in a non-evaluative sense of course. The social context of this relation between description and evaluation has been well expressed by Stuart Hampshire as follows:

> Every reflective person has had the experience of oscillating between two possible descriptions of his own conduct, whether it is actual conduct or only envisaged conduct; one *correct* description makes the conduct

acceptable and not to be despised, and the other *correct* description mentions features of the conduct which make it morally questionable and regrettable. Two competing ways of life, between which a man chooses, explicitly or implicitly, may impose different descriptions on the same envisaged conduct, which may emerge as prohibited in virtue of the descriptions relevant to one way of life and as positively required within another way of life.[17]

The context of the way of life of a person, a social context, may similarly produce rival identifications of what a person needs. It is not surprising, therefore, that what Hampshire calls correct descriptions may well conflict.

Foot herself is somewhat drawn to such a position in some of her writings. Indeed we shall notice that other writers who espouse talk of human needs *per se* are similarly drawn though, together with Foot, they do not give full weight to what they concede is an important aspect of mankind's being, namely social identity. (We have already seen that this is true of Boorse.) Foot, indeed, comes near to finding a role for the imagination in identifying moral concerns reminiscent of Diamond's position mentioned earlier:

> In conclusion it is worth remarking that moral arguments break down far more often than philosophers tend to think, but that the breakdown is of a different kind. When people argue about what is right, good, or obligatory, or whether a certain character trait is or is not a virtue, they do not confine their remarks to the adducing of facts which can be established by simple observation, or by some clear-cut technique.[18]

What is said may well be subtle or profound, and in this sort of discussion of character, much depends on experience and imagination. It is quite common for one person to be unable to see what the other is getting at, and this sort of misunderstanding will not be resolvable by anything which could be called argument in the ordinary sense.[19]

Now what are we to make of this somewhat startling admission? Is she saying simply that actual moral assessments are more intricate than the model she has been considering? This is rather doubtful for argument in the ordinary sense is sufficient to clarify subtleties and complexities. Rather, the difficulties are seen to lie somehow in the role of the facts which are thought to be relevant to moral conclusions. What straightforwardly establishable facts add up to for one person may not correspond to what they come to for another, and one person may not understand another's construction upon the data. This may be true of whether infertility, for example, is regarded as an important need or even a need at all by a given individual.

Basic needs

But may there not be some needs which all people have *qua* people, though others may vary from person to person and be relative to various times and places? This is a recurring theme in the literature. For example, Braybrooke[20] identifies what he thinks is a class of needs which if experienced by any individual endanger the normal functioning of that person considered as a member of a natural species. These needs are contrasted with needs created by adopted projects of individuals. Significantly, however, he allows for needs which individuals may have by virtue of their temperament. But such a distinction between *course-of-life* needs and *adventitious* needs cannot bear the weight it is meant to do. We have already observed in a critique of Foot that an impairment of normal functioning need not be a matter of importance to an individual. Additionally, we should note that it is impossible to draw a clear line between *course-of-life* and *adventitious* needs. Would infertility rank as one of the former or one of the latter group? For those whose temperament identifies as a key feature of human existence the reproduction of their own kind infertility would rank as a *course-of-life* need. We shall see in a moment that such a view is intelligible in terms of the social milieu of the subject. However, for those who regard biological parenthood as an option, infertility will constitute an *adventitious* need. Such a distinction may make a great deal of difference in prioritising the needs of individuals. It would certainly be potentially harmful to the former group to assume that because such a need was not universally perceived it was therefore not one which should rank highly in a health policy. For those for whom few other considerations were more important such a policy would be morally deficient.

MacCloskey[21] is even more ambivalent in his treatment of basic needs. While, on the one hand, he wants to hold on to the idea of basic human needs, i.e. 'the needs of men as men, and the individual needs of particular persons as the unique persons they are (and not as holders of roles or stations)', specific needs which he ranks as secondary arise out of the fact that 'certain social, quasi-natural roles such as those of mother, father, parent become basic to the fabric of most human social organisations, as well as some which are basic only to certain social organisations'.[22] It is not at all clear what the claim to 'natural' status comes to. Certainly the social institutions in terms of which individual perceptions, emotions, desires and identities are created – i.e. persons as opposed to organisms – have a history which predates the individuals concerned and which, in this sense, may be said to have a reality beyond that of the person whose reality is, in turn, realised in terms of them. If this is accepted then the impossibility of biological parenthood may well be seen as a need of individual persons as the unique persons they are. MacCloskey is partially aware of this tension in his account for while, on the one hand, he rejects what he calls 'social and cultural relativity', he acknowledges, on the other, that 'the natural development of man, like that of the oaks, is determined in part by their environment which is both physical and social. This affects what is natural and hence what constitutes a need'.[23]

So here we see more than one possible source of variation in the identity of infertility as a need. First, some societies may have developed an institution of the family making infertility or barrenness a source of grief and even shame, a failure of an important kind. Others may have quite different familial concepts. Thus to imagine, for example, that for Sarai, the wife of Abram (Genesis 16: 1), and for a 'liberated' woman of a twentieth-century western society the status of infertility as a need must be common to them *qua* women is to strain the boundaries of intelligibility. Second, some societies are less homogenous than others. They contain a large variety of social movements and institutions to which individuals have varied allegiances. Moreover some of those institutions may be undergoing quite rapid change – as is the institution of the family in many European countries. Thus the perceptions and awarenesses of individuals vary greatly within such societies, given the mix of social movements passing through them and the flux each of these movements may be subject to between individuals. Thus, as Foot rightly suspected, individuals see and understand different worlds. This reversal of the relationship between the identity of human needs and the concept of human nature from that at the heart of the enterprises of the 'basic needs' theorists is well expressed by Peter Winch in his paper on human nature:

> A child is born within, and grows up into the life of, a particular human society. He learns to speak and to engage in various kinds of activity in relation to other people. In the course of these activities he encounters problems of extremely diverse kinds, problems which change in character as he matures, and problems that bring him into new kinds of relations with other people. Along with this development there comes a growth in his understanding of what constitute problems and difficulties for them. This growing understanding manifests itself in the way he comes to treat people in the course of his daily life, which will include a development in his ideas of what is permissible in his treatment of them and what is ruled out. This growth in his understanding of other people through his dealings with them is at the same time a growth in his understanding of himself, which is in its turn a development of the kind of person he is.[24]

Hence the imposition of one world view on a population in the form of a uniform and inflexible set of health care provisions which are based on some majority view or some ideological theory of needs is morally insensitive. We noted in the previous chapter that this occurs in various kinds of 'maximisation of benefit' models of resource allocation in health care.

It is for reasons such as these that it is proper to resist the proposal to reject the need for children born as a result of assisted conception procedures to know the identity of their biological progenitors on the grounds that the 'need' is socially induced.[25] Katherine O'Donovan had proposed that as this 'need to know' is socially induced we ought rather to be concentrating our efforts on changing society's attitude to the importance of the blood relationship and so preserve the anonymity of donors.[26] This prescribed activity is presumably designed to induce the establishment of a different need because the needs of the infertile, for treatment or for secrecy, may equally well be conceived of as being socially constructed. To demonstrate that a need is socially constructed, however, does nothing to devalue it. One might well ask, in view of our earlier discussion, what human need is not socially constructed. If the importance of socially induced needs for the provision of medical treatment are to be denied then we shall have to deny treatments designed to produce longevity, physical grace and even the avoidance or palliation of pain.

The case made here therefore is that no general theory of human needs entitles us to reject, or indeed establish, the status of infertility as a health need. We have, in the course of the discussion, seen how, for some, the condition of infertility can certainly be conceived of as a need, and indeed a need of a fundamental kind.

Health planning policies

The case outlined above has implied a warning against health policies which trade on assumptions of a general nature in not offering fertility therapies. It remains true that in health planning general policies have to be adopted. Certain matters are properly taken into account in this context such as the incidence of a condition and the demand for treatment, though in the latter case care needs to be taken to ensure that low levels of demand are not themselves due to the failure of provision or of education of the public about what is possible in medicine.

However, we find that other, less desirable, features sometimes determine the levels of service to be provided, and even whether assisted conception services be provided at all. Some of these have figured in the foregoing theories as assumptions which we have called into question. Consider again the health purchasers' disagreement canvassed earlier.[27] Redmayne et al.[28] compared the reasons given by three purchasing authorities in the United Kingdom for refusing to purchase in vitro fertilisation services with the reasons given by three authorities for their decision to purchase the services. One authority refused to purchase the service on the basis that the people demanding the service were not ill. Those who opposed the decision argued that the mental stress of being infertile should be taken into account. Both sides of the dispute therefore accepted a model of health needs which was illness orientated. But why should not infertility be regarded as a serious health need on other grounds? This question was answered unequivocally by two of the authorities who decided to purchase the service. One noted that, in addition to psychological harm that may be caused by the condition, marital difficulties often result. This authority attached great significance to the role of the family. A further authority recognised sub-fertility as a health problem with very definite physiological, psychological, and social implications.

Infertility as a clinical need

Having established the possibility of regarding infertility as a human need we still have some difficulties to address in its classification as a condition which is the concern of health care providers. First, why should such a need be regarded as a clinical need at all?

In order to answer this question let us consider the difference between two senses of having a need. All human beings have need of oxygen in the sense that without it they cannot survive. Yet few human beings have the need to be supplied with oxygen by others, or indeed to make extraordinary provision of it for themselves. It is as free and available as the air they breathe. Others may be said to need oxygen in the more urgent sense of needing to be provided with it either because their situation threatens the supply of it, as when they are buried in an avalanche for example, or when their physical or mental condition is such that they are unable to inhale adequate supplies though it may be freely available in the air about them. It is only those having a need in the latter sense who may be said to have a need which calls for a remedy.

However, the classification of clinical needs cannot be drawn quite as widely as this, because the remedy of the need might not lie in any kind of treatment of the person. It may, for example, lie in education or in environmental measures. For instance, a lack of oxygen may be the result of pollution which in the long term damages people's lungs. Their health may therefore be preserved or improved by treating their environment rather than by treating them. Thus a possible lack of oxygen might denote, in such a case, a health need rather than a clinical need. The well-being of the person is ensured by such a measure or, alternatively, for example, by education about the hazards of smoking. A similar point can be made about childlessness. A husband who resolves his wife's childlessness by impregnating her in the normal way cannot be said to be offering clinical treatment. The use of clinical means comes into the picture where the need cannot be met by natural and morally acceptable means. Most cases would be where a woman or her partner is infertile, or they might together be infertile and desire help to produce a child of their own. There might be more unusual cases where the woman in question might not be infertile but might wish to conceive a child by other than normal means for various reasons. It is hard to see why, where treatments are possible, we can decline to identify the need as a clinical need. This is not to say that we rank the various conditions cited in any particular way. Neither is it to say anything about the priority which should be given to such clinical needs. It is simply to point out that the description is a proper one.

This leads to an interesting practical problem. Where such a need can be met by a variety of clinical means there may be various classifications. These will be determined by the character of the treatment called for: surgical, medical, psychological or whatever. When the need can be met by more than one of these modes of care, or by a combination of them only, can the patient be said to have both psychological, medical and surgical needs? And how should any priority be established in the classification? Should it be according to the most cost-effective, the least intrusive or painful, the least risky, the least expensive or the most readily available therapy? These are questions which purchasing authorities are asking. In the paper cited earlier some of the authorities examined ruled out provision of *in vitro* fertilisation services on the basis of poor cost-effectiveness, and others on the basis of clinical effectiveness. There was disagreement between authorities on the latter point where one authority purchased *in vitro* services because they had the advantage of detecting poor fertilisation and bypassing tubal damage. Clearly, however, this is one sensible way to determine which treatment a person may best benefit from and thus be said to need most.

In the absence of such clinical means of distinguishing the treatments who should decide which kind of need the infertile person has? What role should the patient play in this? Might not a strong preference for IVF prevail over tubal surgery if the woman feels strongly about it? Might this not be good reason for saying that her need is not surgical in the full-blown sense? She might so fear surgery that she would not consider it as a possible solution to her problem. This poses the question of how much room there should be for patient choice in the provision of infertility services.

Criteria of access to services

Before leaving the question of perception of need we must consider the issue of the perceptions of the professional carer. In the United Kingdom the carers' perceptions of need in this area are uniquely safeguarded, save for the connected area of abortion. There exist only two conscience clauses in English medical law which allow a health care professional to refuse to treat a patient on other than clinical grounds. No carer can be obliged to assist in the procurement of an abortion nor in the provision of assisted conception services where such involvement would be against his or her conscience. In the case of abortion it is fairly clear that a clinician who held that aborting the foetus amounted to murder, or at least the killing of a person, could hold that no one could need that such a procedure be carried out. The moral grounds upon which a conscientious objection could be made under the Human Fertilisation and Embryology Act 1990 have not been tested. However, one could imagine, for example, that considerations of unnatural interference constituting a destruction of the unity of the act of procreation will rule out such assistance as an option. A clinician who held such a view would then find it impossible to accept that any patient could need such a procedure, any more than a transplantation surgeon could believe that his patient needed the heart of any particular healthy man, even though he does need a healthy heart. A difficulty then arises as to how far such a clinician should go in making such provision possible by counselling and referral to other practitioners.

A much more difficult set of problems arises where the conscientious objection issues from different non-clinical considerations. They would be considerations about the suitability of the patient to receive such services. These problems have been canvassed elsewhere[29] but we shall pursue them here for a moment as they raise important questions about the application of criteria of access to assisted conception programmes, questions which apply uniquely to these programmes but which have profound implications for the practice of medicine.

What if the moral objection took the form of objecting to the suitability of the patient on the grounds of her lifestyle. Maybe the clinician would consider it improper to assist a lesbian, or a mentally handicapped woman or a single woman to conceive a child. This objection might be couched in terms of his refusal to concede that they need such services. These kinds of occasions might constitute the first time that non-clinical criteria of suitability for treatment have appeared in the ethos of medicine (as opposed to *de facto* applications of non-clinical criteria due to modes of rationing). This change in medical practice would be one to fear, especially in times of scarce resources when patients are expected to take responsibility for their health and where it looks possible that they may, in the not-too-distant future, be refused treatments for conditions they have brought upon themselves. Such restrictions already apply in infertility therapy where services for reversal of vasectomy and reversal of female sterilisation are either not provided, or figure low on the priority scale of infertility services.

The employment of criteria of access to assisted conception services serve another function than facilitating rationing, or protecting the moral sensibilities of the clinician. They draw our attention to the interests of the product of the services offered, viz. the child. For many this is the most disconcerting feature of assisted conception provision. The bringing into the world of another human being, which is the whole point of assisted conception procedures, creates a further set of needs which may be in tension with the needs of the infertile. They are the needs of the new life. Where these needs are located in the need for good parenting, special care will have to be exercised. There is evidence that some of the groups of women mentioned a moment ago might be deemed by providers to be unsuitable as a parent by virtue of their lifestyle or domestic situation. Very firm evidence would be needed to establish such unsuitability, indeed much more than is currently available. Where such criteria were then applied it is important that they be made explicit so that no covert moral prejudices are allowed to intrude into the clinical encounter.

A problematic caveat

It is a peculiar feature of assisted conception services that the need which is met is not primarily met by the treatment, though this is a necessary means to its resolution. In fact it is met by the child who results from the procedure. Achieving a pregnancy alone does not meet the need but birthing a baby does. This is why we earlier referred to childlessness as constituting the need to be met by means of assisted conception services rather than infertility. Certainly the interests of the child cannot be ignored. But now we have identified a further set of puzzles which call for attention once we recognise infertility as a health need. One of the most prominent grounds employed by the three purchasing authorities, referred to earlier,[30] who decided to provide *in vitro* services was clinical. That is, they recognised that the condition of infertility could give rise to psychological and physiological harms. The provision of assisted conception services was then a means of preventing or ameliorating these harms. In other words, the prime motive for providing the service was to provide a unique prophylactic – the child. But now the question arises as to whether this instrumental use of another person, the child, is morally justified. Maybe this note of caution is a suitable one on which to end a chapter which has sought to establish the importance of maintaining moral sensitivity in recognising the possibility of regarding infertility as a health need. In so doing we need to take care that sensitivity to other moral questions is not dulled by enthusiasm for the application of the new and exciting technologies of assisted reproduction.

Conclusion

With so many demands made on health care providers, new areas of care facilitated by advances in knowledge and technology have to compete with traditional demands which arise out of established treatments or treatment types around which teams of expert staff and dedicated facilities are instituted. They cannot simply be added to the menu as resources are short. Thus resources which are provided to make them available have often, at least in part, to be transferred from historically funded services. Managers are then faced with resistance from those services and also with what are often very expensive new treatments. This leads to more fundamental management reflection on the justification for providing funds for a service at all. Such reflection is not a bad thing but often it is limited to finding reasons for not funding the new treatments. In the process of these considerations assumptions about what really are health needs come to the surface. These are not always justified.

Assisted reproduction offers us a perfect example of this phenomenon. We noted in Chapter 1 the erroneous assumption employed by numbers of health providers for not funding this new area of treatment. It was related to the fact that unexplained infertility is not a disease. In this chapter we have looked more closely at the kind of considerations which might be employed in making a positive case for the provision of these services.

The tempting approach is to seek an answer to the general question which forms the title of the chapter. But the example in question dramatically demonstrates the error in this approach. General theories of need tend to consider people simply as typical members of a species. All that remains, for some theories, is to identify what counts as their proper functioning. While this might be possible at the biological level, it leaves the social and spiritual features of human beings untouched. No end for all people as people has been identified or can be. Even where the ability to reproduce is considered an apical goal of people, it constitutes simply a species need and not an individual need. Consequently no general theory, whether it dismisses infertility as a fundamental need because it is better seen as an adventitious need or it identifies infertility as a fundamental need of the species, can provide an answer to our question.

However, the failure to demonstrate that infertility is a need *per se* must not tempt us to find some justification for never treating it as a health need at all by use of specious reasons such as the fact that it is not a disease. Health provision is by no means limited to treating diseases. Among other things it is concerned with the provision of prostheses, the amelioration of socially debilitating biological conditions which are not in themselves diseases such as gross facial deformities arising out of traumas, repairing broken limbs, and so on. Only a little reflection is needed to recognise this yet the providers mentioned in Chapter 1 failed to notice the weakness of their non-disease classification of infertility in their case for not purchasing infertility services. This is particularly surprising given the fact that there was no hesitation on the part of those purchasers of health services to provide clinical means to produce the biological dysfunction of sterility in perfectly healthy people in the form of contraceptives. For the vast majority of those who avail themselves of such services fertility cannot remotely be regarded as a disease condition. It was equally surprising that they were prepared to purchase tubal surgery as a relatively ineffective means of restoring fertility when achieving such a state is rarely if ever divorced from the project of resolving childlessness.

Thus a strong case can be made for regarding infertility as a clinical need in the lives of those people for whom childlessness is a source of suffering and personal and social distress. This is a growing problem in the developed world where levels of fertility are dropping. However, to have established this only makes infertility a candidate for health care funding and places it in the contest with other health needs for a share of the health funds which are available.

Notes

1 J. Wisdom, *Paradox and Discovery*, Oxford: Blackwell, 1965, pp. 137–8.
2 See the earlier discussion in Chapter 1.
3 J. Maritain, *The Rights of Man and Natural Law*, London: Geoffrey Bles, 1945, pp. 34–5.
4 See: C. Diamond, 'Martha Nussbaum and the need for novels', *Philosophical Investigations* 16 (1993), 128–53.
5 Ibid.
6 Ibid., pp. 146–7.
7 Ibid.
8 C. Boorse, 'On the distinction between disease and illness', *Philosophy and Public Affairs* 5 (1975), 49–68.
9 Ibid., p. 59.
10 Ibid., pp. 63 and 68.
11 Ibid., p. 64.
12 P. Foot, 'Moral beliefs', *Virtues and Vices*, Oxford: Blackwell, 1978.
13 Ibid., p. 120.
14 Ibid., pp. 121–3.
15 See: R. Beardsmore, *Moral Reasoning*, London: Routledge & Kegan Paul, 1969, pp. 22–3; and D.Z. Phillips and H.O. Mounce, *Moral Practices*, London: Routledge & Kegan Paul, 1969, pp. 56–8.
16 See: P. Winch, 'Can a good man be harmed?', *Proceedings of the Aristotelian Society* 66 (1965–66), 55–70.
17 S. Hampshire, *Public and Private Morality*, Cambridge: Cambridge University Press, 1978, p. 48.
18 P. Foot, 'Moral arguments', *Virtues and Vices*, Oxford: Blackwell, 1978, p. 109.
19 Ibid.
20 D. Braybrooke, 'Let needs diminish that preferences may prosper', *Studies in Moral Philosophy*, Oxford: Basil Blackwell, 1968, pp. 86–107.
21 H.J. MacCloskey; 'Human needs, rights and political values', *American Philosophical Quarterly* 13 (1976), 1–11.
22 Ibid., pp. 3–4.
23 Ibid., pp. 5 and 8.
24 P. Winch, *Ethics and Action*, London: Routledge & Kegan Paul, 1972, p. 84.
25 D.M. Evans, 'Legislative control of medical practice' *Bulletin of Medical Ethics* 55 (1990), 15–16.
26 K. O'Donovan, 'What shall we tell the children?', in R. Lee and D. Morgan (eds.) *Birthrights, Law and Ethics at the Beginnings of Life*, London: Routledge, 1989, pp. 96–114.
27 Chapter 1, p. 23.
28 S. Redmayne and R. Klein, 'Rationing in practice: the case of in vitro fertilisation', *British Medical Journal* 306 (1993), 1521–4.
29 D.M. Evans, 'Legislative control of medical practice', pp. 15–16.
30 See: S. Redmayne and R. Klein, 'Rationing in practice', pp. 1521–3.

Chapter 6

The child's interests in assisted reproduction

The previous chapter concluded with a reference to a set of puzzles arising out of the results of successful procreation treatments. These cluster around the welfare of children born by such means. Most jurisdictions which have regulations governing assisted reproduction make the interests of the child a matter of great importance. But how are we to implement this concern in clinical practice? What kinds of interests can future people be said to have? Should the doctor offering these services be responsible for the future welfare of the child? And if so, how can he or she ensure such welfare? These are questions to which there are conflicting answers. Our problem will be to determine how independent the welfare of the child, as perceived by the protagonists in the debate, can be from their own various interests.

> To evoke posterity
> Is to weep on your own grave.
> Ventriloquising for the unborn.[1]

We might be sceptical of the whole enterprise of speaking for the unborn, imagining that it is we who put words into their mouths rather than they into ours. If so we would regard reference to future generations as an opportunity to further our interests rather than theirs. But if not we need to ask: how much sense does it make to ascribe obligations of the living to future persons? We might be guided by the 1944 poem of Louis MacNeice entitled 'Prayer before birth'[2] in which he makes requests on behalf of a future human being. Much of the threat to the child perceived by the poet as he wrote when Europe was at war is palpable and the requests subsequently assume plausibility. Here is a taste of them:

> I am not yet born; O hear me.
> Let not the bloodsucking bat or the rat or the stoat or the
> club-footed ghoul come near me.

I am not yet born, console me.
I fear that the human race may with tall walls wall me,
with strong drugs dope me, with wise lies lure me,
on black racks rack me, in blood-baths roll me.

I am not yet born: provide me
With water to dandle me, grass to grow for me, trees to talk
to me, sky to sing to me, birds and a white light
in the back of my mind to guide me.

I am not yet born; O hear me,
Let not the man who is beast or who thinks he is God
come near me.

I am not yet born; O fill me
With strength against those who would freeze my
humanity, would dragoon me into a lethal automaton,
would make me a cog in a machine, a thing with
one face, a thing . . .

But is it sensible to place moral responsibilities on those who are alive to provide goods or protections from harms for those whose existence is as yet only hypothetical? If it is then how do those responsibilities devolve on those who share in commissioning human lives in medically assisted reproduction? And how do we deal with these responsibilities when they conflict with the interests of others which rival those of the child? We shall return to each of the quoted stanzas of the poem as we address these three questions.

The interests of future people

Is there any sense in attributing needs to future people in any context? And if so how can we construe the consequent responsibilities of people who currently exist? In particular how can a clinician providing assisted reproduction services have responsibilities to people who as yet are entirely hypothetical in the sense that even their conception has not occurred but is being contemplated by the commissioning parent or parents together with the clinician. Further, what is the range of these responsibilities if they are conceivable?

Propinquity and contiguity

The problem of identifying moral obligation to future people might be illustrated by reference to the philosophy of David Hume, who was interested in the nature of moral concern and responsibility. He believed that sympathy, a fellow feeling for others, lay at the root of it as a powerful principle in human nature. This fellow feeling facilitates passions in us which move us towards others in need and thus produces moral concern and understanding in us.

But he was aware that distance from the object of our concern in time and space profoundly affects our feelings towards it.

> Our servant, if diligent and faithful, may excite stronger sentiments of love and kindness than Marcus Brutus, as represented in history; but we say not upon that account, that the former character is more laudable than the latter. We know that were we to approach equally near to that renown'd patriot, he wou'd command a much higher degree of affection and admiration.[3]

Diminished propinquity and contiguity could therefore result in a diminished sense of obligation and gratitude. We might compare this kind of case with our obligations to future generations. For example, given that each of us has four grandparents and they had four grandparents each, and so on, each of us had 32,768 great, great, great ... grandparents who were alive fifteen generations ago. Few people realise this let alone sense any relatedness with them or gratitude or blame toward them. They, similarly, never contemplated the possibility of our existence in a world like ours and felt no sense of obligation towards us. It would be difficult to imagine, given the state of knowledge of their time, how they could have been obligated towards us hypothetical descendants who have come to exist as a result of a myriad of unforeseeable accidents of circumstance.

Yet today, given advances in understanding of the possible effects of our actions on potential future generations in environmental contexts and the significance of genetic knowledge, the idea of obligations to those as yet not conceived has some purchase. These obligations figure prominently in the message of the ecology movement[4] and in MacNeice's poem where the child was likely to inherit the desert that war had made of paradise:

> I am not yet born: provide me
> With water to dandle me, grass to grow for me, trees to talk
> to me, sky to sing to me, birds and a white light
> in the back of my mind to guide me.

The unborn and hypothetical persons

But for the doctor engaged in medically assisted procreation the obligation is more immediate. This is not because the hypothetical status of the prospective children is questioned, as it might be if she were dealing with embryos or foetuses. Her obligations are to undeniably hypothetical persons, insofar as the decision to proceed with such assistance concerns the commission of the very conception of a child. However, here the prospect is imminent and the circumstances more readily forseeable than those of future generations. With a prospect so foreshortened it would be difficult to make a plausible case for refusing to recognise the interests of the not-yet-conceived.

An excellent case has been made for the intelligibility of ascribing obligations to future children in this way.[5] We would hold in contempt a terrorist who planted a bomb in a school with the intention of killing or maiming a class of children. It would make no difference whether that bomb was timed to explode within minutes, weeks or years. Given the intent and the predictable harms our condemnation of the act would be as severe as if the interval was as much as four years, by which time children not conceived at the time of the planting occupied the classroom. Murray quotes a legal precedent for recognising such liability from a negligence case where a woman's Rh-negative blood status was misrecorded in her medical file. She later conceived and gave birth to a child with Rh-positive blood. The child was severely damaged as the mother's recorded history did not indicate the prophylactic therapy of RhoGAM, which would have prevented the development of antibodies to Rh-positive blood. The court judgment was based on an illuminating hypothetical:

> Assume a balcony is negligently constructed. Two years later a mother and her one-year-old child step on to the balcony and it gives way, causing serious injuries to both the mother and child. It would be ludicrous to suggest that only the mother would have a cause of action against the builder but, because the infant was not conceived at the time of the negligent conduct, no duty of care existed towards the child.[6]

The interests of commissioned people

But how far is it reasonable to extend the obligations which the living have to potential people? It seems more plausible to call for protections from harm than it does for positive goods. For example, while it would appeal to our sensibilities to refrain from irresponsible behaviour which would commit future generations to hunger and harms, it might appear too much to ask that we ensure for them the provision of delicacies and rich inheritances. While the latter might appear as supererogatory duties even to our own children, the former are surely duties of a more basic kind. Such is illustrated by the balcony case. While the builder was not obliged to provide any such facility to his client and her potential offspring, he was obliged in the provision of the same to ensure that it did not constitute an unacceptable threat to their well-being. The child in MacNeice's poem might be understood as making a plea for such protections rather than supplying a list of desirable goods in each stanza of the work. It is pertinent to our discussion of medically assisted reproduction that such an observation finds a resonance in the dictum of the Hippocratic oath – *primum non nocere* – above all do no harm.

In the case of the doctor engaged in medically assisted surrogacy the object of her concern is even more immediate than the child in the balcony case. She is not obligated to entertain the nonsense of considering the interests of all potential persons, most of whom will never materialise. Rather she considers the interests of a child planned by specific means for specific parents at a specific point in their family history, and, moreover, a child whose existence will result from her intervention. Much can be known about such a child and its prospects and in some cases it might be deemed better that a likely life history remain unwritten. But this conclusion presents numerous problems.

Rival interests

First we have to reply to those who will contend that to entertain such concerns and consequently to deny assistance to the infertile or those unable to carry a child to term constitutes unwarranted discrimination against these groups of patients.

Discrimination against the infertile

We do not currently license normal parenthood and it would be difficult to imagine how this could ever be achieved even if it were thought to be desirable.[7] Yet we know it to be true that some people make very poor parents and that the circumstances of birth of many children are far from ideal. While we may endeavour to improve sex and health education and social services in order to address the problem, we would shrink from tampering with the right of people to found families.[8] Yet in the case of prospective parents seeking assisted procreation services it is received wisdom to make the interests of the prospective child of paramount importance. For example, the Human Fertilisation and Embryology Act 1990 in the UK provides that:

> A woman shall not be provided with treatment services unless account has been taken of the welfare of the child who may be born as a result of the treatment (including the need of that child for a father), and of any other child who may be affected by the birth.[9]

The suitability of candidates as parents therefore becomes one among many considerations in the processing of applications for medically assisted surrogacy or other forms of medically assisted reproduction. But is this fair? The creation of such obstacles to parenthood for infertile couples seems to compound their misfortune.

Some of the arguments in favour of these procedural barriers have invoked the adoption analogy.[10] In each case an endeavour is made to provide children in a non-standard, non-sexual way for parents who wish to raise them. Each involves the intervention of third parties. Each aims to produce social parent–children relationships. But the strength of an analogy is also tested by considering the differences between the analogues. Some jurisdictions such as Sweden are more impressed by the similarities than the differences and thus demand parallel openness in the procedures, so eliminating anonymity provisions for donors of gametes. Others, such as the UK and Norway, see the differences as being more weighty. In adoption procedures loss of family or otherwise fractured bonds with parents present special needs which demand that a secure, stable and caring environment be found to effect repair. Medically assisted procreation, by contrast, is usually concerned with enabling women to become parents by gestating children who have some shared identity in genetic terms with one or more of the commissioning parents. IVF using donated oocytes and sperm would lack the latter and medically assisted surrogacy would always lack the former and sometimes the latter. Nevertheless all but one of these forms of assisted reproduction assume some biological connections and all of them involve the deliberate commissioning of the life by its prospective parents. The differences might be thought to be so profound as to call for somewhat different regulation from adoptive procedures.

Let us imagine that they do make such a difference. Does it then follow that no screening of candidates as suitable for parenthood should occur in medically assisted reproduction? The answer must be no for the crucial similarity of the intervention of a third party remains to be accounted for. It is not only the prospective parents who commission the pregnancy and the new life. *Ex hypothesi* they cannot do so without the assistance of medical personnel. The latter are accountable for foreseeable consequences of their actions and, on the basis of the balcony case, it would be as irresponsible to ignore the interests of the not-yet-conceived child as those of the prospective mother. A doctor would be entitled to refuse to offer such treatment to a woman if in his judgement the treatment constituted an overwhelming threat to the health or survival of the woman. Similarly it would be improper to expect him to proceed with an intervention which would stand an overwhelming chance of producing unacceptable suffering or danger to the child whose conception and birth was the intent of the action.

A state worse than death

Second we have to determine what constitutes an unacceptable life history and how this is determined. Doctors refusing to provide services to the infertile on the basis of concern for the welfare of the prospective children are making a judgement which amounts to saying that such a child's life would constitute a state worse than death insofar as it would be better not to commission it.

One of the major problems in this process is the identification of the child's interests. We have already entertained the idea that protection from harms is the most ready subject of moral obligation for the treating clinician. But which harms are acceptable and which harms are beyond the pale? For example, we might first consider the question of physical harms. Some of these might be inherited in the conception and gestation process. Given that the oocytes of a forty-year-old woman are 40% more likely to produce a Down's syndrome child than those of a younger woman, should such commissioning mothers be refused medically assisted surrogacy or any other form of assisted reproduction employing their own gametes? Or should clinicians insist on the genetic testing of resultant foetuses with a view to termination of the pregnancy? We need to note that an affirmative answer will assume that such a genetic disorder might constitute an unacceptable harm and will imply an evaluation of the worth of a Down's syndrome life. On the other hand, given that it is accepted practice that such a condition constitutes sufficient reason for a prospective mother to choose a termination, should the treating doctor baulk at taking the risk of offering the reproductive service in the first place? And should the knowledge that the commissioning mother would not choose a termination in the event of such an outcome constitute a reason for refusal?

Physical and emotional harms which could occur after the birth of the child might be more likely, foreseeable and manageable. For example, these might be inflicted by a commissioning father with a record of child abuse or a mother with a record of drug abuse and neglect of earlier children. Carefully compiled family histories are needed to facilitate this kind of judgement and their construction might be difficult and intrusive. Given such a history it is likely that attempts will be made to conceal relevant details from clinicians. How far should they go in conducting investigations? Should they consult police records and social services? This kind of detective work might be thought to be beyond the proper remit of medical practice. Should it then be left to other agencies to determine the status of applicants for assisted reproduction services before clinicians proceed with their work? Given the importance of protecting the resultant child such a procedure seems reasonable, though this would constitute a less rigorous screening than that carried out for adoption where details of the economic status of the adoptive parents, their religious beliefs, race and education might play a role.

> I am not yet born; O hear me.
> Let not the bloodsucking bat or the rat or the stoat or the
> club-footed ghoul come near me.

> I am not yet born, console me.
> I fear that the human race may with tall walls wall me,
> with strong drugs dope me, with wise lies lure me,
> on black racks rack me, in blood-baths roll me.

Children as consumer products

Much of the criticism levelled at medically assisted reproductive services has taken the form of allegations that the resultant children are commodified.[11] The aimed-for outcome of the procedure is a healthy take-home child and not a pregnancy. This kind of provision lends itself to the use of language of the market place where issues of the quality of the product arise. These issues can be especially poignant in medically assisted surrogacy where the child suffers some disability. The gestating mother, being the legal mother, might then find herself with a disabled child on her hands which has been rejected by the 'customers' for the service. We might try to avoid this by scrutinising the motives of the commissioning couple. Do they think of the resultant child in these terms – are they seeking only the perfect baby? Are they wanting the child merely to satisfy their own desires as consumers? It is clear that this kind of enquiry will not get us very far. Indeed it might be regarded as imposing meaningless standards of propriety on the applicants. Is there, after all, any sense in saying that one desires a child for its own sake? At this stage the hypothetical child cannot be said to have interests which ought to be satisfied notwithstanding the earlier observation that the interests of future children not to be harmed must be respected. Nevertheless controls in medically assisted reproduction are called for to avoid the dangers of commodifying children. This is most obviously manifested in the field of medically assisted surrogacy where jurisdictions which have enacted controls generally ban commercial surrogacy.

> I am not yet born; O fill me
> With strength against those who would freeze my
> humanity, would dragoon me into a lethal automaton,
> would make me a cog in a machine, a thing with
> one face, a thing . . .

The interests of the child versus others

It was asserted earlier that the interests of the child were paramount in medically assisted surrogacy insofar as no such services should be offered to applicants except they are taken into account. It follows that where those interests are not well served, that treatment should not be accessed. But this is only a part of the story. It would be simplistic to think that the determination of interests is a straightforward matter. We have already seen that rival conceptions of those interests can complicate the issue. In addition it must be noted that those interests do not stand alone and that unless other interests are either served or protected there can be no justification for offering treatment. These interests can come into tension both with each other and, more significantly for the purposes of this chapter, with the interests of the child.

That there is such a tension does not imply that the interests of the child necessarily trump those of the surrogate or the commissioning parent or parents, for the interests of the child might be well served even if they are not best served. Consider a number of scenarios where such tension might arise.

Maternal/foetal conflict

Conflicts of this kind can occur in all pregnancies. Their resolution in current practice is a clear demonstration of the fact that the interests of the child do not generally outweigh those of the gestating mother. The fairly recent British case of compulsory Caesarian section caused great controversy and it has become clear that in future that case will not count as a precedent for the interests of the child prevailing over the interests of the mother.[12] Such a tension seems to present peculiar problems for medically assisted reproduction and for medically assisted surrogacy in particular.

In ordinary pregnancy the interests of the child might not be well served when the mother exercises her freedoms irrespective of her child's interests. But such pregnancies are not banned and while we might morally criticise a mother for disrespecting the interests of her prospective child we do not restrict her liberties in order to enforce such respect. Thus we do not regulate ordinary pregnancy in order to make the interests of the child paramount. Yet this appears to be a goal of legislative control of medically assisted reproduction in most countries where it occurs.[13]

The puzzle is best approached by recognising that the best interests of the child should play a crucial role in the decision to offer medically assisted reproduction services for reasons cited earlier. But the question of ensuring those interests subsequently would be a very different matter. Such an activity would encroach on the civil liberties of surrogate mothers in a particularly intrusive manner. It has to be admitted that this route for providing children for infertile couples or those unable to carry a child to term is fraught with social difficulties. While the surrogate and the commissioning parents collaborate in a most intimate and profound activity, they are placed, nevertheless, in a position of tension with each other of potentially mammoth proportions. The surrogate has custody and responsibility for the care and survival of a life which is of incalculable value to the parents. This puts her in a position of great power. Her behaviour can jeopardise the most cherished hopes of the parents and commit them to a lifetime of grief for a sick or disabled child, or even deny them their child completely. On the other hand the surrogate is placed in a position where her behaviour is subject to extraordinary scrutiny by others with a peculiar and intense interest in her affairs, with consequent loss of privacy and freedoms. Where such relationships go wrong the interests of the child compete with those of the warring parties and they cannot be guaranteed without the introduction of legislative control which would be unacceptable in a free society. For this reason no such treatments should be undertaken without meticulous counselling of all parties in an endeavour to keep the relationship on the best footing and so prevent threats to the interests of the child.

Parent–child conflict

In the evolution of the Human Embryology and Fertilisation Act 1990 the claim was constantly made that the Act was to be child centred. While we have already noted that the Act does emphasise the interests of the child in the decision to offer medically assisted reproduction services, this is insufficient to ensure the intended focus. A good case can be made for saying that the Act is in fact parent and donor centred insofar as it provides both for the maintenance of secrecy of the manner of conception and birth of the child and for anonymity of gamete donors where they are employed.

In the original Bill medically assisted surrogacy constituted a form of assisted reproduction where extraordinary steps were needed in order to maintain the secrecy of the birth circumstances. This was because in both the Act and the Surrogacy Arrangements Act 1985 the gestating mother was deemed to be the legal mother of the child. Thus the commissioning mother, even if she was the genetic mother of the child, would, in the absence of special provision, have to seek an adoption order and be subject to the application of the adoption criteria before being recognised as the mother of the child. This would mean *inter alia* that the circumstances of the birth could not be concealed from the child with such ease. Section 30 of the Act was therefore inserted as a late amendment of the Bill to make this special provision. Under this section gamete donors can make an application for a 'parental order' in order to become the legal parents of the child. Thus the circle of secrecy was closed. If a couple wish to conceal from a child the fact of their infertility, the involvement of a surrogate or a gamete donor they can do so.

In a research exercise in eight European countries in 1995 couples treated in infertility clinics using donated gametes were asked whether they would like their child to know the identity of the donors. Italy returned the highest proportion of 'yes' answers (14.7%), Bulgaria (12.3%), the United Kingdom (11.4%). No other country exceeded 4% and some returned 0% yes answers.[14] Genetic curiosity has been shown to be a powerful force in the case of adoptive children and most adoption laws now provide the right of access to the identity of genetic forebears to adopted children. Numerous countries including the United Kingdom deny this information to children born by medically assisted reproductive services where donor gametes are employed. Sweden and Austria have removed anonymity provisions in the interests of the children. The United Kingdom is currently discussing a move in the same direction. The right of a child to know the identity of its surrogate mother where there is no genetic relation is not a matter which has been canvassed generally.

Present families and future children

One consequence of the lack of openness about the origins of children born as a result of medically assisted reproduction is a tension between the interests of present families which include such children and future children who will be born by means of these techniques.

While medical technology has made it possible for many people to become parents who otherwise would have remained childless, the employment of the technologies also constitutes a very large social experiment. For example, we do not know what the consequences of the employment of donor gametes will be in family life. Nor do we know what the long-term results of Intra-Cytoplasmic Sperm Injection (ICSI) might be. Good clinical practice demands that we base our activities on good evidence and subject it to constant audit and review. This might be at the expense of sacrificing the privacy of parents who have used these services for it will not otherwise be possible to follow up children from whom the details of their origins have been concealed. The criticism has been voiced properly that assertions have been made about the undesirability of homosexual access to infertility services on the basis that it would be harmful to the interests of the resultant children without any good social science evidence to support them.[15] By the same token it should be noted that long-term follow-up of children born by means of new technologies and into new social arrangements is the *sine qua non* of good practice in medically assisted reproduction. How else can possible future harms be avoided? We have no supernatural insight into these matters and must rely on the best scientific methods available to us to protect the interests of the unborn in medically assisted surrogacy and other forms of assisted reproduction.

> I am not yet born; O hear me,
> Let not the man who is beast or who thinks he is God
> come near me.

Conscientious objection

There are few conscience clauses in the law governing medical practice. They occur standardly in laws governing abortion according to which no person shall be under a duty to participate in any treatment authorised by the Acts to which they have a conscientious objection. Outside such provisions, doctors could be guilty of failing to carry out their duty of care if they refuse to treat on other than clinical grounds except for those cases where they are not able to treat due to lack of resources. Where there are laws governing the provision of medically assisted reproduction, including medically assisted surrogacy, a conscience clause occurs. For example, the Human Embryology and Fertilisation Act 1990 contains the following section:

38: (1) No person who has a conscientious objection to participating in any activity governed by this Act shall be under any duty, however arising, to do so.

(2) In any legal proceedings the burden of proof of conscientious objection shall rest on the person claiming to rely on it.

(3) In any proceedings before a court in Scotland, a statement on oath by any person to the effect that he has a conscientious objection to participating in a particular activity, governed by this Act shall be sufficient evidence of that fact for the purpose of discharging the burden of proof imposed by subsection (2) above.[16]

But this raises peculiar problems for the clinician. The section has not yet been tested in the courts though the principle was tested once before the law was enacted.[17] There are considerable uncertainties surrounding its meaning.[18] What counts as an acceptable conscientious objection? It is not part of the ethos of medicine for doctors to make decisions to treat on the non-clinical basis of the moral worthiness of their patients to be treated. Additionally, in New Zealand for example, it would be a breach of the Health and Disability Commissioner Act 1994 to refuse to treat a patient on the grounds of her sexuality. If a doctor holds the view that lesbianism is a morally unacceptable lifestyle, is he justified in refusing access to lesbian applicants for reproduction treatment? The British case might throw some light on this question. In it a woman was refused access to infertility services on the basis of 'her lack of understanding of the role of foster parent'. She was now in a stable relationship but had a history of prostitution. No relevant information apart from her life as a prostitute was provided in the judgment of the court which upheld the refusal at appeal. The history which was sure to bar her from becoming a foster mother was now to bar her from conceiving her own child. The court made it clear that had the hospital's reason been that the woman was a Jew or coloured then the decision might have been regarded as illegal. Presumably the refusal was ostensibly made in the interests of the child whom the providers believed would be born into a context of moral danger. But here it is impossible to separate a judgement about the lifestyle of the applicant from an assessment of the interests of the child. Similarly the clinician's view of the lesbian applicant's lifestyle would determine the hazardous familial context into which the child would be born as a result of the treatment. We are left wondering in this case whether the authentic voice of the unborn is heard in the doctor's decision or whether the child becomes the surrogate mouthpiece of the interests of the doctor.

Conclusion

While it might seem odd to consider that doctors have responsibilities to people who do not exist insofar as they have not even been conceived, it is not impossible to make a telling case for the same. Clearly clinicians are accountable for the consequences of their practice. In providing assisted reproduction services they are intentionally and causally involved in the coming to be of children when the outcomes of the treatment are successful. They cannot therefore wash their hands of responsibility for the children who, as a result of negligent practice, are severely damaged. For example, the birth of children with serious handicaps resulting from multiple pregnancies due to the replacement of too many pre-embryos in the uterus of the mother can be foreseen as a distinct possibility. It is plausible therefore to argue that the doctor can be said to have an obligation not to behave in this way both to the parents and to the prospective children themselves even though desisting from such interventions might result in the fact that the children whose welfare dictate such decisions never come to be. Insofar as this is the case, such prospective children might be said to have interests.

Yet, despite the clarity of the declarations of various legislatures in the field concerning the importance of the welfare of the product of assisted reproduction services, the hypothetical child, it is not easy to determine what would count as a sufficient reason to deny such medical services to prospective parents. Insofar as such reasons would reflect an attitude of the doctor towards the lifestyle or worthiness of the applicants to be treated it constitutes a sea change in the ethos of medical practice.

In addition, this kind of scrutiny of worthiness to become parents seems to discriminate against the infertile with respect to prospective parents seeking to reproduce normally.

Nevertheless if we endeavour to take seriously the injunctions of assisted reproduction legislation on the matter we run into a series of difficulties which complicate the decision to treat in various ways. These are cases where the interests of the child, insofar as they can be determined, come into tension with rival interests.

To regard offspring as commodities would, of course, suggest a tension between parents' interests and those of their child. But the interests of the prospective parents cannot sensibly be contrasted with the interests of normally reproducing couples on the basis of whether their offspring are to be regarded as commodities or not. Other interests of the prospective mother might well be in tension with the interests of the child, such as the desire to enjoy alcohol or smoking during the pregnancy. But guarding against such risky behaviour by clinicians is not possible in normal pregnancies and would, in any case, threaten civil liberties. Thus we might ask why infertile people should be singled out for sanctions, including the ultimate sanction of not being enabled to become a parent at all to avoid damage to a prospective child. Other tensions such as the protections of the parents' interests in the name of privacy might militate against the child's interests as might the interests of a future generation of children produced by these means through preserving a respect for the privacy of the parents. The final problem concerns the difficulty of allowing the treating doctor to honour her conscience by not providing treatment which she believes will be likely to result in a life exposed to danger and harm when she and the parents do not share the same views as to what constitutes harm. Such a freedom on the part of the doctor introduces a difficult criterion of treatment, namely, the worthiness of the patients to receive care.

Notes

1 R. Graves, 'To evoke posterity', *Collected Poems*, London: Cassell, 1959, p. 136.
2 L. MacNeice, (1966) 'Prayer before birth', in *The Collected Poems of Louis MacNeice*, E.R. Dodds (ed.), London: Faber and Faber, 1966, pp. 193–4.
3 D. Hume, *A Treatise of Human Nature*, Princeton: Penguin, 1969, p. 633.
4 See, for example: J. Feinberg, 'The rights of animals and unborn generations', in *Rights, Justice and the Bounds of Liberty*, Princeton: Princeton University Press, 1980, pp. 159–84.
5 T. Murray, *The Worth of a Child*, California: University of California Press, 1996, pp. 98–9.
6 *Lough v Rolla Women's Clinic, Inc.*, 866 S.W.2d 851 (Mo. 1993) 23, 105.
7 H. LaFollette, 'Licensing parents' *Philosophy and Public Affairs* 9 (1980), 182–97.
8 European Convention on Human Rights, Art 12.
9 Human Fertilisation and Embryology Act 1990, London: HMSO, S13(5).
10 K. Ruyter, 'The example of adoption', in D.M. Evans (ed.), *Creating the Child*, The Hague: Martinus Nijhoff, 1996, pp. 177–94.
11 M.J. Radin, 'Market inalienability', in K.D. Alpern (ed.), *The Ethics of Reproductive Technologies*, Oxford: Oxford University Press, 1992, pp. 174–94.
12 *St. George's Healthcare NHS v S* (1998), 3 All ER 673; (1999) FAM 26.
13 See, for example, accounts of law and practice in Norway, France, Austria, Germany, the United Kingdom: Sweden and Norway (Ruyter, op. cit., p.178); France (C. Byk, 'French assisted reproduction legislation', in D.M. Evans (ed.), *Creating the Child*, The Hague: Martinus Nijhoff, 1996, pp. 347–9); Austria and Germany (E. Bernat and E. Vranes, 'The Austrian act on procreative medicine: scope, impacts and inconsistencies', in D.M. Evans (ed.), *Creating the Child*, The Hague: Martinus Nijhoff, 1996, pp. 325–32); the United Kingdom (A.J. Klotzko, 'Infertility, inability and rights: an English legal case study', in D.M. Evans (ed.), *Creating the Child*, The Hague: Martinus Nijhoff, 1996, pp. 341–6).
14 D.M. Evans and M. Dolanska, 'Patient perceptions of services', in D.M. Evans (ed.), *Creating the Child*, The Hague: Martinus Nijhoff, 1996, pp. 291–301.
15 S. Golombok, A. Spencer and M. Rutter, 'Children in lesbian and single parent households: psychosexual and psychiatric appraisal', *Journal of Child Psychology and Psychiatry* 24 (1983), 551–72.
16 Human Embryology and Fertilisation Act 1990, s 38(1–3).
17 *R v Ethical Advisory Committee of St. Mary's Hospital ex p. Harriott*, 1 *Family Law Review*, 1988, 512.
18 D.M. Evans, 'The clinical classification of infertility', in D.M. Evans (ed.), *Creating the Child*, The Hague: Martinus Nijhoff, 1996, pp. 59–61.

Chapter 7

Qualifying as a person

Chapter 6 was concerned with the welfare of hypothetical children insofar as the doctor involved in providing assisted reproduction services has to take into account the interests and well-being of the child which has yet to be conceived. Such children were therefore described as hypothetical persons and were distinguished from embryos and foetuses quite deliberately. This was because for some people human embryos and foetuses are no longer hypothetical human beings but actual human beings.

Nowhere in medicine is there greater disagreement about the facts than in the area of human embryology and reproduction. The advent of *in vitro* fertilisation has brought into bold relief the rival conceptions of the human embryo. But the selfsame dissonance was already well canvassed in disputes over termination of pregnancy as a useful clinical intervention. The disagreement revolves around whether or not either the embryo or foetus or both constitute persons. It is clear that the clinical options for dealing with infertility, contraception, pre-implantation genetic testing, pre-natal genetic testing, and other indications with respect to both the mother's and child's health will be drastically limited if one view rather than the other is taken.

But cannot the remarkable advances in human embryology answer the question for us once and for all? This chapter uncovers the nature of the disagreement and the dismal prospects of resolving it.

The significance of the issue lies beyond the fertility and obstetric clinic. Much has been written about what constitutes a person and some bioethicists have made this the lynchpin of their analysis of the role of values in medicine. Let us examine one of the most explicit bioethical theories of this kind:

> The ultimate question for medical ethics, indeed for any ethics, is also in a sense the very first question that arises when we begin to grapple with moral problems. The question is simply: what makes human life valuable and, in particular, what makes it more valuable than other forms of life?[1]

John Harris is concerned with what it is that qualifies us for the status of persons as such. This he expresses in the form of 'having what it takes to be a person'. Further, armed with this information we shall be enabled to identify others as persons, including aliens, so that 'we will be deciding whether an appropriate response to them would be to have them for dinner in one sense or the other'.[2] This humorous remark is revealing and gets to the heart of what we are concerned with in this chapter. Is our appropriate response to others dependent on having a reason, even the excellent candidate offered by Harris, viz. the ability to value one's own existence, or, indeed, any alternative reason offered by others to perform the same function?[3]

Animals and persons

Harris accepts that some human lives are less valuable than others – for example, foetuses, mentally and physically handicapped individuals, some aged individuals, the terminally ill, and so on.[4] Indeed, on his account, lack of the ability to value one's own life might be a reason for ranking the value of a human being below that of a chimpanzee and for bestowing the label of person on the latter rather than the former.[5]

This view of what marks out the definitive difference between morally valuable lives from others, persons from others, is certainly radical for it entails that the life of a healthy chimpanzee might be more morally considerable than the life of a mentally handicapped human being. Harris is not alone in adopting this kind of view. Many who have opposed the use of animals in research agree with him. The most prominent academic proponents of this position hold that we should behave towards living beings, including human beings, in ways that take due account of their interests which are dependent on their capacity for suffering and enjoyment. Though this is a different test from Harris's, it has similar consequences, viz. that some animals will be seen to have interests which some human beings cannot have because of their relative capacities. It follows that it would be mistaken to be more concerned for the welfare of a senile or insane human being than for a healthy higher primate. This mistake would be evidence of a prejudice against animals which has been labelled 'speciesism'.[6]

There are numerous problems associated with this view which will be discussed in more detail in Chapter 8. For the present let us concentrate on the treatment of human entities which have or do not have a claim to be persons.

Pro-attitudes to pre-embryos

Let us focus our examination on the question of whether it is possible to regard pre-embryos as persons. This issue has assumed fresh importance with the advent of human embryonic stem cell research. It will not be our purpose to determine whether pre-embryos are or are not persons but rather to explore whether such a determination is better understood in a way other than by means of the kinds of theoretical terms employed in Harris's account.

It might well turn out that the deed will count for more than the word in getting clear about the status of the pre-embryo. That is, it might well be that it is by discovering what we are prepared to do with the pre-embryo that we determine what we consider its status to be as opposed to trying to get clear about the matter in order to decide what we shall do. Insofar as this is so then it will be *pro-attitudes* to pre-embryos which are crucial to answering the question rather than seeking for reasons.

The term pro-attitude was invented by Nowell-Smith[7] to describe the logical relation which holds between the reasons one might give for choosing something and the choosing. For example, if you know that someone enjoys ice skating, the question: 'Why do you go ice skating?' would be redundant. There is a logical relationship between enjoying something and choosing it. This relation is not so tight as to make the claim and the decision to do otherwise contradictory for there may be overriding considerations – the skater might have a broken leg. But in the absence of such considerations the claim and the failure to choose to skate would come into an unacceptable tension. Thus the claim is an impeccable explanation of the choice. It is also an impeccable reason for choosing to skate. However, impeccable reasons need not be conclusive reasons.[8]

Nowell-Smith asserts that there is no limit to the possible objects of these *pro-attitudes*.[9] Pro-attitudes may thus be said to provide impeccable though not conclusive reasons for various descriptions of the human embryo. How we are prepared to act towards the human embryo demonstrates our choice of how we shall describe it. However, this is not to provide a moral justification for such a description for, as Nowell-Smith points out, one may have a pro-attitude providing a logically complete reason for morally reprehensible conduct, as when one tortures the cat because one enjoys it.[10]

This phenomenon is well illustrated by the historical disagreements between the ovist and spermatozoist preformation theorists of human reproduction. During the so-called 'embryological revolution' of the seventeenth century the spermatozoists and ovists disputed the relative significance of the sperm and ovum in reproduction. Each thought that the preformed human life was in the preferred gamete and that the corresponding dormant partner gamete either sparked off the growth of the preformed embryo (the role of the sperm in the ovist account) or provided the necessary context for the growth of the preformed embryo (the role of the ovum in the spermatozoist account). What was never disputed between the parties was that the preformed foetus was present somewhere before fertilisation. Some even claimed to have demonstrated the veracity of their account by having observed such a form in sperm by means of the new technology of the microscope. They might not have been perverse in their claims. One's expectations can play a major role in what one claims to observe. However, though one's theoretical framework may produce a certain configuration in the data perceived, it is stretching the bounds of credibility to think of the visual discovery of miniature foetuses in sperm or ova hypothesised by preformation theories. Indeed the later sophistication of the very technology which was supposed to facilitate such a revelation itself enables us to reject the claim with total confidence.

Brockliss[11] has made a very good case for saying that both the emergence of preformationism and its demise were not evidentially based but, rather, ideologically determined. His argument runs thus: the rise of Cartesian mechanism caused the emergence of the theory. No satisfactory account of changes in state could be given in mechanical terms. As a result it was natural to assume that the foetus was preformed before conception. This tied in with the Cartesian theology that God, in one act of creation, had brought a world to be which did not require constant creative acts on his part. Thus all preformed foetuses were created from the beginning of time.[12] This was clearly not evidentially based. Consequently no counter-evidence was responsible for the demise of preformation accounts.[13] Monsters, the traits of the dormant partner, and so on were accounted for by various means, leaving preformationism intact. Nothing could count properly as counter-evidence for the theory was never based on evidence in the first place – it had more the character of a dogma in the light of which observational data were construed. It was the advent of Newtonianism, with its different epistemological implications, which heralded the fall of preformationism, not crucial counter-evidence.

One group of attitudes which might be productive of particular decriptions of the embryo is shaped by religion. Insofar as Brockliss is correct it may be said that the *pro-attitudes* to pre-embryos, which determined how they were described, emerged from prevailing theological or religious considerations. These shaped people's attitudes towards embryos for, despite their differences, the dispute between ovists and spermatozoists never called preformationism into question.

It is precisely this complex relationship between pro-attitudes and descriptions of fact which creates the possibility of radical moral disagreement over the status of the embryo – that is, disagreement which is not resolvable by an appeal to reason. The parameters of what it is reasonable, and even moral, to do are fixed in part by the descriptions we choose; the identity of subsequent acts is determined by our descriptions of the facts in question. Whether we describe the early embryo as a human soul, a human life, a person, human life, or a mass of undifferentiated cells will set down a variety of possibilities of what we would be doing if we experimented on such an embryo to destruction. How we see and describe the embryo will be determined by a whole variety of interests, convictions and preferences. This set of features may be loosely called an ideology but it need not take the form of a tight theory or even of a coherent and comprehensive world view. One may, for example, take the view that life is a gift from God and that man is mysteriously made in

God's image – a belief that is neither necessarily threatened nor undermined by the most detailed description of biological events during reproduction. No amount of embryological investigation could conceivably crack what is held to be an awesome mystery for, by their nature, genuine mysteries are not simply states of ignorance. The description of this mystery is an expression of the awe in which the very fact of human life is held. Such life is not a manufactured commodity but rather a divine gift. Armed with this commitment a person may well, when faced with the question of the status of the early embryo for the first time, choose to describe it as a human soul. If challenged for a reason he might respond that human life is a mystery, a divine gift. This is an impeccable reason for the description insofar as it renders otiose the further Harris-like question, viz. so why do you describe the early embryo as a human soul?

But we must remember that on Nowell-Smith's account pro-attitudes do not provide conclusive reasons, for the pro-attitude may not be shared by some others. For them the world is not as it has been described by this particular believer. They too may be believers yet not cash that out by means of such a description. Indeed many in the Judaeo-Christian tradition have, through the centuries, not so described the early embryo. Such views might also be tempered by other interests and convictions such as that man's intellect should be employed to further understanding and that being in God's image commits man to creative endeavour in God's world. On this view the so-called mystery of life is seen as a state of ignorance, much of which has already been dispelled, awaiting resolution with many other one-time mysteries such as the mystery of flight. These are mysteries which must surrender to the inquisitiveness of the human mind. Given such a context the information provided by the microscope and embryology of the earliest stages of human life may explain the choice of the most radical description of the early embryo as a mass of undifferentiated cells. Certainly for many with no religious conviction and with a profound faith in science and its progress, together with a burden for the suffering of infertile couples, the thirst for knowledge would pitch them towards such a choice of description.

It might seem that this must be a rationalisation of subsequent destructive research on embryos, thinking backwards from practice to description. This would be a mistake. There may be bad faith, of course, but there need not be. How one is prepared to act towards the embryo may demonstrate how one conceives of it. Such a conception may even come as a surprise. How one then goes on to describe one's actions confirms this. Thus researchers might not need to find a justification for taking human lives for the advance of knowledge when they engage in destructive experimentation on early embryos. One may hope that such a price would be too high for any embryologist to be willing to pay. Certainly we know of some who in the name of research have thought human lives worth sacrificing. To tar embryologists with the same brush as the perpetrators of crimes upon humanity in the Nazi death camps would be to ignore the difference in their descriptions of what they were doing. Of course, it remains open to the holder of the conservative view canvassed above to make such an accusation but this vital difference has to be accounted for. The German camp doctors knew that they were sacrificing people for their so-called research, albeit people they despised. The embryologist experimenting on the pre-embryo rejects such a description as do many who support and admire his work. Here we have a moral disagreement about what it is that is being done, a disagreement at the level of the facts, not a disagreement about purported justifications of actions whose descriptions are agreed.

Ideology and crucial evidence

But can't we test this view by an appeal to modern cell biology? Are there not certain very basic biological considerations which today play a crucial role in settling disputes about the status of the human embryo? That is, do not recently discovered facts of human embryology demand that we opt for one description rather than another? On such an account loyalty to some descriptions, though demanded by ideological considerations, would be seen to be maintained only at the expense of being confused or mistaken. If such a view stands then pro-attitudes themselves will be seen to be subject to the test of fact and disagreements arising out of variations between them would be resolvable, given adequate information, goodwill and a concern for the truth. We can test this view by putting forward the strongest philosophical case for not regarding the early conceptus as a human being,[14] a case based on a purportedly crucial biological fact which has come to light in only recent advances in human embryology.

We are told that up to the four-cell stage of cleavage of the early embryo all the cells are pluripotential. That is, as far as we know, there is no means of discrimination between cells which will later form the placenta and those which will form the foetus. We also know that these cells are totipotential. That is, if one of them is separated from the rest, given the right conditions, it too will begin to divide and result in a further embryo which is identical to that which develops from the parent mass of cells. In nature something akin to this occurs occasionally when two primitive streaks develop from one mass of cells and monozygotic twins are produced. What bearing do these facts have upon the descriptions which we choose for the conceptus at this early stage?

The group of cells is sometimes described as an undifferentiated mass. This description is designed to highlight the independence of each cell from the rest save for the fact of their being aggregated together. Separation of one of these from the rest appears to do no harm to those which remain. Neither does it appear to be necessarily harmed itself. The group made up of the four cells does not constitute an organism for there appears to be no functional relation between its parts. Even when cell changes other than cleavage begin to occur this is still the case. Such changes occur before the appearance of the primitive streak but even yet the morula is still capable of developing into two organisms. The appearance of the primitive streak marks the end of this possibility.

It appears that there are two different senses attaching to the notion of being undifferentiated as it may be applied to such cell masses. One we can call the weak sense and the other the strong sense. The weak sense denotes simply that *so far as we know* there is no difference between the cells and there is no functional relation between them. The strong sense denotes that it follows *from what we already know* that, of their nature, the cells are identical and independent of each other – this is demonstrated by their totipotentiality and their pluripotentiality.

What then might be the significance of this strong sense of being undifferentiated? One necessary condition of identifying *a* human life is individuation. An individual mass of cells alone does not constitute an individual life, even though those cells may be human and alive. This is true of a collection of blood cells, for example. Further, individuality must persist through time and structural change. The author of this book is the same individual human being who married Ann, being the son of Aubrey and Mary Evans. No cell in his body remains from the day of his birth, nor even from the day of his marriage, and in some senses he is a very different person. Nevertheless he is the same individual human being. He has no reason to doubt that he developed from an early conceptus. He also knows that his twin developed from an early conceptus, though a different one for they were not monozygotic twins. But if they had been then they would have developed from the same early conceptus. The crucial change, when the one conceptus became two, would be in a different category from all the cellular changes which have occurred in them as individuals. That change would not have occurred in the author, or in his life, in any sense. Neither would it have occurred in his brother's life. It is also very odd to think of all their subsequent cellular changes as changes in some original life from which they sprang. That would be a third human life. It is doubtful that anyone would wish to claim that that was a life sacrificed for the lives of the subsequent twins. Thus the facts of totipotentiality and pluripotentiality of the cells of the early conceptus are obstacles to our identifying that conceptus as *a* human life. While we might retrospectively link a given human life with an early conceptus, we cannot know that any early conceptus will become only one life – or even a life at all as it might develop into a hydatitiform mole or, given that it contains too many chromosomes it must perish. Thus, the argument runs, the very early conceptus, that is the conceptus which is made up of a mass of cells each of which is both pluripotent and totipotent, cannot be properly called *a* human life and that this is not simply because of our current state of ignorance about the nature of the early embryo.

This argument seems to demand, in the name of logic, that all reasonable people agree with its conclusion. Disagreement, it seems, can only be at pain of confusion. But is all as it in fact seems? Would an appeal to the mystery of human life here simply be a refusal to face the uncomfortable facts which have been recently uncovered? A philosophical case can be made which suggests that such a refusal is not a counsel of ignorance so much as an expression of religious wonder at the fact of human life. On this account the inexplicability of factors in the origin of a human life is an important feature of a due respect for that life. In this way the activity of philosophical reflection on the nature of the religious promises a resolution of the apparent clash between the purported biological facts and absolute respect for the fertilised ovum.

In order to develop the philosophical case let us turn to the work of Wittgenstein as an example of a philosopher who reflected on the sense of the religious and who related it to the idea of wonder.[15]

Churchill shows how Wittgenstein's account of religious awareness is tied up with his insistence throughout his philosophy that justification has to come to an end, which in turn is related to his interest in the stopping places for the giving of reasons, viz. human reactions and very general facts of nature. This is the point where he asserts that explanation comes to an end and the business of Philosophy is description. Thus to describe a mathematical rule like addition is all that one can do, there is no justifying such a rule as being correct. This is simply what adding comes to. Though particular additions are justified in terms of this rule, the rule itself cannot stand in need of justification. It is the ground or the boundary of reason giving. Wittgenstein describes[16] a number of disparate commitments that do not rest upon reasons but which form the boundaries of doubt and reason. To question these is not therefore to exhibit caution but rather to be confused. Yet the temptation recurs to endeavour to press beyond these stopping places to press for explanations of why we think as we do rather than rest with the description of what it is to think.

Churchill points out that Wittgenstein sees this temptation as symptomatic of modern, scientific thought. He writes:

> Twentieth century thought, he claims, has substituted the endless quest for explanation in terms of reasons for a willingness to stop when we have a solution. The demand for explanation is a recursive demand, by always seeking a justification that shows why this way is the way, and it functions to block another attitude towards the practice – a wonder or astonishment that it does go this way – happens to go this way – rather than another.[17]

This is a block to wonder at and awe of human life as it is. In the case of the human embryo it may seem that pressing for explanations of the process of reproduction back to the morula and earliest conceptus undermines the sense of wonder of human life. It might then appear that this sense of wonder depends on a certain degree of ignorance. In a way it does, though it would be better to think of wondering at nature as a different form of attention, yet one that is more difficult to attain once explanation has been effected. Churchill helps us with the analogy of Mark Twain's boyhood wonder at the variegated textures and colours on the surface of the Mississippi, which was destroyed by his training as a steamboat pilot:

> The unsignifying glory of the River, its aesthetic beauty, was lost to him forever, and in its place he saw a system of signs, signals of clear passage, shallow water, cross currents, underwater snags.[18]

One might be tempted to think that this philosophical analysis of the religious sense at least should settle any dispute between religious believers about the status of the human embryo. Yet, once again, we have to note that the divide between philosophers about what counts as an acceptable account of the religious is as profound as the differences between views of the status of the foetus, as Churchill eloquently points out. This divide is again determined by pro-attitudes to certain kinds of philosophical activity. Many religious believers see their religious beliefs as involving truth claims and as having explanatory force. Others, in the Wittgenstein mould, may consider that they have missed the point of religion. Yet others, as indeed Churchill intimates, would want to say that there is more than one sort of religion.[19] Philosophy, it seems, is in no position to adjudicate. Thus it leaves us with the kind of rival descriptions of the early embryo we rehearsed above. Pro-attitudes make their presence felt in philosophical reflection too.

So the fine detail of the empirical description of the early conceptus might well be regarded as a threat to the possibility of the sense of wonder at the gift of human life. Things suddenly seem more mundane than they did and human life a poorer thing for it. Such a reaction is not inevitable, however. Indeed one may even come to a wonder at the way things are, by realising that one came to be oneself as one of no less than a myriad of random possibilities. Or, given a certain religious perspective on the case discussed above, one might stand in awe of what one may call the mystery of two or more lives being embodied as one at a certain stage of development. 'Our lives are in the hand of God and if this is how he sees fit to develop them then so be it, thanks be to God' may be a religious response to the facts cited. Critics will retort that the power of God cannot be expressed in defiance of logic, or what makes sense, and such an account will not impress them. But the believer in question may refuse to accept the puzzle as it is presented and feel obliged to question the strong sense of being undifferentiated employed in setting it up. He may feel that there is no onus on him to provide any explanation. He is willing to live with the wonder at what cannot be understood. In other words, it is his commitment to a certain description of the early conceptus which dictates what counts as an explanation.

Conclusion

Harris has provided us with a positive account of personhood. That is, a theory which puts into our hands a method or a tool for determining in every situation whether an individual is a person. This in turn provides us with a means for determining what we should do in the face of specific moral challenges in medical ethics.

But the theory rules out as mistaken many duties and obligations which people believe they have in wide varieties of situations. Maybe Harris is aware of this insofar as he never defends the propriety of eating handicapped persons or human foetuses on the basis of their failing his personhood test, despite the role he ascribes to that test in the dinner invitation aside which was noted at the beginning of this chapter.

Consider the moving case of a patient whom we shall call Jean. Jean was already mother of a son and daughter when she, happily, found herself pregnant again. She was told to expect a daughter. It later emerged that the foetus was anencephalic. Offered the chance of a termination she refused, knowing full well the nature of the problem. Her reason for refusal was that she wished to do as much for her daughter as she had done for her other children. The clinicians respected her decision and she carried the child to term. Her little girl was born, baptised, cherished for a few days and then died. Was Jean mistaken? On the Harris account she certainly was for this was no person which she bore and, had she survived, she would never have become a person. But to the family she was a daughter and a sister. They gave thanks for her, loved her and grieved for her. These are not notions foreign to people outside the philosopher's study. The mother's behaviour was admirable. This is not, of course, to say that she was correct. It is not a question of being mistaken or otherwise about the child's capacities for suffering and enjoyment. It is rather a question of attitude which finds its roots elsewhere than in the baby's apparent lack of qualifications for personhood.

Notes

1 J. Harris, *The Value of Life*, London: Routledge, 1985, p. 7.
2 Ibid., pp. 8–10.
3 For example, consider the following required qualifications: having the concept of a continuous life (M. Tooley, 'Abortion and infanticide' *Philosophy and Public Affairs* 2 (1972), 37–65); being self-conscious (P. Singer and D. Wells, *Making Babies*, New York: C. Scribner's Sons, 1985); being self-legislating (H.T. Engelhardt, Jr., *The Foundations of Bioethics*, 2nd edn, New York: Oxford University Press, 1996, p. 141); having intentional interests (G. Gillett, 'Reply to J M Stanley: fiddling and clarity', *Journal of Medical Ethics* 13 (1987), 23–5); being a psycho-

logically integrated unity capable of morally imputable actions (T.J. Bole, 'Zygote, souls, substances, and persons', *Journal of Medicine and Philosophy* 15 (1990), 637–52).

4 J. Harris, *The Value of Life*, pp. 7–8.

5 Ibid., pp. 19–21.

6 R. Ryder, *The Victims of Science: the Use of Animals in Research*, London: Davis-Poynter, 1975.

7 P.H. Nowell-Smith, *Ethics*, UK: Penguin, 1954, pp. 111–21.

8 Ibid., p.113–14.

9 Ibid., p. 115.

10 Ibid.

11 L.W.B. Brockliss, 'The embryological revolution in the France of Louis XIV: the dominance of ideology', in G.R. Dunstan (ed.), *The Human Embryo*, UK: University of Exeter Press, 1990, pp. 158–86.

12 Ibid., p. 172.

13 Ibid., pp. 175ff.

14 The case is mine though similar cases have been made by others: e.g. P. Singer and H. Kuhse, 'Individuals, humans and persons: The issue of moral status', in P. Singer, H. Kuhse, S. Buckle, K. Dawson and P. Kasimba (eds.), *Embryo Experimentation*, Cambridge: Cambridge University Press, 1990, pp. 65–75.

15 J. Churchill, 'Wonder and the end of explanation: Wittgenstein and religious sensibility', *Philosophical Investigations* 17 (1994), pp. 388–416.

16 L. Wittgenstein, *On Certainty*, G.E.M. Anscombe and G.H. von Wright (eds.), Oxford: Basil Blackwell, 1969.

17 J. Churchill, 'Wonder and the end of explanation', p. 405.

18 Ibid., p. 411.

19 Ibid., p. 391.

Chapter 8

Are animals our equals?

We noted in Chapter 7 that the quest for a theory of personhood has raised the vexed question of the moral status of animals. This is not an insignificant issue in medicine as animals play an indispensable role in medical research. Their role in the development of clinical advances is a topic which has generated major debate and resulted in direct action against researchers by animal rights protesters. There is therefore, even here, a call for health researchers to reflect upon the place of values in these procedures. This is the more so if we give weight to theories of morality in medicine which make personhood the defining factor of what calls for ethical responses from practitioners and which do not restrict the use of the description person to humans. Indeed, as we have seen, the criteria of personhood employed in such theories mean that some animals rate above some humans for ethical concern. Let us look more closely at such claims.

Joseph Wright's celebrated painting[1] conveys all the reactions to the use of animals in research which we confront almost three hundred years later.

The picture depicts a scientist replicating Boyle's experiment demonstrating the need of an animal for respirable air by evacuating the air from a glass jar in which the animal is placed. One reading of the painting is that the demonstration occurs in the home of the audience.[2] The audience is reminded of the slender line between life and death by the presence of the carious human skull, used as a symbol of mortality.

The onlookers, aware that the animal might suffer and die in the experiment, react variously. The demonstrator exercises the power of life and death by means of his left hand on the stopcock which could either provide or deny life-giving air to the bird. The father is eager for his wife and child to learn from the demonstration, whereas the mother cannot bear to look. Is she squeamish or does she hesitate to be party to such cruelty? The serious gentlemen acutely observe the event lest they miss a vital piece of information. The couple on the left glance apprehensively towards each other, torn by doubt about whether they should look and learn at such cost. And, finally, who is the boy who hoists away the cage, sadly resigned to the death of the animal? Is it the son of the house whose pet the bird is?

Figure 8.1 Joseph Wright of Derby, *An Experiment on a Bird in an Air Pump* (1768), oil painting. © The National Gallery, London.

Such reactions can be examined by asking the question: 'Are animals our equals?' following Darwin's celebrated note that: 'Animals, whom we have made our slaves, we do not like to consider our equal.'[3]

The oddness of the question

On the face of it this seems to be a strange question to ask if only because there seems to be an obvious answer to it. We are familiar with public health measures involving the planned destruction of certain animals which pose threats to the well-being of people. We vote for environmental programmes which seek to eradicate whole species of non-indigenous animals from countries which, aside from presenting a threat to public health in some cases, threaten the purity of environmental heritages. Most of us choose which animals to eat and regard them as a major part of our diet to safeguard our health. In this connection we also support a vast industry which informs us of the most interesting and innovative ways to prepare the meat to titillate our palates.

Before the age of mechanical transport we used animals to power our vehicles, pull our ploughs, detect unsafe gases in our mines. We still use them to produce dairy products and some fabrics. Above all, in the area of research, we use them as tools to test our drugs, help us understand the nature of our diseases, cognitive processes and behaviours. We even produce them with compromised immune systems and genetic abnormalities, and inflict injuries and disease conditions on them to further our knowledge about people's health and welfare. So why bother to pose the question at all? Darwin was clearly aware of our reluctance to do so.

Some surprising answers

As we have already noted, there are some who have so reflected and their affirmative answers have led them to draw radical conclusions. Though a small minority their views are well known and include, in some cases, the avoidance, if not banning, of most or all of the above activities.[4] There are others from within the research environment who have also reflected on these matters and have answered with a qualified 'yes'. They have proposed ways forward in using animals in research by recommending 'The Three Rs' approach, which involves efforts to *refine* the use of animals by minimising suffering and distress, *reduce* the numbers of animals used and, where possible, to *replace* the use of living animals by other means in research activity.[5] It took a long time for their message to register in many quarters. For example, the notorious LD50 test used in the pre-Phase1 studies of new pharmaceuticals was widely used up until the OECD recommendation to abolish it in 2000, which became effective in December 2002. This ban covers 30 countries including the United States.

We might still want to ask what these groups mean when they provide their answers to our question as, for others, those answers might still appear to be counter-intuitive. Reflection on the matter might provide us with some useful guidance for approving or disapproving the use of animals in research.

The robust response

As we have seen it is not only animal liberationists who have answered our question with a firm yes.[6] A range of bioethicists concerned with what it is which marks out an individual for moral consideration have gone this way. John Harris's account of personhood considered in the previous chapter provides a robust affirmative answer to our question by providing reasons in some circumstances for valuing animal lives above human lives.

Thus a chimpanzee might be more worthy of our concern than a severely mentally handicapped human being. To adapt a well-known remark, on Harris's account all animals are equal (including human animals) but some are more equal than others (including chimpanzees).

Harris is not alone in adopting this kind of view. Many who have opposed the use of animals in research agree with him. So how much substance is there to the argument that our behaviour towards animals, as well as humans, should be characterised by a respect for their capacity for suffering and enjoyment? We need to keep in mind that the consequence of such an account is that because some animals have greater capacities for either or each of these than some human beings we should be more concerned for their welfare than for that of the human beings in question.

There are numerous problems associated with this view. Not least among them is the counter-intuitive conclusion which, we have noted, follows from it. Such a conclusion might be construed as constituting a *reductio ad absurdam* of the position from which it is derived rather than a compelling case for changing our moral attitudes towards human beings and animals.

It has been argued that to confuse the question of the differences between animals and humans (such as their relative capacities in different circumstances) with the question of the difference between human beings and animals, a pervading difference in attitudes and conceptualisation arising out of the fabric of human life and institutions, affords the position more plausibility than it deserves.[7] Diamond's argument is that the moral difference between humans and animals is not based on our response to their various capacities but rather on our perceptions of what they are, our attitudes towards them. It is this difference which explains why we do not eat human beings and why we conduct funerals at their death, not their capacities to feel distress or pain, or to value their own lives.

Animals can engage in aspects of our lives which call for sophisticated ethical responses, but never in such a way as to erase this difference. But that is because of our relationship with them and not because of innate capacities which they have.

Contrast the example of an anencephalic child, who has no potential to master any skills or enjoy so doing, with dolphins who seem to delight in performing sophisticated tricks and dolphins who are trained to carry out underwater reconnaissance. The question all observers have to answer is which of them makes the greatest ethical demands in terms of what we do with them or for them.

Humans, animals and capacities

Rejection of the equality of humans and animals in the robust sense outlined above does not entail that we should not take seriously the various qualities that living individuals, both human and non-human, have. Those qualities will have much bearing on what we consider to be ethically permissible in the treatment of those individuals. In the sense that many of these qualities will be commonly found in people and animals they will, equally, call for our attention when we make decisions about what it is permissible to do to them. However, despite the fact that they call for equal attention it does not follow that they be given equal weight. For example, should a choice have to be made between the provision of relief for serious pain to a person and a dog then the interests of the dog would clearly take second place. On the other hand the commitment of a fox to a painful and terrifying end in the pursuit of the pleasure of the members of the local foxhunt would, at least, raise the question of its moral propriety. In other words, the infliction of unnecessary suffering calls for moral justification whether it is experienced by a man or an animal, whereas the preference to relieve the suffering of a man before that of an animal does not call for a moral justification.

However, there are various kinds of suffering and pleasure which may or may not be shared between one animal and another and between people and animals. These will carry different weights in considerations of what it is proper or not to do to them. In some cases there may be some doubt as to where to draw the line with respect to the capacities of some animals to experience suffering or pleasure of certain kinds. At the more fundamental level we are able to ascribe certain psychological descriptions to animals because of certain similarities between them and us. What we are prepared to say will vary from animal to animal:

> It is easy enough to extend the concepts of 'sensuous' experience to creatures fairly like human beings, such as cats, dogs, and horses; when we try to extend them to creatures extremely unlike human beings in their style of life, we feel, if we are wise, great uncertainty – not just uncertainty as to the facts, or as to the possibility of finding them out, but uncertainty as to the *meaning* of saying: 'I now know how to tell when an earthworm is angry.'[8]

These lines are drawn with reference to the degree to which animals are able to share in the lives of people. It is here that we run up against the possibility of the sentimentalist criticism. A common reaction to protests against the use of animals in research is that to object to such practice is to sentimentalise the human–animals relation. How much purchase is there in such allegations?

How human beings relate to animals is in part facilitated by the manner in which animals enter into the lives of people. This is not universally the same in either time or place. People of different cultures at different times have developed a variety of interactions with animals which have resulted in a multitude of perceptions about their significance. These range from the worship of animals to, as we have noted, their instrumental use for either food or labour.

The possession of a face is particularly important in this regard, which is why some vegetarians refuse to eat anything with a face. This has little to do with sentimentalising animals. Just try to doubt that a snarling dog baring its teeth is not angry!

However, animals can enter into the lives of people at a more profound ethical level than this. It is here that moral obligation to animals takes on a deeper meaning than simply not causing suffering or distress. Prince

Llewellyn is said never to have smiled after thrusting a spear into the heart of his hound Gelert. He had mistaken the blood upon its jowls for the blood of his infant son, whom the Prince had left in the dog's protection, only to discover subsequently the dead form of a wolf lying beside the unharmed child. Gelert is a byword for faithfulness in Welsh culture and Llewellyn suffered guilt for his lack of trust of the dog. We could enumerate many examples of sophisticated relationships of this sort between man and animals. The pit ponies who laboured in the Welsh coalmines easing the labour of the miners were rewarded with summer holidays in the fresh air and peaceful retirements in the countryside. Why should this be regarded as sentimentality rather than the repayment of a debt?

Animals in the research setting

So how should we relate to animals in the research setting? From what has been said already it would be a mark of moral insensitivity to regard animals in research settings merely as sophisticated tools, as has often been the case.[9]

The instrumental use of animals in research can easily blind us to ethical dimensions of our relationships with them. This is consonant with other instrumental uses of animals as Darwin's observation noted earlier in this chapter. But what did he mean by his ironic use of the word 'equal'? Clearly there are some aspects of our relationship in which we can never be equal. We can, for example, have moral perceptions of them but they cannot have such perceptions of us, nor can they enter into a wide range of the spectrum of emotions which we can experience, due to the fact that they are not language users and do not participate in the host of social institutions which identify our feelings and us. However, to jump from this fact to the conclusion that they are not morally considerable and deserving of our moral respect is to jump too far, even though it might be a convenient move to make. Where we draw the line will itself be a matter of moral dispute. The polarised views which would either demonise animal researchers or ridicule protesters as sentimentalists are each wide of the mark. But where in between can we find ground that respects both the research enterprise and animals?

Darwin's use of the notion of slavery offers us a clue to a partial solution of this problem. Slaves were people who had become the tools of others. Their own independent lives counted for nothing as their sole purpose was to fulfil the designs and wishes of those who had the right to own and employ them. That is not to say that all slave owners were sadistic and heartless exploiters of these lives. Far from it for we have good evidence to distinguish caring and beneficent owners from others. Whether out of concern to preserve the most effective workforce or out of higher motives many owners were willing to house, feed and protect their slaves. Nevertheless those slaves remained slaves with no possibility of leading lives that were their own. In retrospect we do not condone even the kindliest employment of slaves. However, within that tradition the chances of an imaginative relationship between slave and master, in which the independence of the life of the slave would be respected, were almost nil. The idea of respecting the independent life of a slave could not occur to an owner for whom moral obligation ended with the decent treatment of the slave as a slave. The context of the relationship constrained the possibility of a wider sense of concern which would have characterised the relationship between a slavemaster and an equal.

It is this constraint to which Darwin refers. We can see how the analogy fits by considering an example from animal research.[10] Sir Lauder Brunton, a celebrated pharmacologist, was keen to demonstrate the humane character of his research on animals. He cited the example of a dog on which he had made a gastric fistula. The dog showed no sign of pain and, moreover, whenever the dog was examined:

> . . . it showed great delight – just like a dog that has been sitting about the house, and wants to run out for a walk. When it saw that I was going to look into its stomach, it frisked about in the same way as if I was going to take it out for a walk.[11]

Diamond observes that there is another possible reaction to this scene, viz. 'what a miserable life for an animal' as opposed to 'oh good – no pain!'[12] Thinking outside the square of the laboratory setting Brunton would no doubt have deplored such restrictions in a dog's life which the mere absence of pain would not have mitigated.

Diamond observes that this is the reason the charge that animal experimentation makes one callous is levelled. It is a case of special pleading which might result in carelessness in calculating the moral cost of such experimentation. That is not to say that given an awareness of that cost, given a greater moral sensitivity on the part of the researcher, the research would not proceed. Some might not but some might, though with a sense of regret that such a price is demanded by the worthiness of the goal to be achieved.

If we need further stimulation to think of how easy it is to engage in this kind of compartmentalisation of mind, we have only to think back to the beginnings of serious ethical review of clinical research. The Nuremberg Code arose out of the Nuremberg trials in which Nazi doctors were indicted for crimes committed against humanity in the name of medical research. Their attitude to their research subjects was mirrored in the Nazi attitude to slave labour where, for political purposes, people were no longer seen as leading worthwhile individual lives. Some modicum of ethical regard was due them in this political square but its expression might strike us as an inversion of moral consciousness:

> We shall never be rough and heartless when it is not necessary, that is clear. We Germans, who are the only people in the world who have a

decent attitude towards animals, will also assume a decent attitude towards these human animals.[13]

As human beings in a given context can be seen in an ethically restricted frame, as human animals, so animals themselves, in the context of the laboratory, can be viewed in an ethically less imaginative light. They may become laboratory animals, animals to which a whole range of ethically significant attitudes is no longer thought appropriate. This constitutes a blunting of moral sensitivity which might be extended well beyond the laboratory. As Alexander Solzhenitsyn once remarked:

> Nowadays we do not think much of a man's love for an animal; we laugh at people who are attached to cats. But if we stop loving animals, aren't we bound to stop loving humans too?

Conclusion

Apart from the disputes over the moral status of the human embryo and foetus there has probably been no more publicly controversial matter in the area of medical practice and research than the moral status of animals. Each of these disputes has led to violent demonstrations, the former to threats to the lives of abortionists and attacks on abortion clinics and the latter to attacks on animal researchers and animal research establishments. The moral regard each of the groups of protesters accord to the entities of their concern approaches that which we pay to persons. This entitles them to claim rights for those entities, viz. claims to the right to life on the one hand and to animal rights on the other.

Medical science has relied heavily on the use of animals for experimentation to provide leads on the nature and treatment of human diseases. It still does. In this chapter we have identified the case against such practice and determined that there are ethical issues to be faced in the uncritical employment of sentient creatures for human purposes but that ethically responsible destructive research on animals cannot be ruled out *per se*. Nevertheless these subjects of research cannot be properly regarded as persons and thus cannot be regarded as patients whom medical researchers have standard medical responsibilities to protect.

Members of animal ethics committees have to draw some of the difficult lines we have referred to when asked to approve research trials. What kind of suffering can the test animals properly be considered to suffer? And how can it be measured? As they answer these questions the above case calls for a willingness on their part to think outside the square. Such thinking will often enlarge the estimate of the suffering involved. This will increase reticence to approve studies, and rightly so, without hindering good research. Such thinking will be exhibited in the weighing of the moral cost of the experimental treatment against its worthwhileness. Does the gain in knowledge aimed for in the proposal merit such a moral cost? In many cases the answer will be yes, but where the cost is seen to be higher than it might previously have appeared some experiments will be turned down or approved on the condition of significant amendments rather than receive uncritical approval.

Ethical review might then produce an increased sensitivity in researchers which will reinforce the three Rs approach to the research involving animals. This will in part be characterised by a continued search for alternative methods or the more widespread use of alternatives already adopted by sensitive researchers for achieving research aims. For example, *refinement* of the use of animals might be achieved more frequently by using animals which rank lower in the scale of capacities to suffer. *Reductions* of numbers of animals used might be additionally achieved by greater awareness of the moral cost and not simply the economic cost of their employment. *Replacement* of animals in research might be further inspired by the moral imperative to minimise suffering and provide a stimulus to devise *in vitro* methodologies using cells, tissues and whole organs where these are able to achieve objectives currently aimed for in whole animal research.

These measures to keep the suffering and destruction of animals in research to a minimum embody an animal welfare approach. This approach does not rule out the instrumental use of animals in medical research but it does emphasise the moral cost of using them. Those who adopt this approach answer the question examined in this chapter in the negative. This is to be contrasted with the animal rights approach which answers the question in the affirmative and campaigns for the employment of animals in medical research to be banned.

Notes

1 Joseph Wright of Derby, *An Experiment on a Bird in an Air Pump*, 1768, National Gallery, London.
2 W. Schupbach, 'A select iconography of animal experiment', in N.A. Rupke (ed.), *Vivisection in Historical Perspective*, London: Croom Helm, 1987, pp. 346–7.
3 C. Darwin, *Charles Darwin's notebooks, 1836–1844: Geology, Transmutation of Species, Metaphysical Enquiries*, P. Barrett, P.J. Gautrey, S. Herbert, D. Kohn and S. Smith (eds.), Ithaca, N.Y.: Cornell University Press, 1987.
4 T. Regan, *The Case for Animal Rights*. London: Routledge, 1984, pp. 381–2; P. Singer, *Animal Liberation*, 2nd edn, New York: Random House, 1990.
5 W.M.S. Russell and R.L. Burch, *The Principles of Humane Experimental Technique*, London: Methuen, 1959.
6 See the list referred to in Chapter 7, p. 128.
7 C. Diamond, *Wittgenstein, Philosophy and the Mind*, Boston: MIT Press, 1991, p. 354.
8 P. Geach, *Mental Acts: their Content and their Objects*, London: Routledge and Kegan Paul, 1957, pp. 113–14.

9 J.C. Eccles, 'Animal experimentation versus human experimentation', in *Defining the Laboratory Animal*, Washington, D.C.: National Academy of Sciences, 1971, pp. 285–93.

10 C. Diamond, *Wittgenstein, Philosophy and the Mind*. p. 354.

11 S. Paget, *For and Against Experiments on Animals: Evidence Before the Royal Commission on Vivisection*, London: H.K. Lewis, 1912, p. 90.

12 C. Diamond, *Wittgenstein, Philosophy and the Mind*, p. 354.

13 Himmler, Heinrich. Speech to SS-Gruppenführer at Posen, Poland, October 4th, 1943. U.S. National Archives document 242.256, reel 2 of 3.

Chapter 9

Patients and research

The chief advocate for removing animals from medical research laboratories considers that the inability, so far as we know it, of animals to consent to be so used for the benefit of humans is not sufficient to facilitate an ethical distinction between animals and humans as there are some human beings also who are incapable of voluntary participation in research. He refers to some human beings who are too young, too old, too enfeebled or too confused to give or withhold informed consent.[1] He is correct in this assertion. However, it does not follow that animals should therefore be excluded from research. We have questioned both that the status of personhood consists in the possession of a variety of capacities and, relatedly, that differences in capacities are what ethically mark out human beings from other animals. The lack of capacity to consent does not automatically bar human beings from being participants in medical research. However, there are greater protections provided for them than there are for animals in research. These protections are based upon the regard we have for autonomy in human life where decisions either to treat or to carry out research on persons incapable of consent call for an approximation to an informed consent.

In this chapter we shall consider the concept of capacity to consent and the external and internal constraints on this capacity in preparation for an examination of two areas of research involving human participants which threaten respect for patient autonomy.

Capacity to consent

Respect for the autonomy of persons to make decisions, while taking responsibility for those decisions, is closely related to the fundamental Art 1 of the Universal Declaration of Human Rights 1948, which holds that:

> All human beings are born free and equal in dignity and rights. They are endowed with reason and conscience and should act towards one another in a spirit of brotherhood.

That Declaration also underlies many of the succeeding rights to: liberty (Art 3); freedom from slavery (Art 4); freedom from torture and degrading punishment (Art 5); protection from arbitrary arrest (Art 9); freedom from arbitrary interference (Art 12); freedom of movement (Art 13); seek asylum (Art 14); marry voluntarily and found a family (Art 16); own property (Art 17); freedom of thought, opinion and expression (Arts 18 and 19); freedom of peaceful assembly (Art 20); take part in government (Art 21); work (Art 23); choice of education (Art 26); participation in the cultural life of a community (Art 27).

Autonomy is often defined as self-rule and refers to the right of persons to make authentic choices about what they shall do, what shall be done to them and, as far as is possible, what should happen to them. However, there are numerous sets of circumstances where the capacity to exercise autonomy is subject to limits without calling respect for autonomy into question.

External constraints on the exercise of autonomy

Limits to the capacity to exercise one's autonomy need to be carefully defined. Their causes might be either external or internal to the decision maker. For example, with respect to external limits the capacity can be constrained in only rare sets of circumstances each of which involves the protection of the autonomy of others. In some cases authorised personnel can arrest, question and imprison others for breaches of the law within carefully determined and proper limits. In other cases medical personnel can compulsorily detain mentally ill persons for protection and treatment if they constitute a danger to themselves and/or to the freedoms and safety of others. Similarly those who suffer from very serious infectious diseases may be compulsorily removed from their place of abode or work in order to protect the health of others. Such justified restrictions of the liberty of people to choose for themselves are very few and are highly constrained in order to maximise respect for autonomy.

One's ability to make decisions might be improperly constrained by external circumstances in medical practice. For example, some practitioners have extended the power of compulsory treatment unjustifiably, thus making medicine a form of social control to achieve political goals rather than health goals. The psychiatric diagnosis of sluggish schizophrenia was employed by Soviet psychiatrists to impose social control over political dissidents. The diagnosis was used to identify people with non-psychotic symptoms of schizophrenia, people who, it turned out, were deviant in their perceptions of the reality which was the imposed ideology of the day. They were forcibly removed to psychiatric institutions and subjected to compulsory treatments of radical kinds. The groups of psychiatrists involved were pressured to withdraw from the World Psychiatric Association until such improper employment of clinical interventions was removed.[2] Where the law allows medicine to restrict the capacity of people in this way the power is qualified by providing protections to those affected in the form of reviews and safeguards of various kinds.

Internal constraints on the exercise of autonomy

Incompetence is the term commonly used to describe internal constraints on the capacity to consent. It is standardly identified in people who, for reasons internal to themselves, do not have the ability to make authentic choices irrespective of their external circumstances. In this sense incompetence can be defined as lacking the freedom to make authentic decisions because of an inability to make such decisions even when given the opportunity. Various groups of people have been traditionally labelled in this way. They include people with learning difficulties, the mentally ill, children, confused elderly and unconscious people.

Criteria of incompetence

The criteria used to identify the groups of people described as incompetent have included the ability to understand the issues involved in the decisions at stake, the ability to evaluate these rationally, a reasonable outcome of the decision and evidence of a decision being made.[3] While these look like object-ive criteria, there are difficulties in their application. Inevitably the assessment of any judge of the competence of others is made from that judge's perspec-tive of what it is to understand, what is rational and what a reasonable outcome would look like. But there might be disagreement about each of these.

For example, the second criterion cannot discriminate definitively between patients who might be risk takers in life and clinicians who are cautious. What appears to be rational to the former might not appear rational to the latter. People might also disagree about what constitutes a reasonable outcome to a decision. Here there is a danger that informed consent procedures, set up to ensure respect for autonomous decision making, are rendered meaningless if the patient does not choose the outcome preferred by the clinician. We considered some examples of this phenomenon in Chapter 3 in the cases involving the amputation of diseased and healthy limbs. Where this phenom-enon occurs the consent process is compromised. In the first of those cases, if C had accepted the recommended treatment he would have been regarded as competent to consent but his refusal established his incompetence in the eyes of the attending clinician and, but for the court's intervention, he would have received the treatment nonetheless.

Assessing the degree of understanding of data offered to a patient is not an exact science either. Some people demand a more detailed grasp of a wider range of facts than others in accepting that a decision maker understands a situation. To set the standard too high threatens to undermine the freedoms of inexpert patients when judged by their medically expert clinicians.

The general safeguard of the freedoms of patients in these situations is that no judgement of competence should be called for unless there is evidence to undermine the assumption that people are normally competent to decide for themselves. In other words, proof of incompetence is required, not proof of competence. Foolish decisions can be voluntarily made by the most competent people and the freedom to so act should not be restricted by imposing over-strenuous standards of competence.[4]

Let us now consider two areas of patient participation in research where respect for the autonomy of patients is under threat. The first concerns patients consenting to research by default, and thus not being enabled to consent at all to the research in which they are involved. In some innovative treatments considerations external to the patient, namely the provision of inadequate or misleading information about the offered surgical procedure, are responsible for the absence of a proper consent. The second area involves patient research participants who are not capable of providing a consent for reasons internal to themselves, i.e. various groups of patients who are considered to be incompetent.

Innovative treatments

Ethical review of research on human participants is subject to international and national guidelines.[5] The history of ethical review in New Zealand is such that the remit of ethical review committees is wider than elsewhere. New Zealand experienced its own 'Tuskegee study', the *cancer in situ* (CIS) study, which resulted in a scandal not unlike that which surrounded the study of the natural history of syphilis in the group of African Americans in Alabama. The similarities are considerable, such as the scale and protracted period of the studies and the change in the relevant bodies of knowledge during the course of the studies.

In the Alabama study some three hundred patients were observed and offered no clinical intervention for forty years, despite the fact that a treatment of syphilis had been discovered less than half way through that period. The participants in the study were denied information about possible therapies and were not even informed that they were involved in a study at all. In the New Zealand case, a study which stretched over thirty years, a large number of women who had been identified with pre-malignant cell changes in the cervix were observed, some of them over a period of twenty-five years, with no clinical intervention. The aim of the study was to demonstrate that such cell changes were not a precursor of cancer.[6] Even when the study began there were well canvassed opinions that such cell changes were precursors of the disease but within a very short time this became received knowledge in the developed world. Nevertheless the New Zealand women were not told of this and neither were they offered any therapeutic intervention. They regularly visited their hospital for checks but had no idea that they were participants in a study. The consequences were disastrous for many of these women who developed invasive cancer.

As surely as revelations of the Tuskegee study caused political waves – leading to the National Research Act Public Law 93–348, July 12, 1974, and a call for Institutional Review Boards to be set up for all publicly funded research in the United States – so exposure of the CIS study produced a national scandal in New Zealand. A Ministerial Committee of Enquiry chaired by a family court judge, Silvia Cartwright, was set up and this attracted huge public interest. One difference between the two studies was significant. It was a matter of dispute whether the New Zealand women were denied treatment or were simply involved in a conservative treatment regime.[7] Thus when the Enquiry's report called for independent ethical review committees to be set up in New Zealand its brief was to cover not only research on human subjects but also innovative clinical practice.[8]

Almost twenty years have passed since that recommendation was made and a system of ethical review has been established. The Ethics Committees which have been set up constitute in part a reaction to the inadequacy of the Hospital Ethics Committee at the National Womens' Hospital where the cancer *in situ* study occurred. Independence from the providers of care and researchers is now seen to be the *sine qua non* of ethical review of research and practice. Consequently the committees have responsibility both for the review of some aspects of clinical practice, viz. innovative treatments plus provision of advice on other cases and various aspects of service delivery excluding allocation of resources, and for review of research protocols. As such they play part of the role which Hospital Ethics Committees play in some countries plus the role of standard Research Ethics Committees.

There is a National Standard with which these committees are expected to comply. Until relatively recently little attention was paid to the unique responsibility of these committees to review innovative practice. The temptation to evade independent scrutiny of research by labelling it innovative treatment is not open to clinicians in New Zealand. To succumb to such a temptation blinds the patients to what is being done with them. They consent to being treated *simpliciter* whereas they might have been hesitant to consent to precisely the same procedures if they knew that they were experimental. The use of the description 'therapeutic research' is not a satisfactory cover for this practice. Given that in a research activity there is genuine doubt about whether the intervention is beneficial, part of the research question to be answered, the practitioner cannot promise to treat the patient therapeutically by means of the intervention. It might turn out to be therapeutic but it might turn out to be useless, or worse to be harmful. To use the label therapeutic is therefore unjustified and misleading.

But the provision of independent protections in the form of ethical review for these activities runs into conceptual and practical difficulties. Consider an example which presented these challenges and which led to extended reflection by ethics committees on the issue. The example is the use of the CG Clip laminoplasty technique.

Discovery of innovative treatments

In countries such as the United Kingdom, where research on human participants but not clinical practice is governed by ethical review guidelines, ethics committees have sometimes been concerned that some research has not come to their attention because it has been passed off as clinical practice. Such practice can be regarded as research by stealth.[9] By and large, it comes to the attention of ethics committees only when something goes wrong or when retrospective reports of the clinical practice appear in learned journals. This kind of behaviour could be curbed partially if reputable journals, as a condition of publication, applied the same requirements for ethical review of innovative practice as for research trials. However, journal editors and a system of independent ethical review face a common problem, viz. that of discovery.

In an ideal world practitioners would embrace the values embodied in ethical review, primarily to protect their patients but secondarily to protect themselves and their employers, and seek clearance from ethics committees to introduce new techniques, devices and drugs into practice. There are some regulatory constraints already imposed upon such innovation. For example, the licensing procedures for drugs depend on proper testing, which has to be subject to review by accredited ethics committees. Similarly such licences as are issued for certain indications and applications to new areas of practice should be subject to new tests. Latterly the same holds true for the use of new devices in the United Kingdom but this does not yet occur in most other jurisdictions. Insofar as these constraints apply then innovative practice is subject to ethical review. But this leaves large areas of practice untouched, especially in surgery and other disciplines such as physiotherapy. The example we are about to discuss is taken from surgery and involves the insertion of a novel device into the cervical spine of patients. Such procedures have been traditionally introduced without any reference to ethics committees and without adequate testing.[10] In the New Zealand case[11] the surgeon in question took the most unusual step of referring the proposed treatment to his Ethics Committee. This marked the beginning of a steep learning curve for the committee whose subsequent experience has done much to inform the plans for dealing with such applications in the future.

Definition of innovative treatments

Failure to report anticipated innovation to ethics committees is not always perverse or neglectful. There is a genuine problem of identification of innovative practice. For example, in the operating theatre the surgeon has to be prepared to meet unexpected events. In so doing she might attempt to address an emergency by means of a procedure which has neither been premeditated nor previously employed, so far as she knows. It would be wrong clearly to curtail such clinical autonomy in the name of ethical review as patients' lives would be put at risk. The practice is innovative but, at this stage, it could not be subjected to ethical review. However, if we imagine that the patient survives, then the improvisation might take on an appeal as a possible effective intervention which could well be refined and used on a more general basis. Where such an intervention is planned or even provisionally planned then it is possible to refer the matter for ethical review. It is important that this be done for no judgement about either the safety or the efficacy of the procedure can be secured by the one case.

In other settings the implementation of an innovative treatment might creep up on a surgeon by degrees. Each minor modification to a procedure might in itself be so small that it could not be easily tested nor even identified as a new procedure as such. However, given a number of successive modifications the surgeon might end up with what is clearly a different procedure from that which was originally employed. At which point does the evolution call for ethical review?[12] There is no simple rule of thumb which might be promulgated to answer this question but it is clear that it would be wise for the practitioner to consult with the chair of the relevant ethics committee to reach a decision on the matter rather than act as judge and jury for a procedure to which he or she is probably emotionally attached. The possible lack of objectivity on the part of the innovator is a matter with which we shall deal later.

Despite the fact that there will be cases where adjudication on the innovative status of a procedure will be difficult, it remains true that there are many cases where there is no doubt at all about this. Clearly the placement of a novel clinical device into the body of a patient will constitute such a case. Such a procedure must be premeditated given that the device has been designed for such use. This was true of the case presented to the Ethics Committee in question. The clinical problem addressed in this innovation was the narrowing of the canal in the cervical spine which results in pressure on the spinal cord with consequential debilitating pain in shoulders and arms, stiffness, numbness and headaches. Open-door laminoplasty has promised a solution to this problem by opening up the lamina to relieve pressure. Once opened the increased space has been secured by bone grafting until now. The CG clip is a substitute for this latter procedure which promises to cut down on theatre and anaesthetic time, pain and problems with the graft site and possible slippage which would narrow the spinal canal again. There was therefore no doubt that use of the CG clip constituted an innovative procedure.

Justifying treatments

Since the beginning of formalised ethical review it has been clear that the first concern which an ethics committee has when asked to approve a clinical research project or an innovative treatment regime is that the proposed procedures are neither aimless nor unnecessary, and that they are feasible.[13] In the development of new drugs, committees have reference to results of a range of animal studies to help answer these questions in addition to a theorethical justification before Phase One studies on human participants are allowed to proceed. In surgical cases it is rarely possible for such trials to be designed. Committees therefore will have to rely on the theoretical justification offered by the practitioner. In the case in point the above description shows both the reasonableness of the general nature of the intervention and the particular advantages promised by the modification of that intervention employing the clinical device. It also outlines specific gains which would be made in the interest of the patients and health care providers concerned. The nature of the CG Clip device was also explained to the committee and the rationale of its design. Taken together these considerations satisfied the committee that such a treatment regime should be tried.

Here a lesson was learned by the committee in its novel task of reviewing an innovative treatment. It was that the design of the treatment to be tested should be such as to identify precise endpoints, as would a good research design. This demands that very careful baseline measurements be recorded in order for assessments of efficacy to be made. It was at this point that the committee, learning *per ambulandam* to assess innovative treatments, was less stringent in its requirements than it might have been. Thus, many patients later, the data presented were inadequate to assess the efficacy of the innovation. This resulted in a prolongation of the assessment of the treatment which might have resulted in patients being denied what is a very good therapy for longer than was necessary.

Safety of participants

The second, long established, priority of the ethics committee, once satisfied that an innovative procedure should be tried, is the safety of the patients.[14] Phase One drug studies are primarily designed for this purpose where minimal risk is the order of the day. It is very difficult to replicate such procedures in the case of many innovative therapies, such as the case in point. Whether a particular device is safe *in situ* is not something which can be tried on healthy volunteers in the same controlled fashion. Nevertheless there are some parallels with Phase One research which should be taken seriously in the process of review.

While much can be learned about the stability and toxicity of a new drug before first-time-into-human studies, Phase One studies are needed to secure

such information with respect to human recipients. Similar safety information can be collected regarding the safety of devices designed for use in
humans before they are tried in the clinical context. For example, it is known
that the human body will tolerate the insertion of medical devices properly
designed and manufactured. Materials such as nylon, titanium and stainless
steel are known to be safe in this regard and the committee was assured
properly from the start that these materials would be used.

However, there is more to a device than the materials out of which it is
made which needs to be assessed before it is placed in patients. The structure
of the device might render it unsafe. This was the case with the Halifax clamp,
referred to earlier, which produced fatal failures in a number of patients.[15] On
enquiry it was discovered that the clamp had never been subjected to mechanical testing before insertion into the cervical spines of patients. It was withdrawn until such time as modifications had been designed so that the device
was able to withstand the kinds of stresses to which it would be subjected in
the bodies of recipients. Adequate mechanical testing was required before the
device was reintroduced to practice.

With respect to these possibilities the Ethics Committee was to learn
another lesson about the review of innovative treatments. No account of
mechanical testing of the CG Clip was requested of the surgeon and designer.
This was due not only to the novelty of the review which the committee was
undertaking but also to the unfortunate fact that two patients had already
undergone the procedure before the committee was approached and the
prototype stainless steel clips had apparently remained intact in these cases.
Much later, when many more patients had been treated, the Committee
became concerned about the safety issue, having become aware of the Halifax
clamp case. Mechanical testing was immediately called for and sophisticated
tests were designed for the remodelled clip, which demonstrated vastly
superior qualities of endurance. Whereas the original clip failed after 750,000
movements of various kinds, the new clip remained intact after 5 million
such movements. The committee demanded to be satisfied about this aspect
of safety before further procedures were allowed.

Another safety issue arose during the period of further implementation of
the procedure. The Committee expected an annual report on the progress of
the implementation of the treatment as it did with research protocols which it
approved. Application was made to the Committee to conduct further examinations of the patients to prepare an audit report. This was approved but the
Committee was surprised at the number of patients involved – some sixty-five
– and suggested that by now it would have been better to have carried out a
randomised control trial to test the procedure. Here a further lesson had been
learned by the committee with respect to how best to review innovative procedures in clinical treatment. The open-ended permission to proceed with an
anticipated report after twelve months was not a tight enough control to
protect patient safety. Thus the committee concluded that it would have been

better to call for a safety report after a specific number of patients (much smaller than sixty-five) had undergone the procedure. (We shall see later that the same consideration applies to the establishment of the efficacy of a procedure.) This would have been somewhat akin to a Phase One study though it would have involved, necessarily, patients rather than healthy volunteers. The committee now insisted that the results of the sixty-five patients be assessed by an independent expert before further procedures were carried out.

That assessment revealed that a higher than projected number of no less than thirty-two cases of fracture of the device had occurred. None of these device fractures was harmful as it turned out but it would clearly be better to avoid any risk of damage caused by failure of the device in such a sensitive position in the spine. This confirmed the importance of the adequate mechanical testing requirement which had already been set by the committee.

Efficacy of treatments

The independent assessor was asked to address the issue of efficacy as well as that of safety in his review of the results of the sixty-five patients treated. The major concern of the Committee at this point was the safety of the procedure as the Committee had requested the surgeon, on the basis of his previous experience of the procedure, to design a prospective randomised control trial in which the innovative technique would be compared with one or more traditional procedures, given an all clear on the safety question.

The results of the independent review with respect to the safety of the procedure were reassuring and, together with the improved design of the CG Clip, satisfied the Committee's conditions for approving a properly designed Randomised Controlled Trial (RCT). It was at this point that the lesson of precise and properly recorded baseline measures arose for the data proved to be inadequate to facilitate a judgement on the effectiveness of the procedure, despite the surgeon's conviction that his results were superior to those produced by the bone grafting technology. The surgeon's conviction of the efficacy of the procedure gives rise to a number of matters which relate both to the technical problems of designing prospective studies for surgical innovations and to the responsibilities of the ethics committee towards prospective patients.

These matters all revolve around the issue of clinical equipoise. The delays in implementation of further application of the innovative technique and the reported requests from patients to undergo the procedure brought the matter into bold relief. First there was the question of whether the practitioner should be permitted to continue to offer the therapy to patients outside the context of a properly planned RCT. The surgeon's view was that since he was no longer himself in a state of clinical equipoise, having the deep conviction that his innovation was a definite improvement on bone grafting procedures, he was ethically obliged to offer the treatment to patients specifically requesting it. Furthermore he was in difficulty in conducting an RCT for the same reason.[16] He indicated a further argument against the latter proposal, viz. that since the traditional procedure was not itself validated in the manner called for by RCT methodology the proposal was flawed.

Clinical equipoise has been defined as a situation where a practitioner is in a state of genuine uncertainty about the benefits or harms that may result from each of two or more regimens.[17] Furthermore where a practitioner is no longer in such a position he is obliged to proceed with the better therapy. If a clinician knows or has good reason to believe that a new therapy (A) is better than another (B), he cannot participate in a trial of therapy A v therapy B. Ethically, the clinician is obliged to give therapy A to each new patient with a need for one of the therapies.[18]

On this basis it would seem that the surgeon had a point. However, emphasis must be laid on the expressions 'genuine uncertainty' and 'good reason to believe'. Such uncertainty is not dispelled by the holding of a deep conviction alone, and deep conviction does not constitute good reason in and of itself. It is well known that practitioner bias can influence assessments of outcomes, safety and efficacy, hence the call for RCTs. We might be helped to understand this by reference to the null hypothesis which is tested in an RCT. A necessary condition of the null hypothesis is that there is no scientifically validated reason to predict that Therapy A will be superior to Therapy B.[19] Due to this consideration the foregoing definition of clinical equipoise has been challenged and the proposal is that it be amended so that the genuine uncertainty involved is general uncertainty within the expert medical community about the treatment and not simply on the part of individual investigators.[20]

Given such a sensible account of clinical equipoise, the case of the CG Clip was clear. The external assessment failed to support the surgeon's conviction so that clinical equipoise still existed and the Ethics Committee was correct in refusing further elective treatments and in calling for the RCT in line with what has been called the 'uncertainty principle'.

> . . . doctors should always use treatments and management strategies if they are certain that they are effective. Similarly, no doctor should use a treatment which he or she is certain is ineffective. However, if the doctor, in consultation with a patient, is uncertain of the best treatment strategy, given more than one option, the best resolution of this uncertainty is randomization in a well-designed RCT.[21]

The CG Clip case does, however, illustrate the danger of conducting too large a number of pilot cases as this might impugn the null hypothesis sufficiently, on occasion, to threaten the propriety of an RCT.[22] To prejudice the execution of RCTs in this way would be to proliferate untried treatment regimes on the basis of their inventors' enthusiasms and be counter to the current informed practice of evidence-based medicine. Further, such proliferation is not justified by the fact that the traditional therapies, which might serve as the comparators in the RCTs, have not themselves been subjected to such scrutiny.

There was one final matter which occupied the attention of the Ethics Committee. The Committee wished to encourage the testing of what appeared to be a promising innovation. While it wished that patients be protected in this way, it was concerned also that the best possible case could be made for the innovation. It is well attested that growing expertise in the application of a technique produces better results.[23] As the inventor of the procedure was the practitioner with the greatest experience of applying it then the fairest trial would involve him as the lead practitioner. In order to deal with the question of bias as well as possible the Committee therefore required that both pre-operative and post-operative assessments of the participants be independently conducted.

Conclusion of the case

The collaboration between the surgeon and the ethics committee in the case of the CG Clip innovation has ensured greater protection of patients and improvements in the quality of the innovation. Given that the line between innovative practice and research is tenuous, patients would be better protected if the New Zealand remit of ethics committees was adopted widely. The experience of this difficult area of review has suggested the following rules of procedure in such review:

- request theoretical justifications for the procedure together with any relevant safety information to hand before any patients undergo the procedure;
- ensure that precise baselines and outcome measures are established before any procedures are executed;
- approve very small numbers of pilot studies with proper patient consent to assess basic safety questions;
- approve a slightly larger programme with restricted numbers of patients to assess safety and to begin to assess efficacy – each matter to be independently assessed;
- approve a randomised controlled trial.

Research involving incompetent patients

Patients in research might be thought to be vulnerable when they are included in research trials and projects because they are often dependent on the researchers for their therapy. Among these patients are those who cannot be properly informed of the nature of the aims, procedures, risks, and so on embodied in research because of internal constraints such as lack of maturity, confusion and learning difficulties. There are important differences between these constraints which have a bearing on how we might endeavour to preserve a respect for patient autonomy while complying with the imperative of research. Let us consider a number of them in order to illustrate this point.

Neonates

Neonates cannot think like adults – indeed they cannot think at all. It is therefore impossible for them to be able to make decisions, to understand information, to process information rationally or to desire reasonable outcomes. In other words they can satisfy none of the standard criteria of competence. Yet decisions have to be made about them. The best candidates for this role are their parents, on the assumption that above all people they will have the best interests of their child at heart. Sadly, in some cases parents do not make decisions in the best interests of their children. This is problematic in health care settings, especially when the results of the decisions could be very damaging to the health of the child. In most societies provision is made to protect children whose parents are not capable of, or not willing to provide the necessaries of life for their offspring. In those cases it is possible for the state to step in and remove the decision-making role from them. This is done by making the child a ward of the court and placing that role in responsible hands. This step should be one of last resort as it usually has serious negative repercussions in the relationship between the health professional and the parents. Such an outcome bodes ill for the future welfare of the child, who is less likely in future to be presented for health care surveillance and care at appropriate times.

There are health issues relating to neonates which call for research. If we apply the letter of the law as contained in international instruments like the Nuremberg Code we shall have to abandon this group of patients to their fate in respect of these conditions as their consent is impossible to obtain. This applies to all the other groups who are regarded as incompetent. The temptation to resort to proxy consent from the parents is unsatisfactory as their authority to consent ends when the best interests of the neonate are no longer at stake. We noted earlier that researchers cannot promise that their research on any given participant is in the interests of the participant. There are procedures which we can adopt which endeavour to approximate to obtaining the patient's consent. They apply to both neonates and incompetent children.

One crucial safeguard required to minimise loss of respect for autonomy in this connection is the general rule which is applied to all groups of patients deemed to be incompetent, viz. where the research into their various conditions can be carried out by employing competent participants then incompetent participants should not be used. This restriction avoids the problem of obtaining consent from incompetent participants. But what of the many situations where there is no alternative but to use participants who are not capable of deciding for themselves whether to be involved in research?

Many health problems associated with perinatal patients cannot be researched on adults. How then can we preserve respect for autonomy when entering such patients into research?

The approach is best illustrated by using a parallel example, viz. where the question arose about the propriety of carrying out a clinical procedure on a healthy infant for the benefit of his sibling rather than for himself. John was a small baby diagnosed with myeloid leukaemia. He was in a parlous state of health and the only possibility of rescue lay in a bone marrow transplant. But where could a matching donor be found in time? He was not an identical twin but his next best chance was to identify siblings who would be likely to provide the most suitable candidate tissue. He had six siblings whose ages ranged from 17 years to 2½ years. The first five were tested and though some of them would have provided good matches for others of them, none of them provided a good match for John. Finally his youngest brother, a 2½-year-old, was tested and found to be as near an ideal match as could be hoped for. The parents were desperate to see their baby's life saved and would have given immediate consent. But they had a conflict of interest. While it was evidently in the interests of the recipient child for them to consent to the procedure, it apparently could not be said to be in the interests of the donor child. The clinicians therefore did not simply accede to their wishes but reflected on the case together with a class of medical students. It was concluded that despite the facts of the inexplicable, unpleasant and painful few days which the donor would experience in donating tissue the time would come when a mature view of it would likely be formed. The overwhelming chances were that he would be grateful to hear when old enough that he had been the means of saving his brother's life – or at least that he had been the means of giving a brother he was never to know the best possible chance of life.

The consent was therefore called a *hypothetical consent*, that is, a consent which would likely be in accord with the feelings of the donor when mature. Such an outcome would, of course, be less likely if undue risks were taken with the donor's life such as the explantation of a whole organ. Given a carefully minimised level of risk, a child might also be grateful to learn that the use of his data, or his participation in a trial, facilitated the discovery of a new treatment or increased understanding of a dreadful disease. Insofar as this is so, then it might be said to approximate to an informed consent, albeit one which is anticipated, and thus constitute a show of respect for his surrogate autonomy.

Children

Research activities involving children are carried out to learn more about the nature of paediatric development, disease and potential treatments. With young children we face precisely the same problems in obtaining consent as with neonates. They can be tackled in the same way. But there is an extra set of problems researchers will face with many children in preserving respect for autonomy for which the foregoing solution is unacceptable.

It might appear that all children, similarly, by their very nature, are incompetent because they cannot think like adults. While this is certainly true of very young children, as children develop they show marked differences from each other. Fixing a chronological age such as 16 years to mark the attainment of competence is unsafe. The United Nations Convention on the Rights of the Child (UNROC) 1989 asserts that children have the right to say what they think should happen when adults make decisions that affect them and to have their opinions taken into account (Art 12); have the right to get and share information (Art 13); have the right to think and believe what they want and practise their religion as long as they do not stop other people enjoying their rights (Art 14); and have the right to privacy (Art 16). All these assume growing levels of competence which have to be taken seriously.

But when are they capable of making their own decisions? The idea that they will attain a magical common age when this occurs was tested in the courts in the United Kingdom in the *Gillick* case.[24] In that case Mrs Gillick, a mother of teenage daughters, objected to the proposal to make contraceptive advice available to young women without the knowledge of their parents. She challenged the proposal in court and won. However, the matter went to appeal and the decision of the lower court was overturned. In the celebrated judgment made by the Appeal Court the point about the different rates of maturity attained by young people at given ages was considered. The recommendation was that an arbitrary chronological age should be replaced by a test of maturity of the child to understand the nature of the decision to be made and the consequences likely to follow from the selection of the available options. Such a standard has been widely adopted in other countries since the judgment was made. This places an additional burden on the health professional involved in seeking to offer a clinical intervention or advice. However, this is seen as essential in order to safeguard the rights of the child mentioned above.

Clearly some decisions are easier to make than others insofar as they are more readily understood and the consequences of a poor choice are less onerous or dangerous. One might properly apply some higher test of competence for decisions of greater moment. But here it is important to be cautious. This could be a ploy adopted to undermine the rights of mature children to make their own decisions by setting the standards of maturity unacceptably high. Adults too are often competent to make some kinds of decisions but not others and we might devise more stringent tests for the weighty decisions in their case. But the standards should be no higher in the case of children than it is in the case of such adults if we are to have proper regard for their autonomy.

Confused elderly patients

There are growing numbers of patients who once enjoyed the capacity to make decisions of all sorts in their lives but who, sadly, are no longer capable of doing so. Various forms of neurological deterioration including Alzheimer's disease rob people of such powers. Such conditions call for research which no other group of patients can facilitate. How can we respect their compromised autonomy in making treatment decisions or other decisions which involve medical research?

It would be unethical to take these patients any less seriously than fully competent patients. In approaching decisions concerning them we have much more to go on than we do in the case of neonates. These are people who have lived a full life, whose preferences, values and wishes are probably remembered by some if not many who knew them when well. Their offices should be sought when we reflect on what do to for the patient. They should not be asked to provide proxy consents but rather to help build a picture of the life of our patient in which we can locate the decision which we have to make. Insofar as we are capable of doing this then we might be said to be building a *substituted judgement* about what the patient would consent to.[25]

The procedure is well illustrated by the events surrounding the approval of the use of a given patient's case for inclusion in a medical undergraduate curriculum. Susan was in her early fifties. Until just two years previously she had been a very active professional member of the community. She had been a keen amateur opera singer, a senior science schoolmistress and a wonderful wife of a devoted husband. Then suddenly all began to change. Her memory began to fail and she began to repeat herself having forgotten that she had asked the same question but a few minutes before. Within months, conversation became impossible, people were not recognised, ordinary activities were beyond her. She needed constant care for all her needs. Within six months of the onset of her illness she recognised nobody. Hospitalised, she seemed not even to respond to physical stimuli and her joints were rigid. She was painstakingly fed twice a day by her loved ones.

At this stage the local medical school was developing a new curriculum and was seeking good cases. In neurology an Alzheimer's case was needed. Susan was identified as the ideal candidate. The family had wonderful recent home movies of her in full health and engaging in her favourite activities. What a graphic portrayal of the ravages of the disease would be provided by the juxtaposition of those images with a video recording of her daily care as currently provided. But how could such a video be made without her consent? How could her autonomy and dignity be respected were she to be involuntarily placed on permanent video record to be gazed upon by successive classes of young students?

The case against the proposal seemed overwhelming until her husband came forward to offer the following account of Susan's life. She was an accomplished and enthusiastic teacher who was especially committed to medical education. She had been a tireless worker in the community, always putting others before herself. Now there was nothing she could do for learners or for society. Or was there? Yes, there was one last thing. She could be the means of helping young doctors understand something of the human tragedy and the clinical signs of Alzheimer's disease. 'If she was given just one minute of lucidity and asked whether she would consent to the film', he said, 'she would say "Yes, Yes, Yes, please make the video recording. It is the last useful thing that I can do for humanity".' The curriculum committee was moved and convinced. The tape was made and has never failed to deeply impress the students. The circumstances of its making are shared with the class to demonstrate that the school teaches informed consent by both precept and example. The tape was shown at her funeral as a tribute. Here was no proxy consent from the husband but a substituted judgement enabling Susan to speak for herself – surely a mark of respect for her autonomy.

Patients with learning difficulties

It is important not to confuse intellectual impairment with mental illness. This group of people represent a wide range of intellectual ability and no simple standard of competence can be assumed among them. In each case an assessment according to the criteria outlined above is called for in combination with an awareness of the nature of the decision to be made. Only in extremely serious cases will a person with this problem be unable to make a decision about anything. We do not have the benefit of identifying a life previous to the onset of this developmental condition out of which we shall be able to collect sufficient information to build substituted judgements. Neither do we have the prospect of a growing intellectual maturity which we can anticipate in making a hypothetical judgement about what will be regarded by the person as an acceptable decision. Thus in those cases where the impairment is either so great that the treatment decision is too onerous or is too complex to be grasped by the person we have to make a best interests judgement on their behalf. But what about their possible participation in research? We must of course avoid any research procedure which involves risks of adverse events in the patient's life. But the inclusion of such people in research into their condition marks a sign of respect for the group as a whole. They are worthy of concern and attention with respect to their burden of suffering and they are worthy of protection from harm at one and the same time. Though the research cannot be said to be for the benefit of the impaired participant it can be said to be in the interests of all those he represents in the character of his health need and given the light burden of participation the comparative possible relief from suffering offered to his peers is immense.

Mentally ill patients

As with intellectual impairment so with mental illness, we cannot assume that all persons in the group are equally competent or otherwise. On the one extreme people in a psychotic state cannot, by definition, make authentic choices. On the other hand when not in a florid state a person with schizophrenia might be quite clear about how he feels about matters of life and how he would wish to address them. It is the same person with whom we are dealing when he is ill and we must endeavour to carry our memory of him, when well, into our decision-making procedures on his behalf. The same is true of manic depression. When in a manic phase a patient will not always look kindly on apparent interference in his commissioning of various actions. But when restored to his authentic self that person will be grateful that we took note of the wishes he expressed before he became ill. In cases of this sort, once again, we have a wealth of information about the patients which enables us to build an authentic response to a proposal to participate in research as it were in the patient's voice.

Unconscious patients

Treatment decisions and research activities are often called for in the case of unconscious patients. Should we resuscitate? Should we use this or that medication in the early stages of cardiac arrest? These are questions intensive care physicians deal with every day. Clearly their patients are not capable of consenting to or refusing such treatments. We sometimes have the kind of information referred to in the case of substituted decisions to go on. Relatives are our usual source of this kind of information. On the other hand, as time is of the essence in these cases, we might not be able to conduct such enquiries and we choose to err on the side of life. This can turn out to be a disaster for many survivors whose quality of life is dreadful. Is there any other way in which we can preserve respect for the autonomy of such patients?

We might at times, and this is likely to become more frequent, have direct access to what seem to be the express wishes of our unconscious patient – the presence of an Advance Directive or a Living Will. While such documents are becoming more popular, they carry no legal authority in most places. But they might be the most valuable guide we have to respecting the autonomy of the patient.

Such instruments are far from perfect. They have inherent weaknesses which the clinician has to take into account. First they might be old and out of date. How long ago was the wish expressed? Have the patient's views changed over that time? Second they are hypothetical wishes. They are of the form: if I am found to be in such-and-such a state I will regard that state as worse than death and not wish for any extraordinary means to be used to keep me alive. But we often imagine certain states to be unacceptable which, when they occur, are not so. This explains why so many young people who suffer spinal traumas in sport and their resulting paralyses do not want to be taken off their respirators. Even though before the tragedy they might have regarded such a state as worse than death, that is no longer their view. Third, we need to know under what circumstances the documents were produced. Was the person under duress? Was he subject to the pressures of peer groups? The caring doctor with an urgent life-saving decision to make cannot take the piece of paper placed before him as the final word without such facts being established. Thus, while he would be negligent not to consider the document he should not be bound by it.

Individual and communal autonomy

There is a difficulty in aligning the autonomy of individuals with certain cultural settings where communal autonomy might be thought to prevail. This might be thought to impose limits on the capacity of individual members of that community to make decisions. This is a common problem when international bodies wish to conduct research in the developing world. But is it clear that either individual or communal autonomy should be preferred one to another?

It depends on the kind of decision which is at stake. For example, as a member of a particular cultural group a person might be approached to engage in a research project or a commercial enterprise which would provide access by the researchers or the business in question to materials or matters which might be seen as belonging to the group rather than to any individual in that group. Sometimes matters of this kind are referred to as traditional knowledge and cultural treasures. It follows that it is not the prerogative of an individual member of that group to profit individually from communal treasures or to betray such privileged knowledge to strangers without the consent of the group. In such cases, such as the exploitation of indigenous flora or fauna, communal autonomy would impose proper limits on individual autonomy.

However, such cases should not be used as a basis for concluding that cultural considerations can dictate that for members of some groups communal autonomy must always override individual autonomy. For example, if a group is prepared to allow outsiders to carry out research on the community as such, individuals in that community should not be obliged to offer themselves as participants in that research. They might voluntarily devolve the authority to decide for them to the community but this would not undermine respect for their autonomy. This is the import of Art 12 in the Declaration on Bioethics and Human Rights 2005, which asserts that respect for cultural diversity and pluralism should not be used to infringe fundamental freedoms nor any of the principles set out in the Declaration, including Art 5. The scope of respect for individual autonomy cannot be limited by cultural considerations except where cultural knowledge and cultural treasures are involved. Such unauthorised limitations would constitute disrespect for fundamental freedoms.

Conclusion

In this chapter we have considered some occasions in clinical practice where it is impossible for patients to know what it is that health care professionals are doing to them. This ignorance is unrelated to their lack of familiarity with the sophisticated knowledge base out of which that practice springs but rather relates to external and internal constraints on their ability to consent properly to procedures which are pursued in the course of therapeutic interventions. The former constraints are especially interesting when, in the application of innovative procedures, inadequate attention is given to the fact that even the clinician is not in a position to know precisely what his actions will amount to given the total lack of evidence on the matter. His conviction that it is in the interests of the patient to proceed is not evidence based. That same conviction might also be an expression of a lack of objectivity in the practitioner due to various kinds of conflicts of interest. There is need for special protections to be provided for patients in these settings which are akin to research settings. However, in many places it is not expected that these activities be declared or scrutinised by independent bodies. Where this is so it is possible for badly designed research to be executed in the guise of clinical practice where the usual protections afforded to research participants are denied to the patient. Ethical review of innovative practice presents some additional challenges to the review of standard research but we have proposed policies by which they can be met.

We have also noted that for various reasons some people cannot provide informed consents to participate in research. But there are means open to us to demonstrate a fundamental difference in our attitudes towards them and our attitudes towards animals in the research setting. In the first kind of case this is by means of removing external constraints on their autonomy in innovative treatments where the consent procedure is often not even contemplated on the one hand and approximating to obtaining informed consents in various ways in the employment of incompetent participants in research on the other. In the case of animals these protections are not employed. This is not a matter of carelessness or moral turpitude. Rather their employment in these contexts is inconceivable.

Notes

1 T. Regan, 'Ill-gotten gains', in P. Cavalieri and P. Singer (eds.), *The Great Ape Project*, New York: St Martin's Griffin, 1993, pp. 196–8.
2 S. Bloch and P. Chodoff, *Psychiatric Ethics*, 2nd edn, Oxford: Oxford University

Press, 1991; and H. Merskey and B. Shafran 'Political hazards in the diagnosis of "sluggish schizophrenia" ', *The British Journal of Psychiatry* 148 (1986), 247–56.

3 L.H. Roth, A. Meis, and C.W. Lidz, 'Tests of competency to consent to treatment', *American Journal of Psychiatry* 134 (1977), 279–84.

4 For further examples, see: D.M. Evans, 'Ethicist and patient: what is their relationship?', in R. Gillon (ed.), *Principles of Health Care Ethics*, Chichester: John Wiley and Sons, 1993, pp. 394–7.

5 See, for example, the Nuremberg Code and the Declaration of Helsinki reprinted in: *Source Book in Bioethics: A Documentary History*, A.R. Jonsen, R.M. Veatch and L. Walters (eds.), Washington, D.C.: Georgetown University Press, 1998, pp. 11–15.

6 S. Coney, *The Unfortunate Experiment*, Auckland, NZ: Penguin Books, 1988, p. 57.

7 Ibid., pp. 134–5.

8 S. Cartwright, *The Report of the Committee of Inquiry into Allegations Concerning the Treatment of Cervical Cancer at National Womens' Hospital and into Other Related Matters*, Auckland (NZ): Government Printer, 1988, pp. 212–13.

9 D.M. Evans and M. Evans, *A Decent Proposal: Ethical Review of Clinical Research*, Chichester: John Wiley and Sons, 1996, pp. 59–60.

10 See the example of the Halifax clamp: ibid., pp. 56–7.

11 G. Gillett, C.R.P. Lind and A.M. Erasmus, 'CG clip expansive open-door laminoplasty: a technical note', *British Journal of Neurosurgery* 13 (1999), 405–8.

12 Consider the example of the *sling on the string* technique of treating urinary incontinence described in: Evans and Evans, *A Decent Proposal*, p. 56.

13 Principles 2 & 3: 'Nuremberg code', in A.R. Jonsen, R.M. Veatch and L. Walters (eds.), *Source Book in Bioethics: A Documentary History*, Washington, D.C.: Georgetown University Press, 1998, pp. 12.

14 Principles 4–7: ibid.

15 D.M. Evans and M. Evans, *A Decent Proposal*, pp. 56–8.

16 G. Gillett, 'How should we test and improve neurosurgical care?', in A. Zeman and L. Emmanuel (eds.), *Ethical Dilemmas in Neurology*, London: W.B. Saunders Company, 2000, pp. 87–100.

17 J.M. Last, *A Dictionary of Epidemiology*, 3rd edn, Oxford: Oxford University Press 1983, p. 56.

18 L.W. Shaw and T.C. Chalmers, 'Ethics in cooperative trials', *Annals of the New York Academy of Sciences* 169 (1970), 487–95.

19 R.J. Levine, *Ethics and the Regulation of Clinical Research*, 2nd edn, Baltimore: Urban and Schwarzenberg, 1986, p. 187.

20 B. Freedman, 'Equipoise and the ethics of clinical research', *New England Journal of Medicine* 317 (1987), 141–5.

21 R.I. Lindley and C.P. Warlow, 'Why, and how, should trials be conducted?', in A. Zeman and L. Emmanuel (eds.), *Ethical Dilemmas in Neurology*, London: W.B. Saunders Company, 2000, pp. 82–3.

22 T.C. Chalmers, J.B. Block and S. Lee, 'Controlled studies in clinical cancer research', *New England Journal of Medicine* 287 (1972), 75–8.

23 B. Jennett, *High Technology Medicine: Benefits and Burdens*, Oxford: Oxford University Press, 1986, p. 95.

24 *Gillick V. v West Norfolk & Wisbech Area Health Authority*, 3, All England Law Reports, 1985.

25 A.E. Buchanan, and D.W. Brock, *Deciding for Others: The Ethics of Surrogate Decision Making*, Cambridge: Cambridge University Press, 1989, pp. 112–22.

Chapter 10

Ethics, nanotechnologies and health

Emerging biotechnologies offer unprecedented opportunities to bypass individual consent. Their birth is often accompanied by immense promise of multitudes of remarkable benefits so that to be sceptical or even cautious about them seems churlish or small-minded. They facilitate innovative treatments but their essence precedes their applications and these often vary widely. While some of them will be innocent and welcomed, others overtake us unawares and constitute threats to our health and well-being which we would not have chosen to accept had we been able to predict their occurrence or even been aware of their possibility. In addition they often offer great promise to the public interest at the expense of the interest of the individual. In the recent past we have seen two major developments of this kind in *in vitro* fertilisation and DNA genetic technology. Their development has been so rapid that ethical reflection on their introduction and application has lagged behind the technical advances. As a result much of that reflection has been reactive. In this chapter we shall examine the emerging nanotechnologies. They follow hard on the heels of the others but are as yet in relative infancy. Thus a case might be made for endeavouring to anticipate the ethical challenges of these technologies before they are upon us.

Two challenges immediately face us. The first is the identification of the technologies. The second is the problem concerning the difficulty of crystal ball gazing to identify possible developments of the technologies in the face both of exaggerated optimistic claims and exaggerated doomsday predictions of what they might offer humankind. We might best approach the possibilities by means of a consideration of the contrasting accounts of the promises and threats presented by them in respect to individual health, public health, environmental health and cognitive and behavioural development. In each case we can ask the same question which has preoccupied us thus far in the book, viz. what will we really be doing to patients in applications of these technologies?

Learning from precedents

The emergence of new technologies which promise remarkable benefits for health has acccelerated greatly over the last forty years. The discovery of DNA followed by the mapping of the human genome and the invention of *in vitro* fertilisation (IVF) techniques have perhaps been the most notable among them. These have, both separately and together given rise to spin-off technologies and research endeavours which have stimulated much debate about ethical issues.

For example, in the case of genetics we have seen the possibility of matching pharmaceutical agents to patient groups with greater accuracy through the development of pharmacogenetics. This has raised important questions about the collection and use of human tissues and their exploitation in the production of drugs. Issues of privacy, consent and benefit sharing have dominated these discussions. In the case of IVF we have been forced to think carefully about the moral status of early embryos and whether they can be created for and used in research, bought and sold, selected for various qualities, used for the benefit of others. The emergence of stem cell technologies has largely been stimulated by the availability of *in vitro* embryos. Ethical issues such as protecting human dignity, causing harm, and the commodification of human beings, are still being debated on a very wide scale.

These two technologies have also joined hands in health intervention programmes such as pre-implantation genetic testing and screening. Here questions about the notion of a disability and the dignity and value of the lives of people with disabilities have arisen, as well as heated discussions about the differences between restoration of health and human enhancement. Are there important distinctions between making people better and making better people?

Into this already morally contested scene has come this additional group of technologies promising much for the health of people, viz. nanotechnologies.

Claims and counter-claims

There are numbers of peculiar difficulties attaching to the ethical evaluation of these technologies in that in such early days it is not possible to distinguish easily between, on the one hand, the hype of the promises being made and the possibilities, both positive and negative, which are being discussed and, on the other hand, the realities of what is or what might become possible. Insofar as this is the case we have much to learn from its predecessors mentioned above.

In the case of genetics we might note that the new science held out incredible promise for all sorts of stunning health interventions in the form of genetic engineering of cures for conditions such as cystic fibrosis. These might yet emerge but it has turned out to be far more problematic than the early publicity suggested. While we have a remarkable array of diagnostic tools in the field there is little, as yet, that can be done about righting the abnormalities that derive from the genetic faults which are identified, save in the form of avoiding the birth of those who would be so afflicted. The latter intervention is itself a morally contested response to the health problems in question.

In the case of IVF, few people, if any, could have forecast the various developments which have occurred due to the availability of early human embryos in the laboratory. What was essentially a technique developed to relieve the distress of infertile couples has opened the door to vast extensions of knowledge in early human embryology and its various applications such as the use of embryonic stem cells in research, and, it is hoped, therapy.

Extreme optimism and extreme pessimism exist about the potential of nanotechnologies. On the hyper-optimistic side consider the following predictions:

- Nanomedicine will eliminate virtually all common diseases of the twentieth century, virtually all medical pain and suffering, and allow the extension of human capabilities – most especially our mental abilities.
- Consider that a nanostructured data storage device . . . about the size of a human liver cell . . . could store an amount of information equivalent to the entire Library of Congress. If implanted somewhere in the human brain, together with the appropriate interface mechanisms, such a device could allow extremely rapid access to this information.
- But perhaps the most important long-term benefit to human society as a whole could be the dawning of a new era of peace. We could hope that people who are independently well-fed, well-clothed, well-educated, healthy and happy will have little motivation to wage war.[1]

The direst warning about the possibilities of the technologies came from one of its founding fathers, or at least from the scientist who invented the name for some of these technologies, viz. molecular nanotechnology.[2] He envisaged the creation of nano-robots which could be self-replicating and capable of consuming all organic life. While the author of this warning has lately somewhat distanced himself from this prediction[3] his doomsday scenario in which everything would become 'grey goo' has caught the imagination of numerous science fiction writers.[4]

But there are more plausible and likely outcomes which we have to take into account when considering the relationship between nanotechnologies and health. As a sobering corrective to the optimism regarding health benefits, consider the following possibilities envisaged by scientists working at Rice University's Centre for Biological and Environmental Nanotechnology:

One thing we've concluded is whatever these things (nanomaterials) are going to do, they're not inert. What will they do when they get into the environment, and what will they do when they get into people?[5]

Where does this stuff go? What will be its interaction with the environment? Is it the next best thing to sliced bread or the next to asbestos? . . . We know nanomaterials have been taken up by cells. That sets off alarms . . . If bacteria can take them up, then we have an entry point for nanomaterials into the food chain.[6]

A third scientist from this Centre warns that proteins may attach to the surface of nanoparticles in the blood, which could trigger dangerous consequences such as blood clotting. Additionally, she claims, that bacteria absorbing these particles might facilitate the entry of other dangerous materials into the body, and that toxins could similarly be spread in the environment.[7] As we shall see, this area of risk becomes particularly significant when medical interventions might involve the deliberate introduction of nanoparticles into patients.

Setting precedents

There is more that we might learn from the ethical debate which has surrounded both IVF and DNA Genetics. Many of the ethical problems thrown up by these technologies form the heart of ethical concern about nanotechnologies in their health applications. In general it can be said that these are intensified in health nanotechnologies. Thus the debates in this field are not starting from square one as numbers of them did in IVF and Genetics. We can learn from what has been said in those fields in both the identification of ethical issues and their treatment when we come to think about nanotechnologies. Consider a couple of examples.

First, we have already alluded to the development of pre-implantation genetic screening and testing which has arisen out of the joining of hands of the two identified technologies preceding nanotechnologies. It is promised that nanotechnologies will provide us with ways of genetic examination which will be more rapid and vastly cheaper than those currently available. One of the practical limitations restricting the use of these technologies in population screening is its expense and the lack of sufficient expert resources to offer such a service. This barrier could well be removed in the near future by employing information nanotechnology, thus increasing the pressure for such services to be provided. As a result the major ethical problems of privacy and confidentiality, consent and ownership of genetic data, rights to information and dangers of genetic profiling will be greatly intensified.

The second is found in Genetics where, as we have seen, much was promised in terms of engineering out genetic defects in developing human beings. Success in achieving such changes in the early stages of development would ensure better developmental health. But how much engineering is enough? Are we simply endeavouring to restore to an embryo or foetus its 'normal' potential? And how do genetic changes ensure the development of the same individual? Is it not a different person who results from such changes? Nano-technologists have also forecast the remediation of health problems by nano-engineering. For example, it has been suggested, as noted above, that the insertion of intelligent nanoparticles into the brain might help restore a foetus with a developing intellectual impairment to its normal potential. But what is normality? Who is to decide this? If we could go beyond such gains and produce much greater potential for the developing child, should we do so? Questions about the proper role of medicine in this field have been discussed for some time in the context of genetic engineering. Is this eugenics? And if so is this wrong? There is little distinctive about the nano-technological possibilities save for the scale of such extensions. Here we are once again called upon to consider the nature of persons and our moral reactions to engineered human beings, but possibly in the light of more radical possibilities.

In considering the ethical dimensions of the development of nanotechnologies we shall keep in mind the principles of the recently adopted UNESCO Universal Declaration on Bioethics and Human Rights 2005.[8]

Nanotechnology and public health

Let us consider four ways in which the developments in Nanotechnology might impact on public health.

Nanotechnology as a threat to public health

Nanotechnologies present some kinds of ethical issues related to health which do not figure straightforwardly in either genetics or IVF-related technologies. These arise out of the introduction to the environment of nano-substances which constitute environmental hazards. Nanotechnologies involve the production and use of new materials which, by their very nature, might present threats to the health of people. Insofar as this is the case then it is to be marked off from both the science of genetics and the creation of *in vitro* embryos. Here we find ourselves nearer to the development and uses of nuclear science where the physical products produced and employed in the resultant technologies themselves constitute possible hazards to human health.

What are these products and how might they be harmful? Nanotechnologies are concerned with incredibly small quantities of matter, as small as one billionth of a metre. Industry is interested to produce such particles of already existing compounds and such particles of modified materials which do not exist in nature. What is surprising to the person in the street is that these very small quantities of materials behave quite differently from the larger masses with which we are familiar. We might expect them either to retain the qualities of the larger masses or possess them in diminished degrees. In fact we now know that they might possess different qualities, such as colour, or the same qualities in greatly increased degrees, such as strength, chemical reactivity and electrical conductivity. Indeed it is partly the latter fact which makes them so useful.

Whereas genetics has been said to deal with the building blocks of life, these nano-particles have been said to be the building blocks of everything. Their minute character also enables them, when they enter the bloodstream, to cross the blood–brain barrier. They are so small that they can be detected by only the most sensitive of instruments and certainly not at all by ordinary people who might, in one way or another, be penetrated by them.

Their usefulness tempts us to employ them as soon as possible. For example, they are already used commercially in paints and cosmetics. They offer huge potential in being more effective catalysts than are currently used to assist in the refining of oil. Carbon nanotubes provide added strength and are planned to be used in the production of radial tyres. Many companies are producing them by the ton. They are present, for example, in barrier creams to provide resistance to UVF rays. Yet the FDA has no protocols for determining their safety even though all products containing sunscreens are regulated as medicines in the United States.[9] That such products are already for sale does not provide any guarantees that they are safe. The US Government's Food and Drug Administration (FDA) has approved zinc oxide for use in sunscreens without restriction on the size of the particles that can be used, despite evidence that in nano form it has phototoxic effects on cultured mammalian cells and their DNA *in vitro*.[10] The European Commission's Scientific Committee on Cosmetic and Non-food Products (SCCNFP) has recommended that further research *in vivo* be conducted to clarify these findings and to produce reliable data on the absorption of zinc oxide through the skin.[11] European Research has shown that there are grounds for concern in this case.[12] Until adequate risk assessment is performed, there must remain a question mark over the release of these particles into the environment in respect of possible threats which they might pose to public health.

> We consider that producers of nanomaterials have a duty to provide relevant toxicity test results for any new material, according to prevailing international guidelines on risk assessment. Even some 'old' chemical agents may need to be reassessed if their physical state is substantially different from that which existed when they were assessed initially.[13]

Such materials can find ready access to the body. They also can find access into cells. From there on we simply do not yet know what their effects might be. Environmental scientists are concerned because it is already known that some nanoparticles interact with biology in ways which larger materials cannot.[14] It has been proven that nanoparticles which are inhaled from the environment can be translocated to the brains of rats and that this probably occurs via the olfactory nerve.[15] It has been further shown that uncoated 'Buckyballs' (nanoparticles of carbon) cause damage to the brains of aquatic species by causing lipid and protein damage.[16] This kind of tissue damage has been linked to Alzheimer's disease.

Scientists are endeavouring to make such particles safe in some areas of application by coating them. This will be necessary if they are to be of use in the therapeutic field, which we shall discuss later. Policies for providing adequate reassurances concerning environmental risk must be produced before countries rush headlong into indiscriminate production and employment of nanomaterials. In this process of developing such policies due regard must be paid to the following Articles of the Universal Declaration on Bioethics and Human Rights.[17]

> Article 16: The impact of life sciences on future generations, including on their genetic constitution should be given due regard.

> Article 17: Due regard is to be given to the interconnection between human beings and other forms of life, to the importance of appropriate access and utilization of biological and genetic resources, to the respect for traditional knowledge and to the role of human beings in the protection of the environment, the biosphere and biodiversity.

Nanotechnologies as an aid to public health

There are three areas of public health which might benefit greatly from developments of nanotechnologies. The first marks a direct counterbalance to the environmental threats noted above.

First, nanotechnologies might provide us with aids to environmental safety. There are already many pollutants in the environment. Despite the concerns noted above about the possibility of pollution problems being worsened by the development and widespread use of nanoparticles, there is a real possibility that the employment of nanotechnologies could remove pollutants from the environment more effectively than has been dreamed of previously.

The most outstanding opportunity with respect to public health probably lies in the provision of clean water. The lack of clean water in so many parts of the world has been related to more unnecessary deaths than any other single cause. While the developed world might take the provision of potable water for granted, the global cumulative death rates resulting from the consumption and use of impure water dwarfs that of any other single cause, including AIDS and famine, many times over. The World Bank estimates that presently over half the world's population lack basic sanitation and some 1.5 billion people lack access to clean water. The result is that 80% of the diseases of the developing world are water-related. It has been estimated that these lead to 3.4 million deaths every year, the majority of which are children.[18]

The contaminants take a variety of forms both organic and inorganic. Bacteria and viruses play a major role; oil, other organic pollutants and heavy metals also play their part.[19] Various promising nanotechnological solutions have been devised to address this problem. These have been listed by Singer *et al.*[20] as follows:

1   Intelligent membranes can be produced to make affordable and portable filter systems which will remove most contaminants including bacteria and viruses. These materials are 10,000 times more capable of binding bacteria and toxins than activated carbon.
2   Nanomagnets with various coatings can be designed to deal with specific contaminants, including oil, from water. Such dust-like preparations could be spread over wide areas and gathered up affording almost 100% effectiveness. These nanomachines could be recycled and used over and over.
3   Magnetite nanoparticles combined with citric acid could remove heavy metals from water.

The prospect of removing terrible diseases such as cholera and typhus, and common gastro-enteritis from the lives of vast populations of sufferers is cause for great excitement. But will it happen?

Before it is possible there will need to be considerable attention paid by the developed world to the following Articles of the Universal Declaration on Bioethics and Human Rights:

Article 10: The fundamental equality of all human beings in dignity and rights is to be respected so that they are treated justly and equitably.

Article 13: Solidarity among human beings and international cooperation towards that end are to be encouraged.

Article: 14
b) Taking into account that the enjoyment of the highest attainable standard of health is one of the fundamental rights of every human being without distinction of race, religion, political belief, economic or social condition, progress in science and technology should advance . . .
    ii) access to adequate nutrition and water.

Article 15: Benefits resulting from any scientific research and its applications should be shared with society as a whole and within the international community, in particular with developing countries . . .[21]

But it is probable that the financial rewards open to the developers of nano-technologies will tempt them to concentrate on those advances which will show the greatest economic returns for their investors. If this occurs then the gap between the rich and poor nations will grow and a remarkable opportunity to contribute to a better world will be missed. That choice has been starkly presented by Singer *et al.* as follows:

> Will nanotechnology produce the nanodivide? Resources might be dir-ected primarily to nanosunscreens, nanotrousers, and space elevators to benefit the 600 million people in rich countries, but that path is not predetermined. Nanotechnology could soon be applied to address the critical food, water, and energy needs of the 5 billion people in the devel-oping world.[22]

Second, nanotechnologies might provide us with aids to epidemiological studies and public health provision. Epidemiology is focused on populations rather than individuals. It is concerned to make discoveries about the aeti-ology of diseases by studying trends which, in turn, involves having ready access to health data belonging to very large numbers of patients. As such it has a public health interest though, of course, its discoveries benefit individual patients in the long term.

Public health initiatives, similarly, are focused on what has often been referred to as the herd, as in 'herd immunity', rather than individual patients. An example would be the provision of immunisation or vaccination pro-grammes. For example, protection against whooping cough is provided by such means. However, whenever a doctor faces the mother of a child to offer such protection, he or she cannot guarantee that it is in the interests of that individual child to be vaccinated as, sadly, on rare occasions adverse reactions to the vaccine might cause severe brain damage. Nevertheless once a cer-tain proportion of the population has been vaccinated, herd immunity is produced and the possibility of an epidemic is eradicated, which is in the interests of all individual children.

Similarly when population screening programmes are conducted, such as in cervical cancer screening, it is important to be able to follow the unfolding medical history of those involved in the scheme in order to evaluate the schemes' effectiveness. Once again it is not the welfare of individual patients which is the focus of the exercise but the overall success of the population-based programme.

How might nanotechnologies offer support to enterprises of these kinds? There are various possible nanotechnological developments in the field of diagnostics and information technology which, together, would offer great assistance to practitioners. For example the production and insertion into patients of nanocomputer-like particles is constantly canvassed as providing early warnings of the developments of disease conditions. This is not really surprising as proteins might themselves be regarded as nanodevices which perform highly specific functions in virtually all biological sensory, metabolic, information and molecular transport processes.[23] Nanotechnologists seek to replicate such devices at the molecular level. In addition these nanocomputer-like machines can be subject to external control by treating doctors in certain applications, as we shall see later, and be directed to dispense therapeutic substances as needed, and so on. They might therefore also become capable of being tracked by remote sensing devices.[24] If all these possibilities are realised then it is clear that they will constitute a major assistance to audit, public health initiatives and epidemiological research. However, given the dimensions of the particles, people might not even be aware that they are carrying them about in their person and thus might be subject to unwitting surveillance about some of the most intimate and significant features of their lives raising important problems of privacy and confidentiality and consent.

This tension between the interests and rights of the individual patient on the one hand and the interests of public health on the other is not new. There has been much discussion as to how it can be best managed without rendering the public health initiatives impossible. The discussion includes issues about continuing consent, methods of approach to patients in gathering data, the usefulness or otherwise of the distinction between the use of identifiable and non-identifiable data, restrictions of access to irrelevant information or information not canvassed in the original consent of the patient and restrictions of access to unauthorised persons. Given the advent of the technological possibilities canvassed above, all of these issues will arise from some applications of nanotechnology in an extremely focused form as threats to civil liberties are perceived.

In this respect Arts 3 and 6 of the Universal Declaration on Bioethics and Human Rights will need to be taken into account in the formation of public policy in the development of nanotechnological initiatives in the field.

    Article 3:

    a) Human dignity, human rights and fundamental freedoms are to be fully respected.

    b) The interests and welfare of the individual should have priority over the sole interest of science and society.

    Article 6:

    a) Any preventive, diagnostic and therapeutic medical intervention is only to be carried out with the prior, free and informed consent of the person concerned, based on adequate information. The consent should, where appropriate, be express and may be withdrawn by the person at any time and for any reason without disadvantage or prejudice.

b) Scientific research should only be carried out with the prior, free, express and informed consent of the person concerned. The information should be adequate, provided in a comprehensible form and should include the modalities for withdrawal of consent. The consent may be withdrawn by the person concerned at any time and for any reason without disadvantage or prejudice.

Third nanotechnologies might provide us with aids to population screening. This is a further form of population surveillance which deserves separate consideration. This activity, especially at the level of neonatal screening, has been canvassed with increasing regularity over the past ten years or so for various reasons.[25] On the one hand it has been claimed that the wider coverage of such screening would empower people to make sensible lifestyle, social and domestic choices, including reproductive choices. On the other hand it has been suggested that, as more information of this kind is placed in the hands of health care providers, a number of objectives would be realised including a reduction in the number of births of children with major genetic disorders, the facilitation of better planning of efficient and effective health care delivery for the next generation, and assistance in the planning of research programmes.

Laudable as such objectives might appear, each of them poses considerable ethical challenges. However, over and above these, such programmes have been subject to the law of diminishing returns. For example, at present various genetic tests are provided to couples who are deemed to be at risk of having children with genetic disorders. These tests are expensive and highly specific. Expanding such provision to a wider range of people would be likely to return proportionately smaller numbers of positives. The wider the net is cast the smaller the returns would be for much greater investment of resources. Indeed the costs per positive result would increase exponentially, as I noted in Chapter 4.[26] The prohibitive costs of such programmes have been a major deterrent to their introduction. However, nanotechnologies might change this dramatically.

Currently, it has been estimated, it would cost 5 million pounds sterling to map a complete genome – a lengthy process, and 250,000 thousand pounds sterling to map the 5% of the genome which is thought to be significant for medical purposes. Nanotechnologists have been reported to promise vast reductions in both cost and time to the process, opening the door to rapid and affordable large-scale genetic research.

Standard testing methods require large sample sizes and long reaction times to amplify the relevant genetic sequence using polymerase chain reaction (PCR). Microfluidic testing methods that are rapid and that can be performed on small biologic samples (for example, a single human cell) are currently being developed.[27]

Sheremeta refers to published research papers which reveal that microfluidic chips can now be produced to perform PCR,[28] which should make possible high through-put sequence analysis[29] and that it should be possible to read 2 million bases per second, thus enabling an entire genome to be sequenced in two hours.

All of this promise would make population screening of neonates, for example, affordable and achievable. Once the cost barriers are removed it is probable that huge pressure will build up to introduce such programmes and all the ethical and legal discussions, which have proceeded at a relatively leisurely pace while specific genetic testing for very small minorities of patients have been provided, will rapidly become intensified.

So what are these discussions? For convenience we shall group the most notable areas of discussion under three headings. The first group of problems surround the issue of consent, the second concern the long-term benefits for neonates which, it has been claimed, would be afforded by such programmes. The third group concern the nature of the knowledge gained by the screening programme and its consequences for the patients and the patients' families.

If screening programmes are to be fully operationalised and of maximal usefulness then all neonates should be screened. For example, the larger the number of neonates who are not included in the programme, the less likely it is that researchers will be capable of making generalised conclusions about relationships between genetic predispositions and social and demographic data. However, it is clear that there can be no ethical justification for obliging people to be involved either in research enterprises of this sort or in preventive or therapeutic interventions. This is clearly set out in Art 6(a) and (b) of the UNESCO Universal Declaration cited above, together with Art 6(c):

Article 6:
(c) In appropriate cases of research carried out on a group of persons or a community, initial agreement of the legal representatives of the group or community concerned may be sought. In no case should a collective community agreement or the consent of a community leader or other authority substitute for an individual's informed consent.[30]

There are special problems relating to neonatal genetic screening which call for comment here, given the impossibility of obtaining consent from neonates. We have noted that parents are trusted to consent for their children to undergo medical examinations and therapeutic interventions because they are thought, above all people, to have the children's interests at heart. It is not clear that they can consent for their children to be subjected to research, however, because it cannot be said to be executed for their interest specifically. Aside from this difficulty, the creation of a genetic profile of a child at birth allows for possibilities about which it is not possible to build a hypothetical consent on behalf of the children in terms of what they are likely, in later life, to consider was in their best interests at birth. Given the various burdens which knowledge of one's genetic make-up can impose, such as social stigma, restrictions of civil liberties in terms of obtaining insurance, employment and even education of certain sorts, many people choose not to be informed of genetic probabilities which pertain to them.[31] As neonates are in no position to resist such screening, the knowledge will be forced upon them or those who care for them in later life as it will constitute a part of their medical record.

Whenever genetic testing is offered to patients, genetic counselling occurs in order to explain the consequences of being tested and the possibilities of positive results and their consequences. In the light of such information the decision to accept or refuse to be tested is made. No such enabling can proceed in the case of neonates.

While parental consent to pre-natal genetic testing for conditions which could be developmentally important for the child is a proper responsibility of parents, screening for conditions which would, if at all, only develop during the adult life of the neonate are another matter. They could be said to be options for the neonate on reaching maturity.

One of the protections provided for patients who enter clinical trials and who are involved in therapeutic interventions is the possibility of reviewing consent and withdrawing from the trial or refusing continuing treatment. While it is impossible to withdraw specific genetic knowledge from adults who have opted to receive it, it can at least be argued that the possession of such knowledge is voluntary. No such mitigation can be offered in the case of the person who was genetically screened for a much wider range of possibilities as a neonate.

Such negative considerations have to be placed against the benefits promised for the individual neonate who is genetically screened. These might be taken into account when making a 'best interests' judgement on behalf of the incompetent child.

With respect to promised benefits to the neonate we need to consider the nature of the information gathered in genetic profiling. The UK Department of Health's White Paper *Our Inheritance, Our Future*[32] to which the Human Genetics Commission responded in their Report on Genetic Profiling referred to the analysis of a person's entire genome in order to reveal the majority of their genetic variations. The significance of some of these variations is already known but the significance of most of them is not presently known. As the life of the neonate progresses into adulthood no doubt more will become known about these matters. Given the note of the variations in their medical records the persons concerned then will stand to benefit from early warning of their propensity to develop certain conditions, or, possibly, of lifestyle changes which could be advisable in order to avoid triggers for the development of the conditions which they have special disposition to develop. This appears to offer them a considerable advantage. On the other hand it is also likely that the evidence of causal links will not match the progress in identifying the dispositions to diseases which are uncovered. Indeed this is currently true of marker genes which we have already identified. In such cases the knowledge of one's disposition to suffer the diseases might add up to more of a burden than a blessing, except where it might extend one's freedoms. For example, while in some cases, notably Huntingdon's Chorea, knowledge of the certainty that one will develop the condition, or knowledge of being a carrier of the condition, might inform reproductive choices, in most cases the probabilistic knowledge provided by the possession of a marker gene will tend to limit one's civil liberties in ways canvassed earlier.

The development of Pharmacogenomics also promises to assist the well-being of the neonates armed with genetic profiles. More medicines are being matched with groups of patients most likely to benefit from them, or least likely to suffer unacceptable adverse reactions to them, by means of genetic compatibilities. Given the presence of a genetic profile in the medical record arising from a neonatal screening programme, patients will be spared the vagaries of the trial-and-error prescribing which would otherwise occur.

The usefulness of knowledge of a predisposition to a disease for which there is no known treatment has usually been referred to as disadvantageous, save in cases like Huntingdon's as mentioned above. However, given the probable life span of the neonate, treatments which come on line will be more readily matched to them as their health is monitored.

There is still some doubt hanging over whether there is a positive effect on parents who possess knowledge of their child's genetic profile. While it would appear that such knowledge would alert the parent to dangers and thus enable them to provide better care to their children, there is evidence that knowledge of specific dispositions which their child may have to develop a disease tends to make them overprotective. This can have spin-off effects on the welfare of the child who is cast in the patient role.[33]

The more general benefit which is thought to be derived from neonatal genetic screening concerns the planning of future health provision. The more information planners can have about likely disease profiles in a society then the more intelligently, it is claimed, will they be able to plan health service provision to match those developments. Given that genetic disposition is but one feature of disease development it is not clear that this statistical data will be very useful in this regard. It might also militate against the interests of individual neonates who will be likely to develop rarer conditions than those for which explicit provision will be made, given the constant temptation which health service planners suffer to maximise health gain from the investment of health funds. This raises serious questions about distributive justice in health care.[34]

In addition, the possession of genetic profiles by patients might rebound upon health planners and prove a hindrance to efficient provision of health services. The syndrome of the 'worried well' patient will be likely to occur.

This can have a double effect. First, extra demands are placed upon the health service as a result of the anxieties which the genetic knowledge produces. A person who knows of a genetic susceptibility to a condition and develops an ache or pain which might conceivably be related to that condition will be likely to demand investigations in order to deal with the problem early. The number of false alarms will vastly outstrip the number of genuine signs but will place huge additional burdens on providers of care. Second, the anxiety produced by the knowledge might itself produce negative health consequences with which the health service will have to deal.

There are ethical problems which arise out of the very nature of genetic data. These are problems which have arisen in the use of genetic tests irrespective of the employment of nanotechnological aids. They also arise in the case of neonatal screening programmes which are already mandatory in many countries. However, once again, the problems would be considerably intensified given the advent of neonatal screening of the kind outlined above.

There are two major areas of difficulty arising from the nature of genetic information. First, it is information which tells one a great deal about other people than the presenting patient. This shared nature of genetic data raises the question of ownership. Is the genetic profile of the neonate the property of the neonate, and, if so, is it the sole property of the neonate? If something is one's property then one can determine whether and how others can make use of it. One has a right to use that property in any way one chooses within the law and proscribe the use of it by others altogether, even if they have urgent need of it. If that property is shared then it will not be possible to control its use in this way, even if it is used in ways that are against one's interests.

When information contained in the profile of the neonate reveals something significant about the genetic make-up of a relative does not that relative share the ownership of the information? And is not that relative entitled to know it? Consider the example of the child born with a severe genetic abnormality. The condition was the result of a carrier gene of the mother, whose sister was also likely to carry the gene. Should the sister be allowed access to this information in order to guide her reproductive choices? In the case in question the mother refused permission for her sister to be told of the possibility because there were bad relations between the two and the mother hoped that her sister would suffer the same tragedy. What should the geneticist do in such situations? In other cases a child might be discovered to be carrying the genetic mutation for Huntingdon's. Should the 25-year-old mother, whose grandfather died of the disease aged 48, be told this even though she does not want to know if she has the mutation? And how does this affect her 45-year-old mother who has not expressed a wish not to know? Problems of this kind would become much more common given provision of the complete genome of neonates that a general screening programme would involve. Some guidance for practitioners or regulation of practice would be required in order to protect the interests of both the neonate and relatives at the introduction of such a programme but they would not be easy to devise given the vast number of differences which will exist between cases.[35]

The second area of difficulty concerns another aspect of the above cases, viz. the privacy and confidentiality of this sensitive personal information. Where should we draw the line in defining the rights of other individuals and bodies to access the genetic profiles of neonates provided by a population screening programme? It is clear that open access would be detrimental to the interests of the child, especially as he or she grows into adulthood and becomes subject to discrimination on the basis of the stigma attaching to the possibility of developing a variety of disease conditions or disabilities.

One of the motivations for introducing such programmes, as we have seen, is to enable governments to better engage in planning health services. Aside from the question as to whether the probabilistic information contained in whole gene profiles could, in fact, provided bases for accurate prediction and planning, there is the pressure for governments and others to use such profiles for other purposes. We have an excellent precedent in the neonatal screening programme which involves the Guthrie Card, consisting of a spot of blood taken from the heel of neonates and stored on filter paper. It is used to test the child for a series of serious genetic disorders including cystic fibrosis, congenital hypothyroidism and phenylketonuria, all of which are rare conditions. This test is provided because early intervention is in the interests of the children so afflicted. In many places these tests are mandatory. The cards are held in the medical records of the children and so are stored in an identifiable form.

It has been noted that on some occasions these cards have been used for purposes other than those for which the test was provided – for example in police enquiries, and that in some places clinicians have expressed their willingness to release them to insurance companies, employment agencies and law enforcement agencies without subpoena.[36] The use of the data for health research also raises major privacy issues.[37]

The availability of complete genetic profiles would be an even more attractive source of information for both good and bad purposes for governments and other bodies of various kinds and would present the possibility of serious threats to civil liberties. For example, paternity testing for the enforcement of social service benefit provision and child allowance purposes would become a tempting possibility. It is not difficult to imagine much more serious threats arising out of measures of social control in authoritarian settings. The information arising out of the introduction of such programmes of screening would therefore need to be very carefully controlled, if it should be allowed at all.

Nanotechnologies and patient care

There are many nanotechnological clinical interventions in the care of individual patients being promised. Most of these are no more than possibilities at present but others are currently undergoing clinical trials. The pace at which such possibilities are being proposed is remarkable. For example, the following list of working possibilities were reported in the *New Scientist* in the brief period between October 2004 and November 2005:

29 October 2004 Nano structured contact lenses designed to release drugs to the eye as needed to treat conditions like glaucoma.

27 November 2004 Creation of gold nanoparticles to block angiogenesis, which is an important part of tumour development, rather than destroy the results of such development in the treatment of cancer.

7 January 2005 Use of 'smart bombs' consisting of polymer capsules peppered with gold nanoparticles containing chemo drugs and attached to tumour seeking antibodies which will enter cancer cells and be exploded by low energy laser pulses killing the cells and leaving surrounding cells untouched.

31 January 2005 Combinations of magnetic and gold nanoparticles with strands of DNA providing early detection and, possibly, treatment of Alzheimer's disease.

2 April 2005 Use of nano sized laser beams able to detect one precancerous cell from other cells.

17 June 2005 Use of nano particles capable of delivering drugs selectively to cancer cells leaving surrounding cells unharmed.

11 September 2005 Creation of smart plastic films to coat implants like coronary stents and hip replacements and slowly release drugs.

7 November 2005 The creation of new organs by using biodegradable nanotubes containing either liver or kidney cells to create a vascular framework.

Added to these have been announcements about the use of nanotechnology to treat spinal lesions in newly injured patients and the production of hearing implants which will make it possible to listen to music as well as speech. The list is growing by the day.

Clinical innovations

So what are we to say of it all? First, we must say that it is extremely exciting for health carers and patients. The dream of operating at the cellular level seems within our grasp and will make current surgical techniques look crude.

Disease and ill health are caused largely by damage at the molecular and cellular level. Today's surgical tools are, at this scale, large and crude. It is said that from the viewpoint of a cell, even a fine scalpel is a blunt instrument more suited to tear and injure than heal and cure. Modern surgery works only because cells have a remarkable ability to regroup, bury their dead and heal over injury.[38]

But is it safe to proceed with clinical trials at this point? This is the major question to be asked of these realistic, and some of the more ambitious, treatments of promise such as the use of nano-robots called respirocytes which will be 236 times more efficient at delivering oxygen to tissues than a natural red cell.[39]

Here we have to face the research finding that nanoparticles can possibly cause problems of blood clotting.[40] And, further that they can accumulate in organisms.[41] As yet, we do not know how significant these findings are as we consider placing these particles into patients. The enthusiasm to help patients must not mask the need for adequate risk assessment of such innovative practices. Respect for Art 4 of the Universal Declaration is called for:

> Article 4: In applying and advancing scientific knowledge, medical practice and associated technologies, direct and indirect benefits to patients, research participants and other affected individuals should be maximized and any possible harm to such individuals should be minimized.[42]

We therefore have to take care that the introduction of nanotechnological techniques under the guise of innovative clinical treatment does not evade the consideration of such protocols by independent ethics committees. Mention was made in Chapter 9 of some work done of late to provide guidelines for such review in the light of conceptual difficulties of achieving sound evidence for the effectiveness of such innovations by means of gold standard prospective randomised controlled studies.[43,44]

Cognitive and behavioural interventions

This particular category of potential clinical interventions calls for separate consideration as the treatments would raise important ethical issues about the identity of patients. There are two aspects to this identity problem. First there is the question of the enhancement as opposed to the treatment of human beings. Second there is the question of authenticity of choices and behaviour.

What kinds of interventions pose these questions? We referred earlier to discussions about the implantation of nanocomputer-like particles in the brains of patients to enhance memory and, possibly, to remedy deficiencies in the brain's functioning and the behavioural patterns of people. These developments are probably more hypothetical than many of the others we have contemplated in this chapter but it is worth exploring them briefly as some of the issues brought into bold relief by this kind of application are present in the relatively more mundane applications previously considered.

Cyborg (cybernetic organism) is a term which has been coined to refer to beings which are part organism and part machine. It is a term especially applicable to the kind of interaction between machine and human organism which would be involved in the implanting of nanocomputers in the brain. Not only has it been suggested that vast extensions to memory might be achieved by these means but also behavioural modifications – for example the control of criminal tendencies or, at a more detailed level, the control of the impulse to deceive.

If such a programme of interventions became possible should they be subject to limits? There has been much discussion around genetic engineering that there would be a major difference between restorative therapeutic interventions, on the one hand, and enhancement on the other. The former would consist in restoring a person (or a foetus) to a normal state or rectify abnormalities. The latter would be to amplify what would be the normal potential to extraordinary potential. These problems are intensified in the projected applications of nanotechnology.

Even the former kind of intervention has been subject to discussion in that it assumes an understanding of what is normal which could undermine the dignity and interests of human beings. The identity of disability is a contestable issue. Some disability groups believe that it is society which is disabling rather than people who are disabled. In other words, disability is a social construct used to discriminate between people unfairly. Engagement in any kind of system, whether it be pre-implantation genetic screening or antenatal genetic testing on the one hand or interventions such as those currently under discussion on the other, would be ethically suspect on this view. Thus, for example, the termination of 'damaged' and 'irreparable' foetuses reflects on the value of people in our society who live with the difficulties which cause these foetuses to be rejected.

Such difficulties aside, there is a separate concern about whether we should seek to engineer enlarged potential in human beings in excess of what they would, if healthy, have possessed. Once again we are dependent on the idea of a norm before we can identify what enhancement would be. We also have to accept that people are not born equal in terms of their potentialities, whether healthy or not. This latter point is not one of fairness. But when it comes to increasing the potential of prospective people, fairness does become an issue. It is a fact that we already engage in many kinds of enhancement post birth, including education, which are not equally available to people. While some believe this to be unfair, others do not. However, we already have faced this issue in sport where enhancement of performance by means of drugs, such as anabolic steroids, is ruled out on the grounds of fairness rather than the taking of undue risks with health. Life is not a game but people do have to compete to make their way in the world and some are disadvantaged with respect to others in their natural ability so to do. It is doubtful that these would be first in line as recipients of nanotechnological enhancement techniques. Other ethical objections aside, it is predictable that such technological enhancements would widen the gap between the privileged and under-privileged in our world.

The most serious group of ethical questions related to nano interventions at this level have to do with the concept of humanness itself. At what point would we be worried that the intervention was of such a character that it was dehumanising? Here, no doubt, there would be wide disagreement. How could such disagreement be handled?

Some have put the matter in terms of the question of whether cyborgs are persons. The question invites a yes or no answer which, on reflection, is not easy to provide. We have noted in Chapter 7 some approaches to this question from the wide discussions which have ranged about the status of the early human embryo since the advent of IVF technologies. There we examined criticisms of the most popular means which philosophers have employed to answer the question, viz. that of proposing criteria which have to be satisfied in order to identify an entity as a person.

An additional problem with these representative selections of criteria is that according to some of them, nanotechnologically improved people would be more morally considerable as persons than they were before treatment. But we have identified major objections to the recognition of persons on the basis of the application of such criteria.

This is not to say that any one of these criteria fails to mark out important issues which would inform our moral attitude to the nanotechnological alteration of cognitive and behavioural patterns. For example, if the interference with behaviour was of a certain sort, viz. rendering it involuntary, and possibly subject to determination by others, we would not think the resultant behaviour to be either culpable or admirable. We would, however, consider that such interferences with free action were to be condemned.

Yet even here there will be differences between cases. The behaviours of patients are already subject to controls by technological means in ways which enhance their freedoms. For example, the use of pacemakers facilitates all the actions of their recipients whose lives would not be able to continue without them, and the use of shunts avoids hydrocephalus and resulting brain damage. However, there is no interference with intention in such cases, even though the persons are cyborgs insofar as they fit the definition of being a mix of organism and machine. The use of behaviour-modifying drugs like Ritalin in the treatment of Attention Deficit Hyperactivity Disorder, though they do have an effect upon intentional behaviour, are presumed to enable the recipients to behave authentically, intentionally and not impulsively, so freeing them to be themselves. It is interesting that people can intend to take such medications in order to hold down a job or complete a task and remain free to be their authentic selves without the drug when they desire. Witty Ticky

Ray,[45] the Tourette Syndrome patient was such a case. It is debatable which of his selves was the authentic person. Was it the man who chose to take Haldol to enable him to lead the boring, flat life holding down a job from Monday to Friday? Or was it the weekend creative drummer for whom the tics did not matter?

How we react to someone who behaves towards us in an apparently generous or caring way, or in a hostile and aggressive manner, depends very much on what we know about the reasons for the behaviour. If we know that their pacemaker facilitates the behaviour this makes no difference at all to our moral reactions to them. If, however, we were to know that the behaviour itself was engineered somehow and beyond the control or wishes of the person, then our view would, of course, be very different. People can, no doubt, be turned into robots to varying degrees and the more we would perceive this to be happening in nanotechnological interventions the more morally repulsive those interventions would become. It is difficult to see, however, why we should have absolute objections to such technology irrespective of these considerations given the kinds of treatments which are already available and approved which have cognitive and behavioural consequences.

When the time comes to make policy decisions about such developments then care will have to be taken to respect Arts 3a and 5 of the Universal Declaration on Bioethics and Human Rights 2005.

Article 3:
a) Human dignity, human rights and fundamental freedoms are to be fully respected.

Article 5: The autonomy of persons to make decisions, while taking responsibility for those decisions and respecting the autonomy of others, is to be respected. For persons who are not capable of exercising autonomy, special measures are to be taken to protect their rights and interests.

Conclusion

The emergence of new technologies is often accompanied by overblown expectations and promises which dispose people to welcome them somewhat uncritically. Given that it is so difficult to imagine the various applications of the technology which might come on stream later or its negative connotations which might be equally obscure, we are often overtaken by the enthusiasm of their developers and the exploitation of the new tools afforded by the technologies. All these represent potential threats to the well-being of people.

We have many examples in health care from which we can learn when addressing new technologies. In this chapter we have reviewed the ways in which we can learn from the technologies of assisted reproduction and DNA genetics in anticipating and regulating the developments in the nanotechnologies. These latter developments and their application to health provision provide us with remarkable possibilities which are to be welcomed. However, these possibilities should not be pursued without due regard for the welfare and rights of all stakeholders. We have learned from the development of earlier technologies that uncontrolled activity in pursuing worthy goals can have deleterious effects. For example, in pharmaceutical development the well-being of research participants has been compromised in ways which have called for proper regulation and ethical review. In this, and other cases such as genetic engineering, development occurred prior to public ethical discussion of the possible benefits, harms and dangers. In the case of nanotechnologies we have the opportunity to think ahead while the technological developments are at an embryonic stage. Ethical reflection by researchers, manufacturers, consumers and governments should help ensure that unacceptable practices and outcomes are avoided and the most desirable outcomes are achieved.

Notes

1 R.A. Freitas, Jr., *Foresight Nanotech Institute Nanomedicine FAQ*, 1998, California: Foresight Institute. Online. Available HTTP: <www.foresight.org/Nanomedicine/NanoMedFAQ.html> (accessed 25 May 2007).

2 K.E. Drexler, *Engines of Creation: The Coming Era of Nanotechnology*, New York: Anchor Books, 1986.

3 C. Phoenix and E. Drexler, 'Safe exponential manufacturing', *Nanotechnology* 15 (2004), 869–72.

4 See, for example, G. Bear, *Blood Music*, London: Gollancz, 1985.

5 Vicki Colvin, quoted in: D. Brown, 'Nano litterbugs? Experts see potential pollution problems', *Small Times*, Tulsa, Okla.: Penwell Publishing, 2002. Available HTTP: <http://online.sfsu.edu/~rone/Nanotech/NANO%20LITTERBUGS.htm> (accessed 25 May 2007).

6 Mark Weisner, quoted in: ibid.

7 Jennifer West, quoted in: ETC Group, 'No small matter! Nanotech particles penetrate living cells and accumulate in animal organs', *ETC Group Communiqué*, 76, 2002. Available HTTP: <www.etcgroup.org/upload/publication/192/01/comm_nanomat_july02.pdf> (accessed 25 May 2007).

8 UNESCO, 'Universal declaration on bioethics and human rights', *International Social Science Journal* 57 (2005), 745–53. This Declaration arose from requests from developing countries for guidance in policy making surrounding emerging technologies.

9 ETC Group, 'No small matter!'.

10 A. Dowling, R. Clift, N. Grobert, D. Hutton, R. Oliver, O. O'Neill, J. Pethica, N. Pidgeon, J. Porritt, J. Ryan, A. Seaton, S. Tendler, M. Welland and R. Whatmore, *Nanoscience and Nanotechnologies: Opportunities and Uncertainties*, London: The Royal Society and The Royal Academy of Engineering, 2004, p. 44.

11 The Scientific Committee on Cosmetic Products and Non-Food Products Intended for Consumers, 'Opinion concerning zinc oxide (COLIPA n S 76)', Brussels: SCCNFP, 2003, SCCNFP/0649/03. Online. Available at: <www.europa.eu.int/comm/health/ph_risk/committees/sccp/documents/out222_en.pdf> (accessed 25 May 2007).

12 R. Dunford, A. Salinaro, L. Cai, N. Serpone, S. Horikoshi, H. Hidaka and J. Knowland, 'Chemical oxidation and DNA damage caused by inorganic sunscreen ingredients', *FEBS Letters* 418 (1997), 87–90.

13 P.H. Hoet, A. Nemmar and B. Nemery, 'Health impact of nanomaterials?', *Nature Biotechnology* 22 (2004), 19.

14 D. Brown, 'Nano litterbugs?'.

15 G. Oberdörster, Z. Sharp, V. Atudorei, A. Elder, R. Gelein, W. Kreyling and C. Cox, 'Translocation of inhaled ultrafine particles to the brain', *Inhalation Toxicology* 16 (2004), 437–45.

16 E. Oberdörster, 'Manufactured nanomaterials (fullerenes, C60) induce oxidative stress in the brain of juvenile largemouth bass', *Environmental Health Perspectives* 112 (2004), 1058–62.

17 UNESCO, 'Universal declaration on bioethics and human rights', p. 751.

18 These figures are reproduced from: Foresight Institute, *Providing Abundant Clean Water Globally*, California: Foresight Institute. Online. Available HTTP: <http://foresight.org/challenges/water.html> (accessed 25 May 2007).

19 P.A. Singer, F. Salamanca-Buentello and A.S. Daar, 'Harnessing nanotechnology to improve global equity', *Issues in Science and Technology* 21 (2005), 57–8.

20 Ibid., p. 59.

21 UNESCO, 'Universal declaration on bioethics and human rights', pp. 750–1.

22 P.A. Singer *et al.*, 'Harnessing nanotechnology to improve global equity', p. 64.

23 A. Dowling *et al.*, *Nanoscience and Nanotechnologies*, p. 20.

24 J.L. Mertz 'Technological and educational implications of nanotechnology – infrastructure and educational needs', in M.C. Roco and W.S. Bainbridge (eds.), *Societal Implications of Nanoscience and Nanotechnology*, Washington, D.C.: National Science Foundation, 2001, pp. 148–55.

25 See, for example, Human Genetics Commission, *Profiling the Newborn: A Prospective Gene Technology?*, London: HGC, 2005. Online. Available HTTP: <www.hgc.gov.uk/UploadDocs/Contents/Documents/Final%20Draft%20of%20 Profiling%20Newborn%20Report%2003%2005.pdf>.

26 D.M. Evans, 'The limits of health care', in D. Greaves and H. Upton (eds.), *Philosophical Problems in Health Care*, Aldershot: Avebury, 1996, pp. 163–4.

27 L. Sheremeta, 'Nanotechnology and the ethical conduct of research involving human subjects', *Health Law Review* 12 (2004), 47–56.

28 P.J. Obeid, T.K. Christopoulos, H.J. Crabtree and C.J. Backhouse, 'Microfabricated device for DNA and RNA amplification by continuous flow polymerase chain reaction and reverse transcription-polymerase chain reaction with cycle selection', *Analytical Chemistry* 75 (2003), 288–95.

29 A.J. Mellow, 'Microfluidics: DNA amplification moves on', *Nature* 422 (2003), 28–9.

30 UNESCO, 'Universal declaration on bioethics and human rights', p. 750.

31 D.M. Evans, 'Ethics and genetics', *New Zealand Medical Journal* 112 (1999), 109–12.

32 Department of Health, *Our Inheritance, Our Future – Realising the Potential of Genetics in the NHS*, CM 5791, London: The Stationery Office, 2003.

33 N.J. Kerruish and S.P. Robinson, 'Newborn screening: new developments, new dilemmas', *Journal of Medical Ethics* 31 (2005), 393–8.

34 D.M. Evans, 'Limits to care', in Z. Szawarski and D.M. Evans (eds.), *Solidarity, Justice and Health Care Priorities*, Health Service Studies 8, Linkoping: Linkoping University Press, 1993, pp. 28–41.

35 For a series of such cases, see: The New Zealand Independent Biotechnology Advisory Council, *Genetic Testing: An Introduction to the Technology that is Changing our Lives*, Wellington, NZ: IBAC, 2001.

36 J. Elkin and D.G. Jones, 'Guthrie cards: legal and ethical uses', *New Zealand Bioethics Journal* 1 (2000).

37 C. Thomas, 'Guthrie test samples: is the problem solved?', *New Zealand Bioethics Journal* 5(2) (2004), 25–33.

38 K. Choi, 'Ethical issues of nanotechnology development in the Asia-Pacific region', in P. Bergstrom (ed.), *Ethics in Asia-Pacific*, Bangkok: UNESCO Asia and Pacific Regional Bureau for Education, 2004, pp. 337.

39 R.A. Freitas, Jr., *Foresight Nanotech Institute Nanomedicine FAQ*.

40 Reported observations of Dr. Jennifer West of The Centre for Biological and Environmental Nanotechnology (CBEN) Rice University, in: ETC Group, op. cit.

41 Dr. Mark Weisner, Professor of Civil and Environmental Engineering, Rice University, quoted in: Brown, 'Nano litterbugs?'.

42 UNESCO, 'Universal declaration on bioethics and human rights', p. 749.

43 D.M Evans, 'Ethical review of innovative treatment', *Healthcare Ethics Committee Forum* 14 (2002), 53–63.

44 D.M. Evans, 'Ethical Issues in research, part I: research by stealth', Washington, D.C.: *Science*/AAAS, 2002. Online. Available HTTP: <http://sciencecareers. sciencemag.org/career_development/previous_issues/articles/1750/ethical_issues _in_research_part_i_research_by_stealth/(parent)/12098> (accessed 25 May 2007).

45 O.W. Sacks, *The Man Who Mistook his Wife for a Hat*, London: Duckworth, 1985.

Chapter 11

Imagination and medical education

Throughout this book we have been considering the importance of respecting patients as persons with perceptions of their world, including their health needs, which are in turn facilitated by the social milieu in which they are situated and their narratives which are shaped by those contexts. That is, medical practice does not consist simply in understanding and attending to physical or bodily conditions. Rather, patients are understood only when their bodily events and characteristics presented to the doctor are construed in the context of their lives. When this idea was introduced in Chapter 1 we thought about what it was to understand what it is that doctors are really doing to their patients, what are the real health needs of patients and what constitutes the real outcome of a medical or surgical intervention. Science cannot tell us these things though it can contribute to that understanding. The doctor therefore is called upon to develop some fellow feeling for the patient, to endeavour to see the world through the patient's eyes. Empathy is a difficult faculty to instil into people. Some people, we feel, are naturally empathetic and others are not. When it comes to best practice in medicine, however, there is no choice in the matter. Before one can really know what one is doing to one's patients, what they really need and what are successful health outcomes for them one simply must understand their worlds. For some doctors this will be more difficult to achieve than for others but achieve it they all must if patients are to be properly served by them.

It would be a foolish person who thought that these skills could be satisfactorily taught in a medical lecture or a lecture in medical ethics. One can know a great deal about ethical theory and be careless or even gross in one's behaviour. However, it would be as foolish to leave the development of this faculty to chance as it would to deny children a firm grounding in values in the hope that they might happen to pick them up when exposed to the wide world of adulthood. How they see that world will play a major role in how they react to it and live in it.

Given that there is a role for education in the field, as the growing presence of medical ethics in medical curricula suggests, how can it best be achieved? Medical undergraduates, by definition, have a limited range of life experiences let alone clinical experiences. Early contact with patients, long a feature of nurse education, is now seen as an important element in medical education. For many years the standard introduction to medicine was by means of a detailed dissection of a dead body without knowledge of the name, disappointments, family relations, successes and failures, preferences and values of the person whose body it recently was. This impersonal approach together with the important but weighty teaching of medical science could be expected to produce a commitment to what has been called the medical model, where the body is the focus of attention rather than the person. Graduating from dead bodies to living bodies when the clinical phase of medical education began was a natural progression. Early contact with patients, where their fears, relationships, pain and interrupted life commitments soon become visible, is a healthy corrective.

But can more than this be achieved? Learning as you go in early patient contact is important but not sufficient given the wide range of persons to whom the surrogate doctor will be exposed in later life. It is here that we can find a valuable role for imagination. Where better to begin to demonstrate the enlargement of understanding of others than by the employment of imaginative insights achieved in the Arts? Poets, dramatists, novelists and painters have stretched our understanding of the human condition in ways which are both engaging and challenging. Employment of their works offers us windows into human experience which a hundred lives would not give any one of us. This rich vein of understanding is open to exploitation by the teacher of health care practitioners in order to stretch the range of possibilities of human perception and experience that exist in the world students already inhabit and in which they plan to practise. However, there are rival views about the propriety of employing the Arts in this way. We shall look briefly at the discussion of those views before examining an example of a poet's power to illuminate one of the most impenetrable patient narratives and a novelist's ability to throw light on a difficult and demanding activity in medical practice.

Using the arts in medical education

There is an ongoing debate about the usefulness of literature and the fine arts in medical education. The growth of the sub-discipline of medical humanities reflects a conviction that study of the Arts can be beneficial in the practice of medicine. But there is dispute as to how this is possible. Two recent contributors to the discussion have presented rival and incompatible accounts.

One holds that the various principles of good practice are exemplified in a narrative.[1] A critic of that view has argued that reading a novel rather tells the reader something about herself and that in so doing might affect the manner in which that practitioner might approach her practice.[2]

There is something valuable to be learned from each of these accounts. In the case of the former it might be that a principle takes on a new vivacity for the practitioner as a result of her coming across it in a non-threatening context. Stories have traditionally been used in this way to bring home to readers a moral which needed reinforcement. Aesop's fables and the story told by Nathan the prophet to the scheming King David[3] are telling examples. However, the latter view implies that without a personal engagement with the narrative a reading is at best shallow and at worst distorted and doctrinaire. It follows from this view that medical humanities cannot be used instrumentally in medical education insofar as we cannot predict what, if anything, it is that the reader might learn from the narrative. Further, what is learned might be as much a power for either good or evil.

It is certainly true that the former account's usefulness is tempered by the inescapable fact that simply trawling novels for exemplifications of preferred rules of behaviour can become a dead and stultifying activity. The novel might thus become a repository for data of various kinds rather than a compelling tale, and any impact on the reader is lost. The distinction has been well made between these two kinds of reading in a discussion of the assertion: 'When I read a poem or narrative with feeling, surely something goes on in me which does not go on when I merely skim the lines for information.'[4] It is not so much that the words or principles appear in a narrative that counts, as the way in which they are read. A change of emphasis or intonation in the reading of a particular word can make all the difference to its significance. Similar considerations attach to the role and context of the words in the narrative. This is a matter to which we shall return later.

Instrumental uses of the arts

The foregoing reservation does not rule out the instrumental use of literature, contrary to the second account of the matter outlined above. The novelist or poet can fire the imagination of the reader by suggesting new possibilities and understandings which the limited experience of emerging and experienced practitioners precludes. No practitioner's experience is unlimited and such limitations might blind him or her to possibilities which are facilitated by the experience of others. The poet, for example, by use of his gift might open our eyes to realms of experience otherwise closed to us. We might see these for ourselves in his poem or we might be brought to see them by means of sensitive readings and expositions of the poem by others. This growth in imagination can profoundly affect practitioners' understanding of the experience of patients and influence perceptions of their patients' needs and of suitable interventions. We shall consider such an enlargement of the understanding of the life of an Alzheimer's sufferer by reflecting on Philip Larkin's poem 'The Old Fools'.[5] The poet's pathological fear of growing old and of death, together with his mother's affliction, informs his powerful portrayal of the horror of the degenerative disease. Yet it also succeeds in getting inside the head of the sufferer and portrays a significant world which obliges the reader to reassess the question of what is a worthwhile life. While such reassessment does not necessitate any particular principle of behaviour or policy of care, it does at the very least demand justifications for discounting features of the experience of the patient which might otherwise have been overlooked.

The limits of the imagination might be even wider than those of the collective experience of the living and the dead. The work of the novelist and poet might be employed to open up these imaginary realms and, once again, call the reader to reflect upon assumptions and practices which might otherwise appear secure. While the artist creates fictions, even fictions which could not conceivably be realised in fact, it does not follow that they have no bearing on the realities with which we have to deal.

> 'But the fairy tale only invents what is not the case: it does not talk *nonsense*'. – It is not as simple as that. Is it false or nonsensical to say that a pot talks? Have we a clear picture of the circumstances in which we should say of a pot that it talked? (Even a nonsense-poem is not nonsense in the same way as the babbling of a child.)[6]

We observed in Chapter 6 that Louis MacNeice's poem 'Prayer before birth' puts words into the mouth of the unborn child which draw our attention to possible responsibilities that the living might have towards those not yet part of their company. In one sense the poem cannot be said to be true (indeed can any poem be so described?) in that it is not so much a question of how we could possibly detect the wishes of such a prospective person as of how it could make sense to ascribe wishes of this kind. Nevertheless reflection on the poem can be a means to ponder upon the responsibilities which devolve upon the living to protect the unborn from threats and harms which are both predictable and avoidable. Such reflection, as we have seen, is particularly called for among those who play a causal role in facilitating conception and parenthood by medical assistance. The poem was employed to achieve precisely this kind of attention.[7] Insofar as this was successful it was an instrumental use of the work.

The instrumental uses of literature outlined above have something important in common. Literature is not used in either case to support or establish a given line of practice. In that sense the use of it differs markedly from the first account of the use of the humanities in medical education, which is thereby seen at least to be too narrow. Protagonists for the second account might well latch on to this criticism and add that the instrumental use outlined would be most unlikely to effect any change in practice as it would encourage the wrong kind of engagement with the narrative – an engagement rather more akin to that found in proofreading or editing than to that found in the enjoyment of a novel. Insofar as this is true then the imagination of the practitioner would be left almost untouched by the exercise.

On the other hand the outcome for the learner is more predictable than that facilitated by the second account. According to that account the outcome of engagement with the novel would be entirely unpredictable. Consequently the idea of using the literature in an instrumental capacity would be ruled out by the account. In both the examples cited above, however, the aim of the employment of the poems was to inculcate a habit of reflective practice. While such a habit does not guarantee a common outcome in terms of the treatment decisions and perceptions of clinicians, it does, nevertheless, make a difference to their practice. Moreover it is a difference which could not be of negative value.

Imaginative access to the experience of others

The growing proportion of older people in the populations of the developed world presents peculiar challenges in the field of health care provision. Many of these are ethical in character and call for a concentrated effort to increase our understanding of what it is to grow old. In the meantime it is incumbent upon us as morally responsible citizens to ensure that standards of care for the older person are not compromised through ignorance. Moreover it is not in the interests of any of us to neglect this duty for, other things being equal, we too shall arrive at such a place and then be judged and treated according to those perceptions and policies which we have been instrumental in forming, thus making the surprise of old age an inevitably unpleasant one.

Leon Trotsky once wrote that old age is the most unexpected of all the things that can happen to a man.[8] What was true of the turbulent days in which he lived appears not to be true in developed countries in the twenty-first century. Improved standards of health care delivery have ensured that many citizens survive well into their seventies, eighties and beyond. Indeed this fact alone poses considerable problems for governments who find the burgeoning costs of caring for these elderly populations to be among the heaviest demands in their health care budgets. Not only they but also large numbers of the elderly themselves, who have to cope with declining quality of life and multifactorial illness, and their informal carers, who have often to manage with great difficulty these conditions in the context of their family lives, inherit new demands. These various demands presented by the growing numbers of older people pose ethical problems which attach to our views of what it is to be old.

Trotsky's observation still retains a ring of subjective truth. People's perceptions of old age and their acceptance of it varies greatly. As someone has pointed out, old age is always at least fifteen years away.[9] It is certainly not possible to determine at what age one has become old to everyone's satisfaction. These rival perceptions pose ethical issues in the provision of elderly care.

It is here that the subjective truth of Trotsky's observation finds its most eloquent expression. It is not difficult for doctors alone to access the narratives of their elderly patients. We all struggle with the task of understanding one another and the further others are removed from our own orbit of experience the harder this becomes. Rival narratives emerge in tension with each other and it takes considerable effort to access those which do not sit comfortably with our own. These narratives are informed by sets of values, preferences, biographical details and perceptions which do not find a common home among the rivals. For this reason the young often have difficulty empathising with the old and the old with the young. And we might all struggle for meaning in lives which appear to us to be so diminished as to be less than worthwhile. Such is often the case with understanding the elderly when their powers are in decline. But here special care is needed.

It is dangerous to generalise and describe old age as being a phase of declining powers for there are many who live to a great age and retain a wide range of faculties, both physical and mental. Nevertheless it is true that for many others their world becomes a very different place from the one which we inhabit, almost a twilight existence, and this is often marked by a decline in powers of memory. Such is the case with degenerative conditions such as Alzheimer's disease and with disabling conditions such as those resulting from experience of stroke. We shall consider their narratives as the most challenging we have to access in caring for the older patient though much that is true of them will also be true of the less impaired elderly. Here above all other cases we might be tempted to assume that the life of the patient is diminished to the point of being less than worthwhile. Their existence might appear intolerable to us and it is certainly not one which we would choose for ourselves.

Given that we have no first-hand experience of such a realm as that in which these older people live, where might we look for assistance in accessing their stories? We might consult with those who have cared for loved ones in such states, though their accounts might vary considerably one from another. This variety might depend on how well or badly our informers were able to cope with the demands which such care placed upon them. We might also tap the imaginative resources of writers who have endeavoured to get inside the heads of such sufferers and construct their world for us. Each of these approaches is represented by the work of Philip Larkin, an English poet who was faced with his mother's decline. In his poem 'The Old Fools' he first builds a relationship with the reader by sharing his fears and his alienation from the narrative of the Alzheimer's sufferer.[10]

> What do they think has happened, the old fools,
> To make them like this? Do they somehow suppose
> It's more grown up when your mouth hangs open and
> drools,

And you keep on pissing yourself, and can't remember
Who called this morning? Or that, if they only chose,
They could alter things back to when they danced all
                              night,
Or went to their wedding, or sloped arms some
                              September?
Or do they fancy there's really been no change,
And they've always behaved as if they were crippled or
                              tight,
Or sat through days of thin continuous dreaming
Watching light move? If they don't (and they can't), it's
                              strange:
Why aren't they screaming?

Larkin describes the patient's state as it strikes him, an apparently dispassionate observer. The vacant and uncontrolled expressions, the incontinence, the confusion and the physical disability and ungainliness all shock him as intolerable states in which to be. And yet what he finds so unutterably intolerable the sufferers seem to accept without complaint or struggle. Why aren't they screaming?

He soon moves on from what might appear to be a lack of sympathy with the sufferers to an effort to make better sense of their lives than the frightening constructions which he at first imposed on their behaviours. In so doing he offers us a remarkable insight into their narratives.[11]

Perhaps being old is having lighted rooms
Inside your head, and people in them,
                              acting.
People you know, yet can't quite name;
                              each looms
Like a deep loss restored, from known
                    doors turning,
Setting down a lamp, smiling from a stair,
                              extracting
A book from the shelves; or
                    sometimes only
The rooms themselves, chairs and a fire
                    burning,
The blown bush at the window, or the sun's
Faint friendliness on the wall some lonely
Rain-ceased midsummer evening. That is
                    where they live:
Not here and now, but where all happened
                    once.

He now sees that their lives are not completely divorced from reality. They are, rather, lives still lived in the past among people and surroundings which once were but are no longer, mostly unknown to him but features of their biographies. Loved persons and places, familiar actions and aspects vaguely recalled together conjure pictures of some substance to the viewers. The patients' worlds are not entirely unrelated to ours but the connections escape their attention. The dislocation between the past and the present makes their experience difficult to value. But we, the observers, including their doctors, are doubly dislocated from the substance of their thoughts for we never knew the people, places and events which now so often occupy their attention. The question arises are such lives intolerable after all? Are they not worth living? The poet at least gives us pause for thought which might prevent precipitate action to unnecessarily restrict further the lives in question, which restriction might constitute harm to the sufferers, thus accelerating their decline. His work might also suggest some interventions which could, in some circumstances, enhance those lives, despite the frailty of memory.

Such was the case with an Alzheimer's sufferer we shall call Mrs J. Unable to live independently any longer, she had been cared for in a residential home for some years. Her short-term memory was extremely poor though she still recognised family. When it was proposed to take her some hundreds of kilometres to meet her brother and sister, whom she had not seen for many years, her son said that it would be a waste of time as she would not remember it. His wife insisted and it was done. To the surprise of all she recognised her siblings and for a whole weekend chatted incessantly about their childhood, marriages, and babies. On the return journey she fell asleep momentarily and on awaking remembered nothing of the visit. 'I told you so', said her son. 'Ah, but didn't she enjoy herself!' replied his wife. Her point was well made. It had been a worthwhile event in Mrs J's life, remembered or not, for it had facilitated links between the past and present which some had thought long lost and provided an authentic reunion, to everyone's surprise. To have spurned the opportunity would have impoverished Mrs J's life and, on the basis of a faulty assumption, unnecessarily restricted her range of activity.

Imagination in dealing with patients

There are many tasks in clinical practice which call for great sensitivity and what might today be called people skills. These might present daunting challenges as they can be difficult to execute in ways which are of positive value to the people who are involved. One such task is the breaking of bad news to patients. While there is no simple programme which, if followed, will suit every occasion and circumstance, imaginative reflection on the activity can enable practitioners to avoid the grossest faults and enhance the possibilities of good outcomes.

The activity of breaking bad news is commonplace in the delivery of health care. It might consist in the announcement of a death but it is more likely to be the pronouncement of a serious diagnosis or a pessimistic or hopeless prognosis. Whatever the nature of the news, its delivery is something for which candidates for the health care professions should be prepared. But how is this best done? Teachers might feel uneasy at simply presenting students either with a list of rights vested in the recipient of the news: the right to know, the right to dignity and respect, the right to be protected from unnecessary harm, the right to fairness, and so on or with a list of correlative duties the doctor has to respect these rights. Though each of these might be relevant to the activity, acknowledgement of them might fall far short of good care. Indeed unreflective application of any or all of them might produce the most undesirable consultations with dreadful sequelae.

A consideration of an example from outside medicine of good and bad practice in the execution of this task can serve to throw light on what can go wrong when doctors share bad news with patients. The example is nicely presented for us in a dramatised television version of the Charles Dickens novel *David Copperfield*. First read his account of the matter:

> 'You are too young to know how the world changes every day,' said Mrs Creakle, 'and how the people in it pass away. But we all have to learn it David; some of us when we are young, some of us when we are old, some of us at all times of our lives.'
>
> I looked at her earnestly.
>
> 'When you came away from home at the end of the vacation,' said Mrs Creakle, after a pause, 'were they all well?' After another pause, 'Was your Mama well?'
>
> I trembled without distinctly knowing why, and still looked at her earnestly, making no attempt to answer.
>
> 'Because,' said she, 'I grieve to tell you that I hear this morning your Mama is very ill.'
>
> A mist rose between Mrs Creakle and me, and her figure seemed to move in it for an instant. Then I felt the burning tears run down my face, and it was steady again.
>
> 'She's very dangerously ill,' she added.
>
> I knew all now.
>
> 'She is dead.'
>
> There was no need to tell me so. I had already broken out into a desolate cry, and felt an orphan in the wide world.[12]

How can consideration of the Dickens narrative facilitate a growth in the understanding of the nature of the task of sharing bad news in surrogate doctors? In line with the earlier examples of the use of the Arts in education the answer is that study of the narrative can stimulate and extend the imagination in ways which can be productive of better practice, practice which is reflective and consequently more responsible. It is true that such practice might exemplify the values and even principles embedded in rights statements on the one hand and that it might denote an awareness of the self gained from engagement with the novel on the other hand. But, more significantly, the better practice can be attributed in part to the activity of the teacher who employs literature instrumentally to instil habits of reflection in the student, habits which will later inform the behaviour of the practising doctor. The teacher does not tell the student what should be learned from the narrative, poem or painting so much as teach the student how to engage with the piece in a way that will be relevant to practice contexts. This might involve enabling the student to ask significant questions, recognise wider ranges of possibilities, acknowledge personal traits, and so on.

To illustrate how this might be possible let us compare the Dickens narrative of the bad news encounter with that of a BBC dramatisation of the novel.[13] The dramatisation took some liberties with the original text. The changes were not accidental. Rather they were demanded by the need to distil the essence of the story into a manageable timespan. A comparison of this sort facilitates the identification of important issues which need to be taken into account in developing good practice in breaking bad news. It also illuminates those issues and stretches our imagination with respect to the development of practice policies.

According to the BBC account the episode occurred in the schoolroom of Salem House, before the headmaster's desk. David could barely see over the top of the desk, behind which sat the towering figure of the headmaster himself. The child had been made to stand here before. It was the very spot where he had suffered his first cuts from the cane which now sat ominously between him and Mr Creakle. He remembered that occasion when consent had not been sought but when, nevertheless full information had been divulged:

> He told me that if I were famous for biting, he was famous for biting too. He then showed me the cane, and asked me what I thought of that for a tooth? Was it a sharp tooth, hey? Had it a deep prong, hey? Did it bite, hey? Did it bite? At every question he gave me a fleshy cut with it that made me writhe: . . . and I . . . was very soon in tears.[14]

Every waking moment in that institution the boy's eye was alert to the presence of this authority figure whose guest, or prisoner, he was. Salem House was anything but a haven of peace. It continually promised a menu of pain, suffering and fear. And here he stood at the focus of all that, without physical support, alone, to hear the awful truth.

Contrast this setting with that provided by Dickens where David is invited to the parlour, the comfortable, homely setting of the Creakle family. He is led to the sofa and Mrs Creakle sits beside him. The threatening figure of

Mr Creakle, his cane ever before him, lurks in the background as a dark presence, but the parlour is a world away from the schoolroom. A mirror hangs upon the wall into which the child looks later to see how red his eyes had become due to his crying.

The sense of tragic suffering and injustice endured by Copperfield is heightened by the BBC setting which compounds the isolation and vulnerability felt naturally by recipients of such news. The translation of this intriguing juxtaposition of settings to the medical world is not difficult to make. The more humane the context of the sharing of bad news can be made the better it will be. For those working in hospitals there is little sense of threat or foreboding attaching to the institution. They are clearly places of healing where experts with authority to deal with health problems dedicate themselves to the care of their patients. To many patients the hospital appears a very different place. For them it might signify nothing but the threat of disease, the prospect of pain and death and the terrors of clinical intervention. Whether bad news is best shared there or elsewhere, such as in the patient's home, is a question worth asking.

The possibility of moving outside the hospital setting might be too slim in many cases where the patient cannot be transferred in the short term, the home is remote from the hospital, the health professionals cannot accommodate domiciliary visits in their busy programmes, and so on. But in such cases we need to ask whether all settings within the hospital are equally suitable. One of the telling features of the Dickens setting was that the child could be left alone for short periods once the news had been shared. He was allowed to remain there throughout the day, protected from the uncaring bustle and pressures of the life of the school and from prying or uncaring eyes. In the television adaptation his space could have been invaded at any moment by a horde of noisy schoolboys amused, embarrassed or simply untouched by his plight. People generally wish for solitude when trying to absorb or come to terms with devastating news. It ensures privacy as they express their initial shock, grief or relief or whatever combination of these might occur. This might be done alone or with loved ones but out of the gaze of the agents of care, the messengers of the bad news, strangers, helpful though they might have been. There is little opportunity for this in a busy clinic, or in an open ward where a curtain at best might protect the recipients from the attention of further strangers.

In addition to the setting of the incident we are challenged to consider the identity of the bearer of the news. It is tempting to concentrate upon the words used in sharing bad news when we think of what is to be said. But this is to miss much that determines the content of the narrative, the significance of the communication. There is nothing to choose between the Dickens text and the BBC production of the story with respect to the dialogue. The dramatic production remains faithful to almost every word written by the author. But the significance of those words is greatly altered by the choice of the mouthpiece. As surely as it is the case that change in the intonation of a word can alter its meaning, as noted earlier, so too can the identity of the speaker.

Mr Creakle was not a caring soul. Indeed he was a sadistic bully. His dedication to cutting with the cane was almost a matter of professional pride, as David noted:

> I should think there never can have been a man who enjoyed his profession more than Mr Creakle did. He had a delight in cutting at the boys, which was like the satisfaction of a craving appetite. I am confident that he could not resist a chubby boy, especially; that there was a fascination in such a subject, which made him restless in his mind, until he had scored and marked him for the day. I was chubby myself, and I ought to know.[15]

The words which fall from his lips, between mouthfuls of breakfast toast, take on an even more sinister turn, therefore, than they need have done. Following the general excursis on learning about peoples' passing away there follows the progressive torture from the question: 'When you came away from home at the end of the vacation, were they all well?' through the rest. Each succeeding enquiry and statement, punctuated by exaggerated pauses, seems calculated to tighten the screw on the poor pupil's emotions with which the headmaster plays like a cat with a mouse. 'Was your Mother well? – I grieve to tell you that your Mama is very ill. – She is very dangerously ill. – She is dead.' The episode impresses the viewer as a piece of black humour, a sick joke, and, moreover, one designed to cut the child's feelings as surely as the cane had often cut his flesh.

In the Dickens text David is asked to attend the Creakles' parlour by a kindly schoolmaster and on arrival is met by Mrs Creakle, who proceeds to handle the delicate matter of communicating the terrible news. Her manner is warm and friendly. Her tactful acknowledgement of his youthfulness and the inevitability of death serves as an important preparation for what is to follow. We are helped to understand the impact of each stage of the conversation by the child's own commentary. Already he appreciates that something serious is to come as he looks at her earnestly. The mention of his mother and the enquiry after her health focuses his attention even further, causing him to tremble though he did not quite know why. Mr Creakle, who allowed his wife to handle the delicate matter, had little sympathy with the pussy-footing approach.

> He shook his head without looking at me and stopped up a sigh with a very large piece of buttered toast.[16]

The step-by-step approximation to the awful truth further prepares the child for the worst. So much so that once he hears that Mama is dangerously ill he stumbles upon the whole matter for himself.

> I knew all now. 'She is dead.' There was no need to tell me so. I had already broken out into a desolate cry, and felt like an orphan in the wide world.[17]

We do not need to assume that the approach was sensitive for David tells the reader that Mrs Creakle was very kind to him. The truth had certainly dawned upon the lad, which is far from what is often reported to have happened when bad news is shared in the medical setting.[18]

A student in a Medical Ethics class once recounted that as a senior nurse who had worked for many years on a paediatric ward with two consultants, she had observed the contrasting practice of the consultant physicians in sharing bad news. Describing her colleagues' widely different approaches to sharing a poor prognosis with parents she reported that one, a brilliant diagnostician, regularly told the truth as it was, baldly and with the maximum economy of words. This direct approach often caused great distress and ward staff were left to pick up the pieces. Moreover the parents often needed to be faced again with the truth on later occasions, having failed either to register or come to terms with it and all the results of their initial encounter with the clinician. This model of breaking bad news has been dubbed the 'full disclosure model', and has been described as paternalistic since it takes no account of the patient's desires about the timing and amount of information disclosed.[19] His colleague took consultation with the parents more seriously. A number of meetings would occur. At the first the various possible diagnoses and prognoses would be canvassed and written information shared. At the second meeting the feelings of the parents would be explored. How were they coping with the possibilities? How did they find their child was coping with his or her problems? Did they have any further questions to ask? At the third meeting the doctor would ask the parents what they thought was the most likely outcome of treatment. Invariably they produced the prognosis which the doctor agreed with. But it was a truth for which they had been prepared and to which they had come with careful assistance – rather like Copperfield in the Dickens story. This partnership model of breaking bad news has been identified in the literature. It involves negotiation, the development of trust and dedicated time.[20] It would be unwise to lay down a protocol for this activity or even guidelines, given the degree of variation between cases. Breaking bad news according to protocols would be rather like painting by numbers, the results would lack precisely what is called for in each activity, viz. sensitivity to the meaning of what one is doing. Nevertheless the duty to consider carefully the when and how of sharing bad news is incumbent on health care practitioners, and use of the Arts can be of assistance in this regard.

We have identified the relevance of the identity of the speaker with respect to the significance of the words spoken during such encounters. But how should we go about choosing the messenger? Once again consideration of the Dickens tale, while not giving us an answer, will assist us in getting clearer about what is at stake in relation to the various possibilities.

We must not forget what we have already observed in deciding who is best placed to share the news. On the other hand, in many medical contexts it is the person with authority, the person with the most thorough knowledge of the information to be shared who is, at least from that point of view, best placed to perform the task. This might well be why, in some studies, doctors have been found to be the preferred sources of such news by many patients.[21] On the other hand there will be occasions when others will be as well informed and perhaps better placed to serve. David's image of Mr Creakle disqualified the headmaster from being an ideal candidate for the disclosure of his mother's death. The professional dedication to cutting boys got in the way of his caring for this boy. One would hope that no surgeon's practice could be described in the terms chosen by David to describe his headmaster's 'professionalism'. Yet, there is no doubt that the temptation to see patients as interesting cases, as opportunities to pursue research or to innovate, or simply as further ciphers on the managerial spreadsheet of through-put figures or health gain targets can blind practitioners to the human situations before them. There is no easy escape from this problem. To combine adequate knowledge and adequate sensitivity can be problematic. Even if alternative health carers are called in to help, the patients will know that there might be a conflict of loyalties in the last analysis, as surely as there was for Mrs Creakle, who herself stood in a relation of fear to her husband. However, all possibilities of improving this facet of patient care need to be considered for many practitioners have personal problems in tackling bad news which might be difficult to convey and which might betray their failure to live up to the miracle-working myth of modern medicine. Certainly numbers of doctors have been aware of their lack of training in communication skills.[22] While medical schools are now more sensitive to these needs than they used to be, problems still exist.

Conclusion

The foregoing discussion has attempted to show that medical humanities might be instrumental in helping to address some of the difficulties individual doctors have in returning the patient as person to centre stage in medical practice. Recognition of the embeddedness of the patients' condition in the context of their lives, that is, recognition of the patients as persons with narratives, has been observed to be a necessary condition of good clinical practice throughout this book. The use of the Arts to foster such skills of recognition offers a valuable assistance to practitioners to set the highest standards of providing health care, to address the realities of clinical practice, while employing all the resources of science at their disposal.

Notes

1 R. Gillon, 'Imagination, literature, medical ethics and medical practice', *Journal of Medical Ethics* 23 (1997), 3–4.

2 N. Pickering, 'Imaginary restrictions', *Journal of Medical Ethics* 24 (1998), 171–5.

3 2 Samuel 12: 1–7, *The Holy Bible: King James Version*, Nashville: Thomas Nelson, 1989.

4 L. Wittgenstein, *Philosophical Investigations*, Oxford: Basil Blackwell, 1953, 214e.

5 D.M. Evans, *Values in Medicine: What Are We Really Doing to our Patients?* Inaugural Professorial Lecture, Dunedin, NZ: University of Otago, 1998, pp. 59–65.

6 L. Wittgenstein, *Philosophical Investigations*, 97e.

7 D.M. Evans, 'The interests of the child in medically assisted surrogacy', *The International Family Law Journal* (December 2000), 167–72.

8 L. Trotsky, in *The Penguin Dictionary of Twentieth Century Quotations*, M.J Cohen and J.M Cohen (eds.), Harmondsworth: Puffin, 1996, 05–01.

9 B.M. Baruch, 'Sayings of the week', *The Observer*, Manchester: Guardian News and Media Limited, 21 August 1955.

10 P. Larkin, 'The old fools', in *Philip Larkin – Collected Poems*, A. Thwaite (ed.), London: The Marvel Press, 1988, pp. 196–7.

11 Ibid.

12 C. Dickens, *The Personal History of David Copperfield*, Vol. 1, The London Edition, London: Caxton Publishing Company, 1902, pp. 92–3.

13 *David Copperfield*, UK: BBC Television, 1999.

14 C. Dickens, *The Personal History of David Copperfield*, p. 67.

15 Ibid., p. 67.

16 Ibid., p. 92.

17 Ibid., p. 93.

18 K.D. Bertakis, 'The communication of information from physician to patient: a method for increasing patient retention and satisfaction', *Journal of Family Practice* 5 (1997), 217–22.

19 A. Girgis and R.W. Sanson-Fisher, 'Breaking bad news: consensus guidelines for medical practitioners', *Journal of Clinical Oncology* 13 (1995), 2449–56.

20 K. Donovan, 'Breaking bad news', in R.W. Sanson-Fisher (ed.), *Interactional Skills: Doctor/Patient Relationship*. Newcastle, Australia: University of Newcastle, 1990; and E. Matthews, 'Can paternalism be modernized?', *Journal of Clinical Oncology* 2 (1986), 300–3.

21 P.M. Levenson, B. Pfefferbaum, Y. Silberberg and D.R. Copeland 'Sources of information about cancer as perceived by adolescent patients, parents, and physicians', *Patient Counselling and Health Education* 3 (1981), 71–6.

22 C.M. Parkes, 'Communication and cancer – a social psychiatrist's viewpoint', *Social Science and Medicine* 8 (1974), 189–90.

Bibliography

Anderson, J. (1962) *Studies in Empirical Philosophy*, Sydney: Angus and Robertson.

Anscombe, E. (1958) 'On brute facts', *Analysis*, 18: 69–72.

Appleby, J. (1992) *Financing Health Care in the 1990s*, Buckingham: Open University Press.

Ayer, A.J. (1948) *Language, Truth and Logic*, London: Victor Gollancz.

Barthes, R. (1971) 'Rhetoric of the image', *Working Papers in Cultural Studies*, Spring: 49.

Baruch, B.M. (1955) 'Sayings of the Week', *The Observer*, Manchester: Guardian News and Media Limited, 21 August.

Bear, G. (1985) *Blood Music*, US: Arbor House.

Beardsmore, R. (1969) *Moral Reasoning*, London: Routledge & Kegan Paul.

Beauchamp, T.L. and Childress, J.F. (2001) *Principles of Biomedical Ethics*, 5th edn, New York: Oxford University Press.

Bernat, E. and Vranes, E. (1996) 'The Austrian act on procreative medicine: scope, impacts and inconsistencies', in D.M. Evans (ed.), *Creating the Child*, The Hague: Martinus Nijhoff.

Bertakis, K.D. (1997) 'The communication of information from physician to patient: a method for increasing patient retention and satisfaction', *Journal of Family Practice*, 5: 217–22.

Bioethics Council (2004) *Gisborne – Te Turanga-nui-a-kiwa*. Wellington, New Zealand, 13 March.

Bloch, S. and Chodoff, P. (1991) *Psychiatric Ethics*, 2nd edn, Oxford: Oxford University Press.

Bole, T.J. (1990) 'Zygote, souls, substances, and persons', *Journal of Medicine and Philosophy*, 15: 637–52.

Boorse, C. (1975) 'On the distinction between disease and illness', *Philosophy and Public Affairs*, 5: 49–68.

Braybrooke, D. (1968) 'Let needs diminish that preferences may prosper', in *Studies in Moral Philosophy*, Oxford: Basil Blackwell.

Brockliss, L.W.B. (1990) 'The embryological revolution in the France of Louis XIV: the dominance of ideology', in G.R. Dunstan (ed.), *The Human Embryo*, Exeter: University of Exeter Press.

Brown, D. (2002) 'Nano litterbugs? Experts see potential pollution problems', *Small Times*, Tulsa, Okla.: Penwell Publishing. Available HTTP: <http://online.sfsu.edu/~rone/Nanotech/NANO%20LITTERBUGS.htm> (accessed 25 May 2007).

Buchanan, A.E. and Brock, D.W. (1989) *Deciding for Others: The Ethics of Surrogate Decision Making*, Cambridge: Cambridge University Press.

Byk, C. (1996) 'French assisted reproduction legislation', in D. Evans (ed.), *Creating the Child*, The Hague: Martinus Nijhoff.

Cartwright, S. (1988) *The Report of the Committee of Inquiry into Allegations Concerning the Treatment of Cervical Cancer at National Womens' Hospital and into Other Related Matters*, Auckland (NZ): Government Printer.

Chalmers, T.C., Block, J.B., and Lee, S. (1972) 'Controlled studies in clinical cancer research', *New England Journal of Medicine*, 287: 75–8.

Choi, K. (2004) 'Ethical issues of nanotechnology development in the Asia-Pacific region', in P. Bergstrom (ed.), *Ethics in Asia-Pacific*, Bangkok: UNESCO Asia and Pacific Regional Bureau for Education.

Churchill, J. (1994) 'Wonder and the end of explanation: Wittgenstein and religious sensibility', *Philosophical Investigations*, 17: 388–416.

Coney, S. (1988) *The Unfortunate Experiment*, Auckland, NZ: Penguin Books.

Culyer, A.J. (1976) *Needs and the National Health Service*, London: Martin Robertson & Co.

Daniels, N. (1985) *Just Health Care*, Cambridge: Cambridge University Press.

Darwin, C. (1987) *Charles Darwin's notebooks, 1836–1844: Geology, Transmutation of Species, Metaphysical Enquiries*, P. Barrett, P.J. Gautrey, S. Herbert, D. Kohn and S. Smith (eds), Ithaca, N.Y. : Cornell University Press.

David Copperfield, UK: BBC Television, 1999.

Davis, J.A. (1986) 'Whose life is it anyway?', *British Medical Journal*, 292: 1128.

Department of Health (2003) *Our Inheritance, Our Future – Realising the Potential of Genetics in the NHS*, CM 5791, London: The Stationery Office.

Diamond, C. (1991) *Wittgenstein, Philosophy and the Mind*, Boston, Mass.: MIT Press.

Diamond, C. (1993) 'Martha Nussbaum and the need for novels', *Philosophical Investigations*, 16: 128–53.

Dickens, C. (1902) *The Personal History of David Copperfield*, Vol. 1, The London Edition, London: Caxton Publishing Company.

Donovan, K. (1990) 'Breaking bad news', in R.W. Sanson-Fisher (ed.), *Interactional Skills: Doctor/Patient Relationship*. Newcastle, Australia: University of Newcastle.

Dowling, A., Clift, R., Grobert, N., Hutton, D., Oliver, R., O'Neill, O., Pethica, J., Pidgeon, N., Porritt, J., Ryan, J., Seaton, A., Tendler, S., Welland, M. and Whatmore, R. (2004) *Nanoscience and Nanotechnologies: Opportunities and Uncertainties*, London: The Royal Society and The Royal Academy of Engineering.

Drellich, M.G. and Beiber, I. (1958) 'The psychologic importance of the uterus and its functions: some psychoanalytic implications of hysterectomy', *Journal of Nervous and Mental Disease*, 126: 322–36.

Drexler, K.E. (1986) *Engines of Creation: The Coming Era of Nanotechnology*, New York: Anchor Books.

Drummond, M.F. (1980) *Principles of Economic Appraisal in Health Care*, Oxford: Oxford University Press.

Dunford, R., Salinaro, A., Cai, L., Serpone, N., Horikoshi, S., Hidaka, H. and Knowland, J. (1997) 'Chemical oxidation and DNA damage caused by inorganic sunscreen ingredients', *FEBS Letters*, 418: 87–90.

Eccles, J.C. (1971) 'Animal experimentation versus human experimentation', in *Defining the Laboratory Animal*, Washington, D.C.: National Academy of Sciences.

Eliot, T.S. (1940) 'Four Quartets: East Coker', in *The Complete Poems and Plays of T.S. Eliot*, London: Faber and Faber.

Elkin, J. and Jones, D.G. (2000) 'Guthrie cards: legal and ethical uses', *New Zealand Bioethics Journal*, 1.

Emery, J. (1995) 'Silent Suffering', *British Medical Journal*, 311: 1647.

Engelhardt, Jr., H.T. (1996) *The Foundations of Bioethics*, 2nd edn, New York: Oxford University Press.

ETC Group (2002) 'No small matter! Nanotech particles penetrate living cells and accumulate in animal organs', *ETC Group Communiqué*, 76. Available HTTP: <www.etcgroup.org/upload/publication/192/01/comm_nanomat_july02.pdf> (accessed 25 May 2007).

Evans, D.M. (1978) 'Photographs and primitive signs', *Proceedings of the Aristotelian Society*, LXXIX: 213–38.

Evans, D.M. (1990) 'Legislative control of medical practice', *Bulletin of Medical Ethics*, 55: 15–16.

Evans, D.M. (1993a) 'Ethicist and patient: what is their relationship?', in R. Gillon (ed.), *Principles of Health Care Ethics*, Chichester: John Wiley and Sons.

Evans, D.M. (1993b) 'Limits to care', in Z. Szawarski and D. Evans (eds), *Solidarity, Justice and Health Care Priorities*, Health Service Studies 8, Linkoping: Linkoping University Press.

Evans, D.M. (1996) 'Pro-attitudes to pre-embryos', in D.M. Evans (ed.), *Conceiving the Embryo*, Dordrecht: Martinus Nijhoff.

Evans, D.M. (1995) 'Infertility and the NHS', *British Medical Journal*, 311: 1586–7.

Evans, D.M. (1996a) 'The clinical classification of infertility', in D.M. Evans (ed.), *Creating the Child*, The Hague: Martinus Nijhoff.

Evans, D.M. (1996b) 'The limits of health care', in D. Greaves and H. Upton (eds), *Philosophical Problems in Health Care*, Aldershot: Avebury.

Evans, D.M. (1998) Values in Medicine: What Are We Really Doing to Our Patients? Inaugural Professorial Lecture, Dunedin, NZ: University of Otago.

Evans, D.M. (1999) 'Ethics and genetics', *New Zealand Medical Journal*, 112: 109–12.

Evans, D.M. (2000) 'The Interests of the Child in Medically Assisted Surrogacy', *The International Family Law Journal* (December).

Evans, D.M. (2002a) 'Ethical Issues in research, part I: research by stealth', Washington, D.C.: Science/AAAS. Online. Available HTTP: <http://sciencecareers.sciencemag.org/career_development/previous_issues/articles/1750/ethical_issues_in_research_part_i_research_by_stealth/(parent)/12098> (accessed 25 May 2007).

Evans, D.M. (2002b) 'Ethical review of innovative treatment', *Healthcare Ethics Committee Forum*, 14: 53–63.

Evans, D.M. and Dolanska, M. (1996) 'Patient perceptions of services', in D.M. Evans (ed.), *Creating the Child*, The Hague: Martinus Nijhoff.

Evans, D.M. and Evans, M. (1996) *A Decent Proposal: Ethical Review of Clinical Research*, Chichester: John Wiley and Sons.

Evans, D.M. and Price, N. (1999) *Ethical Dimensions of the National Waiting Time Project*, New Zealand: Health Funding Authority.

Feinberg, J. (1980) 'The rights of animals and unborn generations' in *Rights, Justice and the Bounds of Liberty*, Princeton: Princeton University Press.

Foot, P. (1954) 'When is a principle a moral principle?', *Proceedings of the Aristotelian Society*, Supplementary Volume 28: 95–110.

Foot, P. (1958) 'Moral arguments', *Mind*, 67: 502–13.

Foot, P. (1959) 'Moral beliefs', *Proceedings of the Aristotelian Society*, 59: 83–104.

Foot, P. (1978a) 'Moral arguments', in *Virtues and Vices*, Oxford: Blackwell.

Foot, P. (1978b) 'Moral Beliefs', *in Virtues and Vices*, Oxford: Blackwell.

Ford, N.M. (1988) *When Did I Begin?* Cambridge: Cambridge University Press.

Foresight Institute, *Providing Abundant Clean Water Globally*, California: Foresight Institute. Online. Available HTTP: <http://foresight.org/challenges/water.html> (accessed 25 May 2007).

Freedman, B. (1987) 'Equipoise and the ethics of clinical research', *New England Journal of Medicine*, 317: 141–5.

Freitas, Jr., R.A. (1998) *Foresight Nanotech Institute Nanomedicine FAQ*, California: Foresight Institute. Online. Available HTTP: <www.foresight.org/Nanomedicine/NanoMedFAQ.html> (accessed 25 May 2007).

Geach, P. (1957) *Mental Acts: Their Content and their Objects*, London: Routledge and Kegan Paul.

Gillett, G. (1987) 'Reply to J. M. Stanley: fiddling and clarity', *Journal of Medical Ethics*, 13: 23–5.

Gillett, G. (2000) 'How should we test and improve neurosurgical care?', in A. Zeman and L. Emmanuel (eds), *Ethical Dilemmas in Neurology*, London: W.B. Saunders Company.

Gillett, G., Lind, C.R.P. and Erasmus, A.M. (1999) 'CG clip expansive open-door laminoplasty: a technical note', *British Journal of Neurosurgery*, 13: 405–8.

Gillick V. v. West Norfolk & Wisbech Area Health Authority (1985) 3 All England Law Reports.

Gillon, R. (1997) 'Imagination, literature, medical ethics and medical practice', *Journal of Medical Ethics*, 23: 3–4.

Girgis, A. and Sanson-Fisher, R.W. (1995) 'Breaking bad news: consensus guidelines for medical practitioners', *Journal of Clinical Oncology*, 13: 2449–56.

Golombok, S., Spencer, A. and Rutter, M. (1983) 'Children in lesbian and single parent households: psychosexual and psychiatric appraisal', *Journal of Child Psychology and Psychiatry*, 24: 551–72.

Goodman, N. (1968) *Languages of Art*, New York: Bobbs-Merrill.

Graves, R. (1959) 'To evoke posterity', in *Collected Poems*, London: Cassell.

Greaves, D. (1996) *Mystery in Western Medicine*, Aldershot: Avebury.

Greaves, D. 'The historical conceptualisation of impaired capacity and some ethical implications', unpublished paper for the European Commission research project on Decision Making and Impaired Capacity, 1997.

Griffin, J. (1986) *Well-being: Its Meaning, Measurement and Moral Importance*, Oxford: Clarendon Press.

Hampshire, S. (1978) *Public and Private Morality*, Cambridge: Cambridge University Press.

Hare, R.M. (1960) *The Language of Morals*, Oxford: Oxford University Press.

Hare, R.M. (1963) *Freedom and Reason*, Oxford: Oxford University Press.

Harris, J. (1985) *The Value of Life*, London: Routledge.

Harris, J. (1987) 'QALYfying the value of life', *Journal of Medical Ethics*, 13: 117–23.

Harrison, T.R. (1980) *Harrison's Principles of Internal Medicine*, 9th edn, K.J. Isselbacher, R.D. Adams, E. Braunwald, R.G. Petersdorf and J.D. Wilson (eds), New York: McGraw-Hill.

Himmler, Heinrich. *Speech to SS-Gruppenführer at Posen*, Poland, October 4th, 1943. U.S. National Archives document 242.256, reel 2 of 3.

Hoet, P.H., Nemmar, A. and Nemery, B. (2004) 'Health impact of nanomaterials?', *Nature Biotechnology*, 22: 19.

Hokusai, K. (1988) *One Hundred Views of Mount Fuji*, London: Thames & Hudson.

Human Fertilisation and Embryology Act 1990, London: HMSO.

Human Fertilisation and Embryology Authority (1995) *Fourth Annual Report*, London: HFEA.

Human Genetics Commission (2005) *Profiling the Newborn: A Prospective Gene Technology?*, London: HGC. Online. Available HTTP: <www.hgc.gov.uk/UploadDocs/ Contents/Documents/Final%20Draft%20of%20Profiling%20Newborn%20 Report%2003%2005.pdf>.

Hume, D. (1888) *A Treatise of Human Nature*, L.A. Selby-Bigge (ed.), Oxford: Oxford University Press.

Jachuck, S.J., Brierly, H., Jachuck, S. and Willcox, P.M. (1982) 'The effect of hypotensive drugs on the quality of life', *Journal of the Royal College of General Practitioners*, 32: 103–5.

Jennett, B. (1986) *High Technology Medicine: Benefits and Burdens*, Oxford: Oxford University Press.

Jonsen, A.R., Veatch, R.M. and Walters L. (eds), (1998) *Source Book in Bioethics: A Documentary History*, Washington, D.C.: Georgetown University Press.

Kerruish, N.J. and Robinson, S.P. (2005) 'Newborn screening: new developments, new dilemmas', *Journal of Medical Ethics*, 31: 393–8.

Klotzko, A.J. (1996) 'Infertility, inability and rights: an English legal case study', in D.M. Evans (ed.), *Creating the Child*, The Hague: Martinus Nijhoff.

Kripke, S. (1972) 'Naming and necessity', in G. Harman and D. Davidson (eds), *Semantics of Natural Language*, Dordrecht: Reidel.

LaFollette, H. (1980) 'Licensing parents', *Philosophy and Public Affairs*, 9: 182–97.

Larkin, P. (1988) 'The old fools', in *Philip Larkin – Collected Poems*, A. Thwaite (ed.), London: The Marvel Press.

Last, J.M. (1983) *A Dictionary of Epidemiology*, 3rd edn, Oxford: Oxford University Press.

Levenson, P.M., Pfefferbaum, B., Silberberg, Y. and Copeland, D.R. (1981) 'Sources of information about cancer as perceived by adolescent patients, parents, and physicians', *Patient Counselling and Health Education*, 3: 71–6.

Levine, R.J. (1986) *Ethics and the Regulation of Clinical Research*, 2nd edn, Baltimore: Urban and Schwarzenberg.

Light, D.W. (1991) 'Observations on the NHS reforms: an American perspective', *British Medical Journal*, 303, 568–70.

Lindley, R.I. and Warlow, C.P. (2000) 'Why, and how, should trials be conducted?', in A. Zeman and L. Emmanuel (eds), *Ethical Dilemmas in Neurology*, London: W.B. Saunders Company.

Lough v Rolla Women's Clinic, Inc., 866 S.W.2d 851 (Mo. 1993) 23, 105.

Lower, A. and Setchell, M. (1993) 'Should the NHS fund infertility services?', *British Journal of Hospital Medicine*, 50: 509–12.

MacCloskey, H.J. (1976) 'Human needs, rights and political values', *American Philosophical Quarterly*, 13: 1–11.

MacIntyre, A. (1966) *A Short History of Ethics*, New York: Macmillan.

MacNeice, L. (1966) 'Prayer before birth', in E.R. Dodds (ed.), *The Collected Poems of Louis MacNeice*, London: Faber and Faber.

Maritain, J. (1945) *The Rights of Man and Natural Law*, London: Geoffrey Bles.

Matthews, E. (1986) 'Can paternalism be modernized?', *Journal of Clinical Oncology*, 2: 300–3.

Mellow, A.J. (2003) 'Microfluidics: DNA amplification moves on', *Nature*, 422: 28–9.

Merskey, H. and Shafran, B. (1986) 'Political hazards in the diagnosis of "sluggish schizophrenia" ', *The British Journal of Psychiatry*, 148: 247–56.

Mertz, J.L. (2001) 'Technological and educational implications of nanotechnology – infrastructure and educational needs', in M.C. Roco and W.S. Bainbridge (eds), *Societal Implications of Nanoscience and Nanotechnology*, Washington, D.C.: National Science Foundation.

Mill, J.S. (1874) *Utilitarianism*, London: Longmans, Green, Reader, and Dyer.

Mooney, G.H. (1986) *Economics, Medicine and Health Care*, Brighton: Wheatsheaf Books.

Mooney, G.H., Russell, E.M. and Weir, R.D. (1986) *Choices for Health Care*, 2nd edn, London: Macmillan.

Moore, G.E. (1962) *Principia Ethica*, Cambridge: Cambridge University Press.

Murray, T. (1996) *The Worth of a Child*, Berkeley: University of California Press.

New Zealand Health and Disability Commissioner Act 1994.

Nowell-Smith, P.H. (1954) *Ethics*, London: Penguin.

Obeid, P.J., Christopoulos, T.K., Crabtree, H.J. and Backhouse, C.J. (2003) 'Microfabricated device for DNA and RNA amplification by continuous flow polymerase chain reaction and reverse transcription-polymerase chain reaction with cycle selection', *Analytical Chemistry*, 75: 288–95.

Oberdörster, E. (2004) 'Manufactured nanomaterials (fullerenes, C60) induce oxidative stress in the brain of juvenile largemouth bass', *Environmental Health Perspectives*, 112: 1058–62.

Oberdörster, G., Sharp, Z., Atudorei, V., Elder, A., Gelein, R., Kreyling, W. and Cox, C. (2004) 'Translocation of inhaled ultrafine particles to the brain', *Inhalation Toxicology*, 16: 437–45.

O'Donovan, K. (1989) 'What shall we tell the children?', in R. Lee and D. Morgan (eds), *Birthrights, Law and Ethics at the Beginnings of Life*, London: Routledge.

Paget, S. (1912) *For and Against Experiments on Animals: Evidence Before the Royal Commission on Vivisection*, London: H.K. Lewis.

Parkes, C.M. (1974) 'Communication and cancer – a social psychiatrist's viewpoint', *Social Science and Medicine*, 8: 189–90.

Phillips, D.Z. and Mounce, H.O. (1969) *Moral Practices*, London: Routledge & Kegan Paul.

Phoenix, C. and Drexler, E. (2004) 'Safe exponential manufacturing', *Nanotechnology*, 15: 869–72.

Pickering, N. (1998) 'Imaginary restrictions', *Journal of Medical Ethics*, 24: 171–5.

Radin, M.J. (1992) 'Market inalienability', in K.D. Alpern (ed.), *The Ethics of Reproductive Technologies*, Oxford: Oxford University Press.

R v Ethical Advisory Committee of St. Mary's Hospital ex p. Harriott 1 *Family Law Review*, 1988: 512.

Re C (Adult: refusal of treatment), (1994) 1 Weekly Law Reports, 290–6.

Redmayne, S. and Klein, R. (1993) 'Rationing in practice: the case of in vitro fertilisation', *British Medical Journal*, 306: 1521–4.

Regan, T. (1984) *The Case for Animal Rights*, London: Routledge.

Regan, T. (1993) 'Ill-gotten gains', in P. Cavalieri and P. Singer (eds), *The Great Ape Project*, New York: St Martin's Griffin.

Roth, L.H., Meis, A. and Lidz, C.W. (1977) 'Tests of competency to consent to treatment', *American Journal of Psychiatry*, 134: 279–84.

Russell, W.M.S. and Burch, R.L. (1959) *The Principles of Humane Experimental Technique*, London: Methuen.

Ruyter, K. (1996) 'The example of adoption', in D.M. Evans (ed.), *Creating the Child*, The Hague: Martinus Nijhoff.

Ryder, R. (1975) *The Victims of Science: The Use of Animals in Research*, London: Davis-Poynter.

Sacks, O.W. (1985) *The Man Who Mistook his Wife for a Hat*, London: Duckworth.

Sassoon, S. (1961) 'The one-legged man', in *Collected Poems (1908–1956)*, London: Faber and Faber.

Scharf, A. (1974) *Art and Photography*, Baltimore, Md.: Penguin.

Schupbach, W. (1987) 'A select iconography of animal experiment', in N.A. Rupke (ed.), *Vivisection in Historical Perspective*, London: Croom Helm.

Shaw, L.W. and Chalmers, T.C. (1970) 'Ethics in cooperative trials', *Annals of the New York Academy of Sciences*, 169: 487–95.

Sheremeta, L. (2004) 'Nanotechnology and the ethical conduct of research involving human subjects', *Health Law Review*, 12: 47–56.

Singer, P. (1990) *Animal Liberation*, 2nd edn, New York: Random House.

Singer, P. and Kuhse, H. (1990) 'Individuals, humans and persons: The issue of moral status', in P. Singer, H. Khuse, S. Buckle, K. Dawson and P. Kasimba (eds), *Embryo Experimentation*, Cambridge: Cambridge University Press.

Singer, P. and Wells, D. (1985) *Making Babies*, New York: C. Scribner's Sons.

Singer, P.A., Salamanca-Buentello, F. and Daar, A.S. (2005) 'Harnessing nanotechnology to improve global equity', *Issues in Science and Technology*, 21: 57–8.

St. George's Healthcare NHS v S (1998) 3 All ER 673; (1999) FAM 26.

Stevenson, C.L. (1944) *Ethics and Language*, New Haven, Conn.: Yale University Press.

Taylor, P. (2000) 'My left foot was not part of me', *The Observer*, Manchester: Guardian News and Media Limited (6 February), 14.

The Holy Bible: King James Version, Nashville, Tenn.: Thomas Nelson, 1989.

The New Zealand Independent Biotechnology Advisory Council (2001) *Genetic Testing: an Introduction to the Technology that is Changing our Lives*, Wellington, NZ: IBAC.

The Scientific Committee on Cosmetic Products and Non-Food Products Intended for Consumers (2003) *Opinion Concerning Zinc Oxide (COLIPA n° S 76)*, Brussels: SCCNFP. Online. Available at: <www.europa.eu.int/comm/health/ph_risk/committees/sccp/documents/out222_en.pdf> (accessed 25 May 2007).

Thomas, C. (2004) 'Guthrie test samples: is the problem solved?', *New Zealand Bioethics Journal*, 5(2): 25–33.

Tipene-Matua, B. (1999) 'A Māori response to the biogenetic age', in R. Prebble (ed.), *Designer Genes*, Wellington, NZ: Dark Horse Publishers.

Tooley, M. (1972) 'Abortion and infanticide', *Philosophy and Public Affairs*, 2: 37–65.

Toulmin, S. (1950) *The Place of Reason in Ethics*, Cambridge: Cambridge University Press.

Trotsky, L. (1996) in *The Penguin Dictionary of Twentieth Century Quotations*, M.J. Cohen and J.M. Cohen (eds), Harmondsworth: Puffin.

UNESCO (2005) 'Universal declaration on bioethics and human rights', *International Social Science Journal*, 57: 745–53.

Wellman, C. (1975) 'Ethical disagreement and objective truth', *American Philosophical Quarterly*, 12: 211–21.

Wiles, R. and Patel, H. (1995) *Report of the Third National Survey of NHS Funding of Infertility Services*, London: College of Health.

Williams, A. (1985) 'The value of QALYs', *Health and Social Service Journal*, supplement: 3.

Winch, P. (1965–66) 'Can a good man be harmed?', *Proceedings of the Aristotelian Society*, 66: 55–70.

Winch, P. (1972) *Ethics and Action*, London: Routledge & Kegan Paul.

Wisdom, J. (1965) *Paradox and Discovery*, Oxford: Blackwell.

Wittgenstein, L. (1953) *Philosophical Investigations*, Oxford: Basil Blackwell.

Wittgenstein, L. (1961) *Tractatus Logico Philosophicus*, London: Routledge & Kegan Paul.

Wittgenstein, L. (1969) *On Certainty*, G.E.M. Anscombe and G.H. von Wright (eds), Oxford: Basil Blackwell.

Wittgenstein, L. (1974) *Philosophical Grammar*, R. Rhees (ed.), Oxford: Basil Blackwell.

Index